Distinctly
I Remember

The Author—1943

Distinctly
I Remember

a personal story of Burma

Harold Braund
M.B.E.,M.C.

with a foreword by
Brigadier Sir Bernard Fergusson
G.C.M.G.,G.C.V.O.,D.S.O.,O.B.E.

Wren

ING PTY LTD

toria

© d 1972

First publis. 1972

National Library of Australia Card Service Number
and International Standard Book Number
ISBN 0 85885 006 0
Registered in Australia for transmission by post as a book
Text set by Trade Composition Pty Ltd, Melbourne
Printed and bound by Wilke and Company Limited,
Clayton, Victoria.
Designed by Derrick I Stone.

To
the peoples of Burma
who gave me these years;
and to comrades
who did not survive

Contents

List of Illustrations

Foreword

In the course of the last war, I found myself serving with men of whose existence I had been only dimly aware. These were the British employees of the Burma firms, which had been engaged for three-quarters of a century in developing and handling the resources of that rich and beautiful country: timber, rice, mines, waterways and the like. By the time I came to know them, these men were all in uniform; but the characteristics which they had in common shone and shimmered through the anonymity which the donning of uniform sometimes involves.

They were all quite remarkably resourceful, and no wonder. I soon discovered that almost without exception they had lived up-country for long periods on their own. They had become accustomed in early youth to being self-sufficient, to taking major decisions without troubling their superiors, to dispensing rough medicine and even rougher justice, and to being, in short, responsible far beyond their years. They did not always take kindly to being bossed around by people like me. They were not 'sweir', as we say in Scotland — the English have no better word for it than 'loath' — to point out to us, their military superiors, what we were doing wrong, and in what manner we ought to mend our ways. Yet at the same time they were the most loyal of officers. Casting my mind back, I cannot recall one single 'dud'.

I never met H. E. W. Braund, the author of this book. It fell to him to serve with the Chin Levies, who operated in a different part of the Burma theatre of war from that in which I was slogging around with my pack on my back. The Chin Levies built up a formidable achievement and tradition of their own, and became a legend in their short lifetime. But among my Burma officers, men drawn from the same background, that *corps d'elite* of 'Burma hands', there were plenty who knew him, and none who did not speak highly of him. It is pretty obvious from his book that he conformed precisely to the description I have offered above of those young men who served the various Burma companies. Most were Scotch; some, like 'Elephant Bill', whom I did know, were Cornish; a few privileged Englishmen were allowed to be of their number.

Authenticity rings through this book from start to finish. This preface from me is really unnecessary, since the book speaks for itself, both of the days of peace and the days of war, when Braund and all the others rose so splendidly to the occasion, and brought to it their virtues of knowledge, experience, confidence, enthusiasm and guts. But it does give me a chance to pay my own private tribute to this select group of men, whose endowments and achievements and contributions are not as widely known as they should be. Among these, incidentally, was the extraordinary loyalty which they inspired in their subordinates from the many races that inhabit Burma. When Britain's sun had dipped far below the horizon and all was dark, hundreds of native employees some of whom had served the companies for three generations, ranged themselves with their former *Thakins*. They shared their faith and their fate, hiding them, guiding them, and sharing all the risks, because they had learned to trust them. Many of these were killed, and must not be forgotten.

Braund's own story is remarkable enough. Others have parallel tales to tell, but he has proved himself an excellent mouthpiece for them all. To seek to recapture the atmosphere of those pre-war days might seem like trying to catch the rainbow with a butterfly net; but I think he has done it. Certainly he has done much to explain to me why the 'Burma hands' who became my trusted friends and comrades in those unexpected and gruelling years were so outstandingly good.

Ballantrae, 1972   BERNARD FERGUSSON

Introduction

Child and man I was based in Asia for thirty-eight years. I do not expect ever to return.

During the post-war approach to my final leavetaking, when the career Briton was progressively giving place to the short-term specialist or consultant, I was often saddened by reflection on the swiftness with which the *mores* of the 'Eastern hand' were slipping into limbo so largely unchronicled.

After my *vale* in 1965, I listened one day, in the Australian Club in Melbourne, to a member who was holding forth on the dearth of recorded history in his own country. His theme was that each of us owes it to his heirs and successors to commit to paper some account of his own life and times, no matter how sketchy.

In some measure, perhaps, I am beholden to this gentleman, since he unwittingly pointed the way to a less ambitious goal than publication as a spur to the putting together of the personal story I was already contemplating. I have enjoyed the writing of it for its own sake; it has involved me in some colourful reliving; and it should account to my children for some of their father's possible idiosyncrasies.

More than this, however, it is the story of a way of life that is no longer open and, as such, may perhaps have wider — even historical — value. No longer do young Britons 'go East' for motives of romance and adventuring or of family tradition — to a manner of living that speeds their maturing and tests their wisdom, their morals and their fortitude in a way that no 'domestic' career ever can.

The story spans the whole of my Burma service, though this accounts for only thirteen of my thirty-four years with Steel Brothers and Company Limited. I was eighteen when it opens and I leave it at thirty-two. It is therefore a young man's tale, covering the years of decision and self-revelation that should be each man's road to the maturity that would 'see life steadily and see it whole'.

That I can depend on much more than memory for my writing is due, firstly, to my father, who, of his own volition (and unknown to me for many years), preserved all my weekly letters home, filing them chronologically with their miscellaneous enclosures in hard-cover binders. These letters, propped open at will on a carved Koran holder, have been worked on at a window commanding a view of Australian skies, which factors may have added to the necessarily nomadic aura of the narrative.

The letters themselves, their substance as distinct from their content, have, I hope, livened the tale. They were speeded from the pen by launch, by runner, by raft and by elephant; they have survived stranding by water and disaster by air; they bear the scars of the censor's blue pencil and scissors; they have reflected the flickering flames of the arson that goes with communal rioting; they have been written in sickness and in solitude, to the sounds of bombing and mortar fire and, in one case at least, in the fear that I might be writing my last; they have lain temporarily secreted in the jungle under enemy pressure and have been delivered during air raids. During the years of war, when I wrote in duplicate, posting last week's carbon copy with this week's original, on two occasions only did neither original nor duplicate get through. In no case did the surgery of censorship perform the same excision on both copies. I had thought to destroy such raw material as superfluous when my task was done but, as with Poe and his raven, it is with me still.

Secondly, as a work of reference, I have had the benefit of a complete set of *Steels House Magazine*, which has been published continuously (albeit with some departure into wartime garb) since 1939. And thirdly, I have my personal war diaries and maps on which to draw for that side of the tale. In only a small minority of cases have I thought it necessary to conceal the names of persons who are or may still be living.

That my story was not written nearer to the years of which it treats is due to the fact that only now, since my arrival in Australia, are my data and I sharing the same roof. Distance can lend enchantment, and it is for this reason that I have chosen to quote from contemporary letters and reports with regard to events where presentation in the original colours may command greater credence.

I offer my thanks to the Director-General of the Imperial War Museum in London for permission to reproduce the wartime study by Anthony Gross Esq., A.R.A., of 'Captain Braund with "B" Levies of the Kamhau Tribe'.

I thank the United Service Institution of India for permission to quote from my *Three Years with the Chin Levies*, published in the October 1946 and January 1947 issues of the Institution's journal.

To Steel Brothers and Company Limited I am grateful, *inter alia*, for the photograph of the guide wall at Lanywa; to Mr Brian Palmer, of Melbourne, for his preparation of Maps '5 and 6'; to Mr and Mrs C. K. Baldwin, of California, for the photograph of the Burmese girl 'dancing' with the hamadryad; to the then Major Fry, of the Punjab Regiment, for his pencil sketch of a Chin Levy, executed in bivouac on Army-issue toilet paper; and to the Royal Air Force (presumably) for the silk escape maps, presented to me by a rescued pilot, sections of which have met my present needs most adequately.

To a number of British (ex-Burma and India) and Australian friends in Victoria I am indebted for their reading of the first draft of my story. Revisions and corrections, a distillation of their collective suggestions, permeate the final presentation. If I have rejected some proposed expansions, it is because they lie outside my personal ken; and if I have left unaltered the occasional patch of rawness, it is because I believe this should be a 'warts and all' story if it is to be fairly balanced.

Last, but hardly least, I thank the great and now distinguished 'Chindit' who has honoured my story with a
foreword.

Melbourne 1971

Names

Names have a thistledown habit of fluttering in out of history,
    The facets, that is, of events we endeavoured to mould.
Be it feast or a fight, was it death or some unresolved mystery,
    Each stealthily grappled its deeper than realized hold.
Names are our masters, unheeding of time or occasion,
    And, ever their servants, they call and we go where we're told.

    (*Ooozie* and *peijeik*, artists in concert,
        Indaw to Lawtha enthroned on Pu-bay;
    Jenny the veteran — peace on her tusklessness,
        Phalomay-gyi and Phalomay-galay!)

Convalescent reflection is always fair soil for invasion,
    In fact that is how this stray theme ever came to unfold.
When the mind is at slack there is little it needs of persuasion,
    To seek out old paths, knowing well that the scent has
        grown cold.
Names can deprive us of sleep and rob dawn of its welcome,
    They also reprieve dying memories of singing and gold.

    (White's Mergen and a titled beachcomber,
        King Island in an island-studded sea;
    Mangrove, the phosphorescence and the fireflies,
        Beik-myo, mi-gyaung, kya-na-bin and *nga-pi!*)

On occasions I think that this theme holds some deeper potential,
    A two-way exchange when the carpet of Time is unrolled.
That when memory pulses at large on the edge of the *taung-ya*,
    Some well-trusted *lu-gyi* is roused by an echo of old.
Names, though we take them for granted, are keys to a kingdom
    Of personal riches that cannot be bargained or sold.

    (Suanglangsu Vum to the Bungvun Va,
        Patrol at midnight when the moon was low.
    Fever, leeches and Lord knew what to follow,
        Nang-ma na dam maw? Bawi-pa ka dam ko!)

In hospital, London, 1954

Glossary

*of Asian words and phrases not to be found
in the Shorter Oxford English Dictionary*

Bur — Burmese	Chin — Chin	Jap — Japanese
Mal — Malay	Shan — Shan	Urdu — Urdu

Asoya (Bur) — The Government

Atap (Mal) — Palm leaves

Atta (Urdu) — Wheat flour

Basha (Urdu) — A grass or leaf hut

Bawi-nu (Chin) — A woman, a wife

Bawi-pa (Chin) — An officer, one to whom respect is due

Beik-myo (Bur) — Mergui

Bo-gyi (Bur) — A big chief

Bolo (Urdu) — Say, tell

Bombine (Bur) — The Bombay-Burmah Trading Corporation (slang)

Chalaki (Urdu) — Cunning, deceitful

Char (Urdu) — Tea

Chaung (Bur) — A stream, nullah, creek (alternatively a school)

Durwan (Urdu) — A watchman

Dushman (Urdu) — An enemy

Galay (Bur) — Small, a child

Gyi (Bur) — Big

Indaing (Bur) — Forest of hardwood trees

Jawan (Urdu) — A soldier, other rank

Kempeitai (Jap) — Military, or secret, police

Koi hai (Urdu) — Anyone there? (Fig. 'an old *koi hai*' — an Eastern 'hand')

Kya-gyi (Bur) — A tiger

*Kya-na-bin*r) (Bu — A hardwood timber

Lugalay (Bur) — A young man, a personal servant

Lu-gyi (Bur) — An old man

16

Lundwin (Bur)	A country boat
Ma de (Bur)	He is well
Mali (Urdu)	A gardener
Maro (Urdu)	Kill
Mat (Urdu)	Do not
Mi-gyaung (Bur)	A crocodile
Nang-ma na dam maw? ⎱ (Chin)	⎰ Are you well?
Bawi-pa ka dam ko. ⎰	⎱ Yes Sir, I am.
Nat (Bur)	A spirit
Nga-pi (Bur)	Rotted fish
Nikalo (Urdu)	Take out
Ooozie (Bur)	Elephant rider
Oung (Bur)	To push with the head
Pahit (Mal)	A measure of gin
Panji (Bur)	A sharpened bamboo stake
Peijeik (Bur)	An elephant helper or attendant
Phongyi (Bur)	A Monk
Phongyi-chaung (Bur)	A Monastery
Pyaw zaya (Bur)	A conference
Pwe (Bur)	A dramatic performance, a play
Sigri (Urdu)	A bee-hive shaped basket over a charcoal brazier, used for drying clothes.
Singaung (Bur)	*Sin* — elephant, *gaung* — headman
Stengah (Mal)	A measure of whisky
Taung-ya (Bur)	Shifting cultivation
Taw chet (Bur)	A jungle fowl
Tawmaw (Shan)	A temporary rest house
Thakin (Bur)	Master (honorific)
Thit bo-gyi (Bur)	A Forest officer
Thit kok-thu (Bur)	A woodcutter
Twin za (Bur)	A well owner
Wa de (Bur)	He is fat
Zayat (Bur)	A small rest house
Zu (Chin)	Rice beer
Zu-riel (Chin)	Rice spirit

1 London Apprenticeship

February 1932 to June 1934

When 'Kep' Brown slipped and fell to his rocky death in the remoteness of the Upper Chindwin, I was twenty years of age and fretting impatiently at my London office desk in anticipation of a Northern Ireland bird-watching venture that was to consume my fortnight's ration of holiday for the year.

Alas for plans frustrated! That expedition went forward without me.

A day or two after the tragedy I was tremulously closing the Chairman's door behind me, committed in three weeks time to boarding at Marseilles the Bibby Line's *Cheshire* due to sail for Rangoon on 15 June 1934. Sadly but verily I was off to fill a dead man's shoes.

Steel Brothers' office of those days, and until Goering's Air Force demolished it, stood in the narrows of Lime Street where, sullen and grey, it competed on unfavourable terms, even in sunshine, for a fair share of the available daylight. Except during the release of the lunch hour, artificial light ruled our labours.

Somewhat akin to those sackcloth-secret night clubs, where the proverbially whispered 'Joe sent me' admits the stranger to the furtive frolic beyond, the front door of the office, with its impassive air of mercantile gloom, gave nothing away.

The venturer's goal in this case, however, lay not on a sensual dance floor or at a shaded gaming table, but in eastward flowing sea lanes that had as their staging-post the shadow of the Shwedagon Pagoda and as their destinations the teak forests, the paddy fields and the Native States of what must then have been one of the choicest places on earth—the land of Burma.

The London office was staffed by three cadres, so distinct as often to be self-identifying on the briefest appraisal.

The senior managerial chairs were the preserve of the *Bo-gyis*, men who, having completed an oriental stint of twenty-five years or more, had returned home as departmental managers, with a possible directorship as their remaining goal. The hallmarks of these demi-gods tended to be the Burma cheroot, a duodenal ulcer and a habit of attending funerals of Eastern contemporaries who had died from one or other of these causes. By and large they were good men to work under—tolerant and encouraging of those who were destined to follow their own chosen path.

At the other end of the scale were the 'trainees', young men, mostly from public schools, who, with or without a clear idea of what they were letting themselves in for, had been actuated by a desire for many years of tropical exile when they joined the House of Steel. It followed that many of this band fell by the wayside for one reason or another— one in favour of the life of a professional wrestler—before climbing the gangway at Liverpool. Of twenty-three awaiting passage at the time I joined only seven actually sailed.

Midway between these poles was the permanent 'Secretariat', men with no taste for voyaging but content with home service for the period of their working lives. These were not without their own realms of ambition: the best of them could look forward in time to becoming office managers, company secretaries and so on. Their attitude towards the juniors was generally one of firmly benevolent overlordship that lasted until the latter's first leave, when a gloss of maturity in the exile balanced or overweighted the scales. Those who stood to me in this relationship were of the generation that provided the air raid wardens and ambulance drivers in London's hour of need not many years ahead, and inevitably some of them did not survive.

So varied a staff could not be without its characters. Old Walter Frames, whom we used to bait mercilessly, unfailingly put us to shame when we sailed for Rangoon by presenting each of us with a copy of *The Pilgrim's Progress*. Willie Milne, under whose expert tutelage I learnt to express opinions on rice samples once a week, suffered fools more gladly and spoke more slowly and distinctly than any other man I have known. Sam Shelley had his eternal tip for the three-thirty, which was conveyed to the Chairman in the same raucous whisper as used to jar the humblest of us—interested or not. These are but three of the many whose contributions to the tapestry of Steels must continue discernible while memory of them remains.

Entry to Steels was usually the outcome of a personal introduction. A preliminary to the round of directorial interviews was a written exam for which one 'sat' in the Board Room. The only question that I can recall is—'What are the four main ports of Burma?' Down went Rangoon and then, ten pen-sucking minutes later, I remembered that the summons to the ordeal was in my pocket and that the letter-head catalogued the lot.

The interviews usually took the form of a brusque questioning of short duration, since reminiscence tended to take over at an early stage. It was then left to the candidate to interject monosyllabic indications of interested attention into a tale, it may be, of what happened in Bhamo in 1910.

The interviews over, one was passed on to the Company's medical adviser who, as might be expected, was himself an ex-Eastern hand. Old Spence's craggy Scottish eyebrows dropped lower and lower down his brow as he thumped and prodded my torso.

'D'ye smoke?' he asked with an air of doom.

'No Sir,' I replied truthfully.

(A tragic case of unsuspected TB?)

'Wull, that's a pity—for theer are the cheroots and theer the cigarettes.'

Collapse of fear-crazed party!

And so, on 1 February 1932, at a salary of eighty pounds a year, I took my seat in the Rice Department under the guardian eye of George Stanwyx, who for two years was to coach me in the distinguishing of Medaung Super from Kanoungtoe Loonzain. That this agricultural training was

21

to bear little relevance to my subsequent posting to the Burma oilfields was nothing unusual. On an Eastern vacancy occurring, shall we say, in the Rice Department, the senior trainee would be sent off to fill it, regardless of what department had been his in London.

My princely salary, over thirty pounds of which went on rail fares, was supplemented by a luncheon voucher which entitled me to the run of my teeth up to a limit of half-a-crown—first at 'Pimm's' and later at 'The London Tavern'. I don't recall what it was that thrust the first of these eating-houses out of favour but both were later demolished by bombing.

The luncheon voucher scheme is now common—an insurance that lower-paid staff do not skimp on their mid-work sustenance. I have always understood, however, that Steels pioneered the idea. Certainly, we of their number were an envied race apart in both establishments; and the possible permutations and combinations of two-and-sixpence-worth from the menu involved us in weighty discussions and decisions—and a pretty varied fare.

Two or three days a week, after a quick lunch, I used to wander off to listen to organ or string recitals in one or other of the old city churches; or else I would join the throng round one of the speakers on Tower Hill. At the outset my Christian faith was not notably alive, but to this two-year routine, during which time I listened to the preaching of such men as 'Tubby' Clayton, Donald Soper, Tom Savage and Cuthbert Bardsley, I owe as much as to anything else a conviction of Christ that no subsequent shortcomings have ever wholly undermined.

Of the four men I have mentioned, incidentally, the first has become something of a legend in his lifetime, the second a Peer of the Realm and the other two bishops: so my mentors were men of calibre.

It is a strange reflection that an occasional companion in these post-prandial seekings after Truth was later to die a traitor's death. It was hidden from me also that several of those old, history-packed churches were to be destroyed or damaged by the *Luftwaffe*. I would not aspire to the mind of a seer in the times in which we are living.

During this period I boarded with my parents at Guildford, footloose and fancy-free. This state made it the easier for me to continue my education after office hours. The Eastbourne College Mission at Bethnal Green, a course in journalism and story writing at the London Polytechnic, Toc H, Shakespeare at the Old Vic and Sir Henry Wood's Promenade Concerts at the Queen's Hall all combined to ensure that I was ever mindful of the time of the last train home.

Weekends were devoted to bird-watching in the summer (Thursley Common, near Guildford, harboured a range from curlews to Dartford warblers) and in the winter, to rugby football, and the subsequent pub crawl, with the Guildford R.F.C. Every fourth Saturday an office roster system provided me with a full day off. To these long weekends I owe, among other things, my introduction to the Stone Curlew on Swincombe Down near Oxford and to potholing in Yorkshire (a pursuit, however, for which I found a mild claustrophobia disqualified me).

The Stone Curlew, I fear, must long since have fled before the onward march of pylons: but oh! the thrill, after hours of vigil, and during the rotational withdrawal of my companions for lunch in the pub at the foot of the hill, of being the sole witness of the hen warily sidling onto her eggs!

Another occasion was a fruitless search for a pair of ravens that were reputed to be nesting on a Yorkshire crag. This involved me in cliff-climbing well beyond my capability as I had judged it until then. Only the objective drove me onward.

Yet another memory is of a camping-cum-cycling holiday with an old school friend. We included in our itinerary a pilgrimage to Gilbert White's Selborne in Hampshire. The weather was exceptionally warm and I had converted my flannel slacks into shorts by cutting off the legs above the knees with a pair of nail scissors. The result was a curiously serrated garment, wearing which, without any option and at the Vicar's insistence, I took up the offertory at Holy Communion on the Saint's Day that happened to follow that on which we had arrived and pitched our tent above the village.

Gilbert White's memory is perpetuated in his church by a beautiful stained glass window of St Francis and the birds. His lineal successor—our host at breakfast after the service—was a man of wealth and erudition. His house was a marvel of good taste in furnishing, and his library a memorable concentration of the best that man has penned.

The period of preparation for exile, from which these anecdotes are culled, had a curious *interim* quality to it. One avoided anything in the way of long-term commitments and it was well that I suffered no serious romantic attachment. Steels used to sponsor our study of Burmese at the London School of Oriental Languages, and the evening train journey provided an obvious occasion for homework—sometimes to the puzzlement of curious fellow-passengers. Burmese is a language that few Europeans have truly mastered. Old Stewart, who taught us, was an outstanding exception.

A coincidence that was to affect my life in Burma arose out of a sudden enthusiasm for research into the history of my forbears—the Braunds of Bucks Mills in Devon. Having taxed to exhaustion the memories of the older generation of the living who were known to me, as well as the memoirs of some of those who had passed on, I selected from the London Telephone Directory a Mr H. B. L. Braund, Barrister, of Lincolns Inn Fields, as a possible repository of further information.

On the day I set aside for a call on this gentleman I received my marching orders for Rangoon. I abandoned the projected visit in the light of this momentous development, but only until the evening of the same day when, opening the *Evening Standard* in the train, I saw portrayed the said Mr Braund on the occasion of his appointment as a Puisne Judge of the High Court of Rangoon! I 'made my number' without delay, established the precise nature of our relationship, and subsequently was to owe much to the hospitality extended to me in Rangoon by Ben and his wife and daughter.

These stray musings are intended no more than to provide some idea of the memories that were to be mine in Burma: nothing epoch-making or earthshaking; nothing even to rank in importance with other occasions that somehow lost their gilt in retrospect. They survived because they must have had deeper roots, or perhaps because they had a quality of responsiveness to echo in other climes and settings. Whatever it be, they have floated to the surface in fever and in ambush, on shikar and patrol, on broad waterways and mist-shrouded heights, in silent jungle and tangled mangrove swamp—a man's private memories, some of which can haunt but most of which should sustain.

So to shipboard at Dover, in the betraying company of tin trunks and cabin baggage that obviously had never travelled, but which nevertheless conferred on my cross-Channel passage a longer-term import than that of a mere Continental holiday.

Cheshire was already some days southward out of Liverpool. In view of the urgency with which Rangoon had represented the need for a replacement, Steels had insisted on my going by this particular sailing. Hence, to gain time, I had arranged to join the ship at Marseilles.

This device provided the time-honoured vista of the white cliffs as my parting view of England. Released now from the farewells that had been so much harder to say than anticipation had warned, my feet were set, if not precisely upon 'the golden road to Samarkand', at least on a compass course to imagined paths of mystery and independence.

The cliffs dropped astern. The packet bucked to a stiff breeze and to white-capped waters. I was on my way to five and a half years of merchant adventuring.

2 In the shadow of the Shwedagon

June 1934 to October 1934

Cheshire was steaming eastward out of season. In June anybody who could would be travelling westward to the English summer in flight from the Burmese hot weather and monsoon. Hence, with a passenger capacity of over three hundred, we numbered little more than sixty out of Marseilles. Of these about half, mostly of the Sudan Political Service, disembarked at Port Sudan, while from Colombo onwards we were eight, all males!

At Port Said I sought the full treatment, from the 'gulli gulli man' to Simon Arzt. The conjurers were to continue to display their craft at least until Nasser closed the Canal in 1967. I was to see the store, owned by Selfridges at the time of my visit, decline over the years to a tawdry relic of its former glory. On this occasion, however, it provided me with a topi for five shillings and sixpence. This contemporary headgear, likewise, was to suffer virtual extinction during my time out East.

The Suez Canal, of which I had childhood memories, received mention in my letters now for its bird life and for the Anzac Memorial, which impressed me in its sandy solitude. Port Sudan I noted for its welcome swimming pool and a tour in a glass-bottomed boat to view the fantastically coloured life of the coral; the Red Sea for its intense heat— I don't think I ever again knew it so grilling; and the monsoonal run from Cape Guardafui to Colombo for the seasickness that utterly prostrated me.

On arrival at Colombo (my birthplace, incidentally) for an overnight stay, I was met on board by Kenneth Youngman, a relative by marriage, who took me ashore after breakfast and dropped me off at Hirdiramani's on his way to the office. In this famous establishment I was measured for a couple of white drill suits at a cost equivalent to fifteen shillings and ninepence each—'which', as I wrote home, 'seems reasonable enough'. I called back for a fitting after lunch and the suits were delivered to me at Kenneth's chummery that evening! I wonder where such service survives.

Shipboard company from Colombo to Rangoon was monastic and sparse as I have already indicated. I best remember Barrett ('Ba Yit', as he was known to the Burmans) of the Bombay-Burmah Trading Corporation, a colourful character by any reckoning; 'Sugar' Williams, the Editor of the *Rangoon Times*; Ritchie Gardiner of McGregors, a winner of the George Medal in an unsuspected future for his part in a remarkable epic of the trek from Burma to India ahead of the Japanese in 1942; and Major 'Ted' Cartmel of the Burma Frontier Force whom, with even less predictability, I was next to meet as my Commanding Officer for a few months before the Japanese invasion.

It was Ritchie, I think, who introduced me to 'the green flash'—that phenomenon of tropical seas associated with the disappearance behind the horizon of the last sliver of the sun's rim. Though my father had spent many years out East, I had never heard him mention this hoary leg-pull; and I fell like a ton of bricks!

The Bibby ships had deck space flanking the forward hatches that lent itself to a specialized game of skittles, so absorbing as probably to have cost the Line's less fortuitously endowed rival some loss of passenger custom. Traditionally, when our sister-ship *Yorkshire* passed us homeward, we played an inter-ship match. Results were radio'd across at the end of each hand so that the scoreboard on each deck could be kept entered up to the minute. The losers paid for the winners' drinks, and the bill, likewise, was settled by radio (our opponents being many miles astern by this time). We were the winners on this occasion, doubtless because of the unlimited opportunities for practice that our small numbers afforded.

Yorkshire was torpedoed during the war, but *Cheshire* lived on and in later years I found myself astern of her at Port Said. She then wore the garb of a troopship but I imagine that she must have gone to the knacker's yard by now.

Came the day—Saturday, 7 July 1934. We were moving up the Rangoon River, a major artery of the Irrawaddy delta, muddy, studded with floating islets of water hyacinth and as barren of welcome as the featureless banks that were gliding past us. After so much personal build-up, Burma, I felt, should at least have had the red carpet out for me! Even my first glimpse of the Shwedagon Pagoda was something of a disappointment: it looked smaller than I had expected, and drab. The monsoon weather that overhung our approach could do nothing that day for the serene, golden beauty that I was later to seek out and wonder at. Soon came scattered huts, then riverside villages, and isolated sheds of which one but guessed the purpose.

At an increasing tempo the pugmarks of industrialization multiplied, and finally we were edging in to the Sule Pagoda wharves.

My luggage lay on skittle alley awaiting the unloading slings. I paid a last visit to my cabin, ostensibly to make sure that nothing had been left behind, actually to satisfy myself, in front of the mirror, that my topi was set at my idea of a seasoned tilt. Then up on deck as the shore boys piled aboard.

It was probably no more than a happy coincidence that the Bibby ships regularly berthed at about noon on alternate Saturdays. It certainly provided a popular first rung on the ladder of weekend drinking for all who had been nursing a growing thirst during the week. Soon the bar was crowded with a noisy throng of those having occasion, good or nebulous, to come aboard as soon as the gangway was up.

My own reception committee comprised five whom I had known in the London office and who now had variously from six to eighteen months of Burma service behind them. Even six months seemed a long start to a newcomer with five and a half years stretching out ahead.

After a suitable intake of brandy and ginger ale, which seemed to be the fashionable drink for the occasion, I was shepherded ashore, through the Customs and along to the office. Here one of my colleagues made it his business to take me on a hurried round of such *Bo-gyis* as were still at their desks. These included Robert Howison, the General Manager, who welcomed me affably enough and confirmed that I was being posted to the Company's Oil Department, which administered the affairs of its subsidiary, The Indo-Burma Petroleum Company Limited.

Despite my training in the Rice Department, I had done enough 'homework' on I.B.P. to know that their sphere of activity comprised oilfields at Yenangyaung, Lanywa and Indaw. Of these the first two were located one on either side of the Irrawaddy some four hundred river miles north of Rangoon. Indaw, much further north yet, was up the Chindwin, remote, difficult of access and notoriously malarious. It was to contribute much to my experience of life in due course. At Seikkyi, some miles down-river from Rangoon, stood the Company's Refinery, which processed the crude oil from the Fields. One day I was to see it die.

Rangoon itself was the base for the marketing organization in Burma while in India there were marketing branches and filling installations at Calcutta, Bombay and Chittagong. An ocean-going tanker, the *Shwedagon*, completes a brief picture of the framework of the organization.

From the mild inquisition of introductions I was conducted to the top floor of the office, where were accommodated in a chummery the six most junior Assistants stationed in Rangoon. A board at the front door proclaimed the name of the establishment 'Merry Helenside'; but somewhere along the road the joke had palled for it was more commonly known as 'Office House Chummery' or even 'Office House'. The accommodation comprised six horse boxes, a communal dining room and a lounge, plus the usual 'offices'. The horse boxes surrounded a well giving a view of the departmental floors below: in some cases individual residents were able to gauge from on high the volume of telegrams awaiting decoding on their own desks early in the morning.

29

The furniture was sparse and advisedly of poor quality, since it tended to require replacement on Mondays that followed a Saturday evening party. This accommodation was conspicuously sub-standard, and would have been rejected out of hand by any to whom it was offered in the post-war era. At the time of which I write, however, Eastern jobs were regarded as glamorous and were certainly more easily lost than secured: it was a case, therefore, of 'beggars can't be choosers'.

My initial companions in this eyrie were those who had met me aboard *Cheshire*, save that one of them, by my arrival, had been elevated to 'another place', to wit Kandawgalay House, the senior chummery, widely known—even beyond Burma—as 'the Gin Palace'.

When someone comes to write, as someone surely should, of the role of the chummery in Britain's commercial tenure of the East, 'the Gin Palace' can undoubtedly claim title to pride of place. It was indeed a notable establishment. Built in recent times, and specifically for the purpose, it provided on three floors bachelor accommodation for eighteen of Steels' junior Assistants. Each quarter was self-contained and the communal rooms were well appointed. The grounds were spacious and included tennis courts. The building stood outside the hubbub of the bazaar and was everything that 'Office House' was not. It sheltered some memorable characters in any sense of the adjective. It also earned its measure of notoriety as readers of Maurice Collis's *Trials in Burma* will recall. The parties that those walls have witnessed they must be re-echoing yet! *Eheu fugaces!*

The gulf between 'the Gin Palace' and 'Office House' was wide and significant. None from the latter might visit the former without invitation.

Steels' insistence on their staff becoming proficient in the languages of the country—and in Rangoon this meant Urdu to start with, since the Burmese were then a minority in their own capital—carried a veto on ownership of a car or membership of any club until the Government exam in colloquial Urdu had been passed—and that within six months! This fence cleared, you were allowed to join one club in which, even then, it was politic not be to seen with such frequency as to suggest that your cramming for the Lower Burmese Commercial exam (which included the written script) was less than 'flat out', since this had to be passed within two years. Verily the shades of the prison house heavily overhung the junior domain!

This rigorous exclusion from the leisure pursuits that the normal heart desired was defensible in its design but occasionally near-tragic in its results. Barred from the company of their kind—and none but Steels were as exacting in this respect—young men with normal social appetites and interests were thrown back on avenues of questionable entertainment when it came to the weekend let-down from hours of work that are no longer countenanced as normal anywhere. Most survived the experience and in the long term, possibly, benefited from it. Some did not.

One of my earlier Saturday evening crawls round Rangoon's seamier haunts involved a meeting at a bar with an elderly Scot. Temporarily I had become separated from my guides and guardians and here he was, next to me, gazing moodily into his drink. He was an old *koi hai* all right, with embattled features, and cheeks that invited a probe with a forefinger to see if the whisky would seep out. His choice of habitat and his general appearance shed no light on his eligibility or otherwise for club membership. He looked like a man who would have scorned the notion of applying. Suddenly and gruffly he introduced himself. Gratified, I reciprocated.

'Ye've juist arraived?' he asked.

'Yes Sir.'

'An' whoor ye with?'

'Steel Brothers, Sir.'

'Steel Brothers! Steel Brothers! Aye, they're a michty fine furrm. Ye'll find the furrst thurrty years are the wurrst.'

And here he reverted to his crystal ball; he did not speak again!

The magnificence of the observation never left me. Thirty years later, on the anniversary of my arrival in Burma, still with Steels but elsewhere by a couple of thousand miles, I threw a party to celebrate my release from the old man's conception of bondage. As guest of honour, alas, he was present only in the shadows.

It should not be thought, however, that our restricted role in the social scheme of things necessarily left no doors open to a wider sphere. Some found them by fortuitous advantage; by some they had to be ventured; by others they were not sought. I was fortunate in my new-found and well-placed second cousin, Ben, who showed me hospitality in Rangoon on a number of occasions. Through him I came to know that I had in Burma another second cousin in the person of Billy Rivers, a former regular officer of the Burma Rifles and now manager of a large private grant of paddy land near Pegu. I was soon to meet him, and he and his wife, Judy, were very good to me on a number of occasions. I have kept in touch with them ever since.

In the Rangoon office itself I received a helping hand from 'Bill' Matthew, the Manager of the Shipping Department, a bachelor, and, like me, an Old Eastbournian (though of widely separated generations). Bill was a rare character. Upright, philanthropic and the soul of integrity, he was said by an earlier General Manager to have failed to rise higher than he did because of his insistence on trying to run his department on Church of England principles. There are worse epitaphs!

Bill had a happy knack of inviting a number of young people to a party at the Gymkhana Club, and disappearing as soon as they had all taken to the dance floor.

I became a regular worshipper at the Anglican Cathedral, to which fact I owe, though a little later in the story, a close but short-lived association with 'Stooky' Seagrim (later G.C., D.S.O., M.B.E.), that remarkable man who is unlikely to be displaced as 'the most unforgettable character I have ever met'. His immortal wartime story of valour in isolation and self-sacrificial death has been enshrined for posterity in Ian Morrison's *Grandfather Longlegs*.

'Stooky' and a brother officer used to motor-cycle in from Mingaladon Cantonment to Evensong. As often as not, after the service, they would come back to my rooms for a drink

MAP OF BURMA showing locations of Maps Numbers 2, 3 & 4

CENTRAL BURMA

and sometimes a bite of food. In my copy of *Grandfather Longlegs* I have this pencilled note:

'. . . we always got involved in discussion, sometimes religious, sometimes not, but usually serious—despite which, Stooky's manner of arguing promoted laughter sooner or later.'

He was a dynamic, infectious character; and, had he survived the war, there is little doubt that he would have carried out his oft-declared intention of leaving the Army and becoming a missionary in Burma.

Having been a member of Toc H in England, I joined the Rangoon Branch—at this time somewhat riven by an influx of Oxford Groupers, to whose philosophy likewise I was no stranger, though reserving my adherence. Here, in due course, I met John Hedley and Victor Morton, two more who were to influence me in their various ways.

Of the newly-commissioned John, in 1941, a fellow officer-cadet prophesied to me, 'That madman will either be killed or win a D.S.O.' The colourful manner in which he achieved the latter is well told by John Masters in *The Road past Mandalay*. Victor, to describe whom is to define the word 'gentleman', died as second-in-command of 'The Glosters' while trying to clear a Japanese road block on the Prome Road in 1942. His wife, Joan, co-opted as a G.H.Q. cipher clerk, had been flown out a few days earlier. With her had gone Victor's valuable collection of Burmese butterflies, which tipped the scales at what she was permitted to take out in the way of personal luggage.

Steels' office, and 'Office House' with it, fronted on to Merchant Street in the commercial heart of the city. The environs were noisy and odious, and even to go for a walk in the evening involved begging or hiring a lift to and from a reasonably salubrious starting-point. The noise you could not exclude, noise incessant and varied, dropping perhaps to a near-lull in the very early hours of the morning, but reviving with the dawn chorus of expectorations to a crescendo that mocked that last hour of potential sleep, by which time the crows had taken over anyway. Of one of many such clamorous occasions, somewhat immaturely perhaps, I wrote:

... this evening a tremendous rabble lurched past in a procession in honour of some wretched food festival. They were banging on gongs, tins, pots and drums and blowing through bugles and weird looking trumpets, clattering cymbals and castanets, and all the while shrieking and chattering like monkeys.

and of another:

... the building opposite our windows, and only about thirty feet away, has hitherto been untenanted: but now it has been taken by a wealthy broker who moved in yesterday with seemingly ten or twelve wives and Heaven alone knows how many children. Last night at about 11.30, just as we were pushing off to bed, this platoon of wives set up a sort of wailing chant to the gods, calling down health and strength on their lord and master. At 1.00 or 2.00 a.m. I dropped off to sleep through sheer weariness, although the racket was still going on, and at 5.00 a.m. I was woken up by it!

Hours of work I have referred to. Typically they were 6.00 to 8.30 or 9.00 a.m. followed by bath, shave and breakfast. Then from 10.00 a.m. to 5.30 p.m. or later, with a fifteen-minute break for a snack lunch. Saturdays differed only to the extent that it was a bad day if you stayed as late as 5.30 p.m., while on Sundays 7.00 to 10.00 a.m. was the normal.

To start with I had a somewhat obscure time as Assistant in charge of I.B.P. stores purchasing. Owing to the reshuffle occasioned by 'Kep' Brown's untimely death, the desk had been unoccupied for several weeks prior to my arrival. Thus there was no one from whom to take over in the normal manner and I had to depend heavily on a forbidding, betel-chewing Hindu head clerk whose attitude was clearly one of distaste for his task!

The Sunday office session tended to terminate with a descent on 'Office House' by such denizens of 'the Gin Palace' as had nothing better planned for the morning. They would bring a generous supply of beer with them, but the closure was seldom applied until late in the afternoon, by which time our stocks had been exhausted also.

Rugby football was the saving grace of my early months in Burma. I wrote home:

This Rugger business is the first inconsistency I have struck in Steels. Punctually at 5.15 on match days R. B. Howison takes his seat on the touchline, and if there are only fourteen Steels men on the field, next time the team list comes round the office there is a sarcastic footnote on the subject of unpunctuality. If the choice lies between Rugger and an urgent telegram—then the telegram can wait.

The fact is that Steels took the greatest pride in being the only merchant firm East of Suez that regularly, twice weekly during the rainy season, put its own fifteen into the field. Elsewhere the enthusiast could turn out for his Gymkhana Club or for 'the Civil' or 'the Military' or for 'the Planters'; but we played for Steels. Any trophies that we won stood in 'the Gin Palace', not anonymously behind a club bar.

Even the most dedicated adversary of anything that might offend the god of unstinted hard work might be seen slipping unobtrusively away from his desk on match days in time to be at the ground for the kick-off. Since the Rangoon Gymkhana provided the playing field, compromise had to be—and was—found to overcome the disability of non-membership of the Gym. of those of us who were still struggling with Urdu. We were made rugby-playing members, with the right to a hot shower and a quick shandy before we returned to the blighting company of our *munshis*, the Indian language teachers.

Playing time, normally, was twenty minutes each way, this being extended to twenty-five minutes for tournaments or major matches and half an hour for finals. In that climate it was enough!

I was admirably suited by all this. Rugby is the only game I have ever played well and I soon found myself an automatic choice for England in the Burma International series and for Steels first seven in the Seven-a-Side Tournament. I had my fill of the game and it kept me fit and reconciled to deprivations in other directions. One of the fifteens playing in my first year was the King's Royal Rifle Corps, stationed at Mingaladon some miles out of Rangoon. The leader of their pack, with whom I often rubbed shoulders in the literal sense, was John Hunt of Everest fame to come.

Little more than two months after my arrival in the country, the time came to select the Burma fifteen for the

All-India Tournament, to be played that year in Calcutta. Though I learnt early that my name was on the list of those required, I had no thought of being given permission to go. It was unheard-of in one so newly arrived and would be straining managerial enthusiasm too far, even though I had just skidded through my Urdu exam.

Perhaps this latter counted; perhaps it was because there was only one other Steels representative making the trip; perhaps it was because the decision to transfer me away from the rugger playing scene had already been taken, and this was recognized as possibly my only opportunity. Whichever it was, my inclusion was approved by Howison, though against the scandalized advice of Gordon Nicoll, the Manager of I.B.P., who left me in no doubt about his views on the matter before I sailed!

We left for Calcutta towards the end of September in the British-India Steam Navigation Company's *Ekma*. As soon as we cleared the Rangoon River we ran into wild seas; and by the time I got on to my feet as we sailed up the Hooghly three days later, my stomach for rugger had gone the way of my attempts to keep food down; and I was cursing the dispensation that had allowed me to make the trip. What a revolting affliction seasickness is! However, I was bludgeoned into parading for the last of a series of daily PT sessions which a surprising number of my team-mates had attended regularly.

We were met on docking by a fair-sized crowd, which included my host for the duration of our stay, a young banker of about my own age. He drove me to his chummery for tiffin and some badly needed sleep, and in the evening took me along to a mammoth cocktail party that had been laid on to enable all the visiting teams to meet and mingle before doing battle.

The following morning, Monday, I reported at I.B.P's Calcutta office where, among the British staff of four, I already knew one who had been with me in the London office and had been posted to Calcutta a month or two before I sailed for Rangoon. Thence I hunted out Frank Preston, who for two years had been a fellow traveller of mine on the seven-fifty from Guildford to Waterloo; and Reggie Youngman, an elder brother of Kenneth in Colombo. The East in those days was an astonishing network.

In the afternoon we kicked a ball about in preparation for our first match on the morrow. And here a word about the Tournament is called for.

The 'All-India' of those days was held by rotation in Calcutta, Bombay and Madras, with Colombo added at some later date. The official programme provided this historical note.

Rugby is not indigenous to India and we have never yet discovered that it possessed any playing interest for Indians as a whole. The game is imported and was played originally and exclusively by players whose sojourn in the country was but temporary. But it has made steady and remarkable progress during the half-century that men have been chasing the elusive ball across the greensward of India and in a climate that could hardly be deemed suitable for so strenuous a game ... Their efforts have been rewarded in so far as their example has brought into being a number of local clubs and thus an Indian tradition has been built up.

One may say there are now two main nurseries of indigenous rugger and they are located in Bombay and Khargpur. In the former place the Cathedral High School provided a fine training ground for youngsters who have found their way later on into other clubs and in the result a flourishing old boys' team has been a factor in Western India rugger for some years. Khargpur owes its record to the keenness and enthusiasm of one or two men who have turned the talent of the railway settlement to good purpose. From small beginnings Khargpur can now field several fifteens and the Bengal Nagpur Railway team always provides Calcutta's best with strong opposition. Acting on the example of Khargpur other local teams have sprung up in Calcutta, and the Customs, Police, la Martinere and other local fifteens are evidence of the good work of the original pioneers of the game in India.

Still the 'All-India' survives. Sooner or later, I fear, it must die for lack of regular playing contact with its source. With it will go one of those minor but wholesome repudiations of the 'never the twain shall meet' philosophy; for Ceylonese in particular, Indians and Burmans were progressively being attracted into the game.

On the present occasion nineteen teams had entered and, by customary procedure, the four with the furthest to travel had been 'seeded' into the last eight, to reduce to a reasonable minimum the duration of their absence from home. The four so treated were Madras, Cawnpore, Bombay and Burma (we, incidentally, being the only side to travel by sea).

Our first match was against the Bengal-Nagpur Railway, which had possibly the heaviest pack I have ever played against. They ran us off our feet to begin with and we were soon five points down. However, we then took a lasting grip and ended as winners. Our semi-final encounter was with the Duke of Wellington's Regiment, which had already beaten two strong sides in the Durham Light Infantry and Bombay. We lost an excellent game by three points to eight, both 'The Duke's' tries being scored by their centre three-quarter captain, Lieutenant Moran, by the sale of superb dummies. In the final 'The Duke's' went down to a Calcutta side of such talent as could seriously have challenged the best of Britain's club sides of that year.

My time in Calcutta off the rugger field was variously spent. I.B.P's Manager took me down-river one morning to look over the Company's installation at Budge Budge. Here I watched four-gallon cans being manufactured for the packing and distribution of *Shwedagon's* cargo throughout Eastern India.

Part of my childhood up to the age of seven had been spent in Calcutta. We lived in Camack Street as ground-floor tenants of our landlord, Eric Studd, who lived above us. All these years later he was still there. I had intended to call on him anyway, but was flattered and strengthened in my resolve when I heard that he had recognized my name among the invaders and had been inquiring for me. The door was opened to me by the selfsame butler—a real patriarch now—as we had known as kids. Eric himself was very pleased that I had called. His name was a household word in Calcutta for his many-sided philanthropy. He came of a remarkable family: one brother, C.T., who captained Cambridge University at cricket and played for England, was of the 'Cambridge Seven', that distinguished band of cricket, rowing and football 'Blues' who collectively made the China Mission Field their life. Another brother, Kynaston, became Lord Mayor of London. Eric possessed the qualities of both in notable measure. There is no conflict between commerce and Christianity when men of his calibre stride the market place.

During the few days left to us after our defeat by 'The Duke's' we were off training, and life was a round of unstinted hospitality by the rugger devotees of Calcutta. We were entertained in a seemingly unbroken circuit of cocktail parties, dinners and dances, culminating in the All-India Rugger Dinner at the Great Eastern Hotel, a memorable debauch with countless repercussions all round the town during the next few hours.

I recall in particular the fate of a member of the Madras side, a character with enormous 'Jimmy Edwards' moustaches. Unknown to himself, of course, a prize had been offered to whomsoever produced the largest portion of his whiskers after midnight. The unsuspecting victim was closely but unobtrusively trailed by quite a crowd of contestants until, as midnight struck, he went down to his doom before a horrific display of drawn penknives and nail scissors!

We sailed back to Rangoon in the *Ellenga* on the morning after the dinner. Our departure was delayed briefly while two members of our team were located and carried aboard, dinner-jacketed and inert. As we drew away, a rugger ball was passed between shore and ship until distance ensured its watery grave. The return journey to Rangoon was no happier for me than the outward trip had been. This time, however, no one displayed the least interest in my powers of recuperation and I was left alone to my misery.

I was hardly ashore in Rangoon when I received the startling news that the staff programme had had another working over, as a result of which I was required to leave for Lanywa in forty-eight hours on long-term transfer. This left me less than no time for all that I had to do before I could get away—including two brutal sessions in a dentist's chair—and I felt very ill-equipped as I was seen off on the night train for Prome. Not the least of my worries, the result of my passing the Urdu exam, was that I had paid off my Hindu 'bearer' and replaced him with a Burmese *lugalay* without time even to get to know the newcomer. However, he appeared to know the ropes and there was little I could do but place myself in his hands.

My 'Office House' companions on the station platform dropped out of sight, and soon the train was straining for the darkness of the Burmese countryside and the unknown.

3 The Burma Oilfields

October 1934 to May 1935

The train journey I was now making had something in common with my overland short-cut to Marseilles to intercept *Cheshire* from Liverpool. The Irrawaddy Flotilla Company's river steamer, which I was to board at the railhead at Prome, was already on its way up from Rangoon with such passengers, if any, as had the leisure to extend their trip in this delightful way. Usually they would be tourists or residents of Rangoon taking a lazy cruising holiday. On this occasion there were none but an American driller and his wife and child returning from leave. Actually I had been a fellow-passenger with them in the *Ellenga* from Calcutta but, for reasons that I need not repeat, I had been in no condition then to make their acquaintance.

I was the sole first class boarder at Prome, so we were a small party in the saloon when we moved off soon after daybreak. As travelling companions between decks, of course, there was a noisy, heterogeneous throng of two or three hundred of the peasantry going about their various occasions.

The trip up-river had an enchantment for me that I was never to lose. Nothing was hurried. The day's run was short, allowing plenty of time at the ports of call for barter, family reunions, meals ashore, bathing and a babel of conversation that never flagged. In the saloon beer was drunk, meals were consumed, books toyed with, and one's feet spent most of the time tucked into the rail at about eye-level.

Typically the scenery was a backdrop of hills, to a mid-stage of teak or *indaing* jungle, and a foreground at the water's edge of palms, mango and banana trees, irregularly disposed to accommodate groups of stilted dwellings. Always, on peak or promontory, there would be the graceful beauty of the pagodas, most of them a dazzling whitewash against the green, a few gold-leafed and gleaming in the sunshine. Sometimes there would be an open stretch of paddy, with water buffaloes and small boys in attendance providing the only movement. At other times, dependent on hour of day, or time of year, or slack or flood season, it wouldn't look like that at all. It really was a stage, subject to a theatre's every change of scenery. No matter how often you travelled, there was never a sense of repetition but always of unpredictable variety.

We tied up for the night at Sinbaungwe, a small village midway between the larger centres of Allanmyo and Magwe. Our day's run had been about a hundred miles.

Over the years I was to know and delight in many nights like this when, moored alongside a jetty or a steep embankment, I became for twelve hours or so an appendage to a Burmese village, or something akin to a nomadic caravan dweller who camps alongside his kind at dusk but moves on with the dawn.

While daylight lasted, the air would be filled with the strident cries of domestic commerce, the cheerfulness of exchanged greetings, the angry protests against obstruction that came from over-laden coolies staggering ashore along spring-board gangplanks, and the shrieked criticism, ridicule and advice flung into the ring gratis by a band of slate-carrying school children, who had interrupted their home-ward way to squat down in a line along the top of the bank to enjoy the free entertainment.

As night fell, not suddenly but progressively, the children would depart, unloading would cease, and friendly reunions would be transferred to distant hearthside bowls of rice. The clamour of noise would give place to the symphony of sound.

Gradually the ear would attune to the lap of current-borne waters against the hull and to the undisturbing thud of a tautening hawser. From afar a gong would ring out with benediction from a *phongyi-chaung*, firmly launched, but quavering to a dying fall that the senses followed even beyond full silence. From the top of the embankment you might hear the 'plop' of an expectoration that followed the sudden lowering of a glowing cheroot; the persuasive argument countering ridicule at the suggested price of a few bags of rice or a water buffalo; the low, provocative laughter of illicit flirtation; the slurred imprecations of drinking gamblers; the song and music that betokened a household celebration; and, from further afield perhaps, the ribald acclamation that greeted a particularly bawdy passage of a *pwe*.

As a listener to all this, reclining, bathed, full-shirted and trousered against the mosquitoes, in a long-sleeve chair in the prow of the ferry with a drink on the deck beside me, I would be contemplating the pathway of moonlight seemingly resisting the flow of the waters. Every now and then it might liven to the silent intersection of a dug-out gliding down with the current. Overhead would be the stars, and in the air the aroma of spices and the allure of frangipani. Sometimes there would be the company of one of my kind, to whom I warmed the more he kept silent. More often I would be learning to live alone and discovering the magic of it.

Sailing early in the morning from Sinbaungwe, we reached Yenangyaung, the hub of the oilfields, early in the afternoon. Here my American companions disembarked and I carried on alone. Some of the wells were clearly visible from the river, and I can recall vividly my first contemplation of pumpers 'on the beam'. From afar they looked like the solution to perpetual motion and, even on such scanty evidence, I scented that I was entering upon one of life's more fascinating and unpredictable occupations.

As night fell, a blaze of lights up-river proclaimed our approach to Chauk and Lanywa on the east and west banks respectively. Had I been told that somewhere along the line we had gone about and were approaching Rangoon again I would have had little to dispute, for any oilfield, anywhere, is nothing if not well lit.

We pulled into Chauk for the night after dark. My impatience to get on to Lanywa and journey's end was allayed by the arrival alongside of I.B.P's launch *Cicala* to

take me across forthwith. On board were Wilfred ('Hutch')
Hutchinson, whom I was to relieve, and Bill Grant, the
Assistant Drilling Superintendent. In a few minutes my
luggage had been transhipped and we were away. If I had
thought to satisfy my immediate interest in the scene by a
barrage of questioning, I was beaten to it by the cross-fire I
encountered on the subject of the All-India Rugger Tournament, which obviously had not lacked for enthusiastic
followers in these parts.

The run across and up to Lanywa took us about forty
minutes. The river here, some four hundred miles from
Rangoon, is still two to three miles wide and we were
pushing against the current. Disembarking at Lanywa,
almost at the foot of a drilling rig but with no encouragement
to linger, I was hustled off by 'Hutch' to his bungalow for a
quick bath and change, and thence to Bill Grant's where the
latter, in the absence of his wife in England, was modestly
celebrating his wedding anniversary. The fourth for the
party was my new *Bo-gyi*, Armour McGilvray. (I never did
learn whence came his only and improbable Christian name
but as he was never known as anything but 'Mac' the
question did not arise.)

There was little ceremony but, once again, this time for
Mac's benefit, I had to give a ploy-by-ploy account of the
matches in Calcutta. The Burma Press had done me proud
over that trip; my listeners knew nothing of my inability to
leave my bunk either way, so I was accepted as having hair
on my chest from the day of my arrival—which helped!

I was frequently to cross trails with these three men in the
years ahead. 'Mac' was a Scot of the Scottish: red-haired (or
at any rate haloed) and massively eye-browed, with a
forbidding countenance (the Burmese knew him as the 'Red
Dragon') that nevertheless had a delightful way of crumpling
into mirth; and he was a demon for work. He and Mrs 'Mac',
whom I was soon to meet, were the kind of people a mother
in England, fearing for the fate of her twenty-year-old in
'Darkest Burma', would be relieved to know had charge
of him.

Grant was a London Scot, artificially polished, capable,

self-confident, generous, helpful and bombastic. 'Hutch' was an Englishman, sincere, conscientious, impeccably mannered and aching for his second leave next year when he was due to be married. I could have fared worse for company.

Lanywa, of which I obtained my first daylight view next morning, was originally an insignificant riverside village, prompted as to location by a break in the line of low sandstone cliffs created by a scouring sweep of the Irrawaddy. The village lies within Burma's dry zone, which cuts a wide swathe across the waist of the country and embraces all the Irrawaddy oilfields. Gone was the jungled panorama I had absorbed from the river steamer coming up from Prome. Here now were cactus and scrub trees such as survived on an annual diet of twenty to thirty inches of rain, most of which fell in a brief monsoon season in May and June.

The oilfield was unique. It had long been the thesis of the I.B.P. geologists that the oil-bearing structure lay wholly under the Irrawaddy, either as an extension of the Chauk Field, which the Burmah Oil Company was developing successfully on the east bank, or as an independent anticline. This interpretation was rejected by the B.O.C. geologists, the chief of whom is alleged to have undertaken to drink every drop of oil the I.B.P. got out of Lanywa!

As far back as 1913 the I.B.P. theory had been tested by the drilling of a well on a sandbank exposed during the low-water season. This well had not reached the postulated oil-bearing horizon before the river rose and called a halt to operations for that year. Then disaster struck when a river craft ran foul of and carried away the well-head, causing the Government to place a ban on any renewed attempt at off-shore drilling not backed by what were bound to be very costly protective measures.

So, after the first World War, the I.B.P. fell back on an inevitably less attractive alternative and drilled five wells above the high water mark. Of these the first yielded a small, non-commercial quantity of oil and the fifth some gas from a deeper horizon. These unprofitable results, nevertheless, were enough to steel the Company's resolve to drill off-shore again despite the cost of the protective works insisted upon.

The measure adopted took the form of a guide wall built out into the river from the mainland along the outer edge of the inshore sandbanks. The top of the wall had to be higher than the highest recorded rise of the river, and the whole strong enough to withstand the full force of the river in flood. None without experience of a major river in spate can appreciate the magnitude of such an undertaking.

The project was submitted to the vetting of the highest engineering talent before it received Government approval. The design required a wall a hundred and fifty feet wide at the base, forty-five feet high and fifteen feet broad at the crown. Protection of the weather slope called for a minimum thickness of two and a half feet of heavy stone facing and, running out from the toe of the embankment, an apron of stone one hundred feet wide by four feet thick. Construction started in the low-water season of 1925-1926 with a labour force of five thousand, and the original length of five thousand feet took three low-water seasons to complete. The cost was about a million pounds sterling, which in those days represented a gamble of frightening proportions.

Fortune favoured the brave, however, and I.B.P's seventh well struck oil in a manner that set all doubts at rest. Four subsequent extensions of the wall carried it to a total length of over two miles, but the original construction had so denuded the near countryside of suitable stone that the extensions were faced with bricks burnt in an immense brickyard established at Lanywa for the purpose. The bricks measured twelve by twelve by six inches and, as far as was known, were the biggest bricks ever burnt for any occasion. Ultimately the wall shielded from the flow of the river something over a hundred oil wells.

To begin with, of course, the wells were still being drilled in water exposed to the rise and fall of the river. The wall diverted the flow: it did not dam it. As they were completed they were connected by walkways, while the concomitant paraphernalia of tank batteries, pumping stations, power sub-stations and so on were likewise 'waterborne'. A decision followed, therefore, to fill in the area behind the wall. To this end a diesel-electric dredger, the *Margaret*, was bought and, over many seasons, achieved an area of reclamation that embraced even the outliers of the oil wells and permitted a network of roads that brought every corner of the Field within easy motorable compass. For its day the whole project was a magnificent feat of engineering and the completed cost was about five million pounds.

The guide wall, though it started almost at right angles to the river bank, had had to follow a curving course that finally brought it nearly parallel with it. For all that it had made possible, therefore, the wall had narrowed the flowing width of the Irrawaddy to only a small degree—by something less than twenty per cent in fact. Nothing more was technically possible in this direction. Thus most of Lanywa's oil still lay under the river and its recovery called for some other technique.

This took the form of a line of wells drilled along the top of the wall itself and deliberately inclined from the vertical so that they 'bottomed' at considerable distances out under the river. Fortunately the nature of the formation favoured inclined drilling and, with the aid of special equipment, ultimate deviations of up to seventy degrees from the vertical were obtained.

Even this still left much to go for and, had the second World War not intervened, there is no knowing which of various improbable-sounding courses might not have been explored seriously. Even shaft mining as distinct from drilling had its advocates.

When I arrived in Lanywa all was being got ready for the penultimate extension of the guide wall, while *Margaret* was already hard at work consolidating what had been gained by the previous season's extension.

The overseas staff at Lanywa numbered about twenty. 'Mac' had charge as Field Agent (the conventional term in Burma for an administrative manager on the oilfields). There were about half a dozen drillers, some of them Americans, and about as many engineers. A civil engineer had charge of the guide wall construction, and there were a resident geologist and a petroleum technologist. The stores superintendent and I, as assistant agent, provided the tail.

At any given time something less than half the number would have their wives with them and usually there were up to half a dozen children.

Lanywa was isolated in the sense that no motorable roads left it. Our 'metropolis' was Chauk on the other side of the river. Here the B.O.C. worked one of its more prolific oil-fields, and an Anglo-American community of about a hundred and fifty went with it. The amenities included a church, a hospital, a club—with a twice-weekly film show—a swimming pool, a golf course, and cricket, football and hockey according to season. A good motorable road led to Yenangyaung, forty-five miles to the south, where there was an even larger community, and polo as an additional pursuit if you were that ambitious.

Transport between Lanywa and Chauk was provided by I.B.P's two launches, *Lawtha* and *Cicala*, which ran at fixed times, with no more than ten minutes grace allowed for latecomers. An involuntary night on the wrong shore was the likely price to be paid for that last 'one for the road'!

The principal extra-curricular activity for 'Hutch' at Lanywa had been for some months the creation of a nine-hole golf course on wholly unpromising terrain. Grass there was as an occasional phenomenon: mostly it was stony soil and cactus. The greens were 'browns', surfaced with a compound of sand and 'tank bottoms', the vernacular for petroleum sludge. Local rules proliferated of stark necessity, since no ball was ever likely to come to rest in a playable lie.

Chaungs fissured the fairways and, where they plunged down to the river, it was possible for a pulled tee shot to bound for half a mile or more before coming to rest on the sand of the foreshore. It is at least possible that the most devastating of these deviations established a world record for distance travelled from the tee—even though it assured beyond question the loss of the hole and the ball.

The completion of this creative task I inherited when 'Hutch' left for the Chindwin. It was to my advantage, I think, that I had no previous knowledge of the game or of the minimum attributes of a golf course. What my borrowed labour thought of it all I can only guess. They used to carve

The Rangoon Gymkhana Club
Lanywa—The Guide Wall

Views of Popa
Burmese Girl and Hamadryad

out fairways and tamp down 'browns' with impassive mien. At least I did not have to bother with bunkers: they were the provision of Nature in abundance.

In its completed form, the golf course provided an amenity that transformed the leisure life of the 'camp'. The most unlikely candidates for initiation progressively made an appearance, club in hand, on the first tee. The cost of the venture raised the eyebrows of neither accountant nor auditor: it was 'lost', a drop in the mammoth bucket of expenditure on the guide wall; and the benefit to morale must have made it cheap at the price.

Tennis was less of an excavatory problem. We had two or three cement courts, one of them floodlit; and, as a minimum commitment, I took over 'Hutch's place in a seriously contested weekly four.

Bird life abounded. I remember the fascination of the first moonlit night when I lay abed listening to the 'tonk tonk' of that strange night watchman, the Coppersmith. Soon I was patiently locating the nests of the Little and River Terns that bred on the sandbanks in the river, and delighting in the aerobatics of the Bee-Eaters that I could watch from the verandah of my bungalow. These were but a few of many.

For all this colourful curriculum I received a 'jungle allowance' that increased my emoluments by about a third! The systematic study of Burmese, however, I found to be much less easy than in Rangoon. There was no dearth of office clerks keen to earn a few extra rupees by coming up to the bungalow for an hour or two in the evening, but their teaching methods were far removed from those of the seasoned practitioners available in Rangoon, and I found this aspect of my liabilities very tough sledding; but I really worked at it.

Two or three weeks after my arrival 'Hutch' left by river on the seven days journey to Indaw in the Upper Chindwin. Here I.B.P. worked a small jungle oilfield, of evil repute by reason of the high incidence of a particularly virulent strain of malaria that had proved itself a killer on several occasions. I had already learnt that I was to follow 'Hutch' up in six months time, this being a normal tour of duty in the circumstances.

With my mentor gone, I had to learn to run my own establishment. The mysteries of the cook's book, the short-comings of the dhobi, the absence of the *mali* at times when I was most likely to be around to supervise his modest activities; all these and more aspects of the gentle art of taking the newcomer for a ride had to be experienced and countered. The periodical social duty of throwing a dinner party was practically a day's work of apprehensive super-vision, and it took me months to learn how to stage such an affair at an hour's notice. One of my earlier ventures in this field was the occasion of my twenty-first birthday. None among my guests could recall a precedent, as I had come out to Burma exceptionally young.

Borrowing of tableware for these occasions was arranged unofficially via the kitchen door and without reference to the owner. No eyelid was batted on either side if you found yourself pouring wine for the owner of the glasses. She would probably have her best set under lock and key anyway.

Up to the time of the departure of 'Hutch' I was a non-smoker. Living on my own, however, I soon found the lure of the Burma cheroot to be irresistible. In due course I rang the changes by adding a pipe to my armoury of self-indulgence. In a day and age when Raleigh's contribution to the processes of quiet contemplation may be facing social outlawry, I nevertheless look back on the frequent solace of the 'weed' with gratitude. The cigarette does not answer the same call and, with a certain ex-Indian Army Colonel—a caricature of his kind—I share the opinion that 'cigarette smoking is like kissing your sister—there's nothing in it'!

Compared with the sordid outlook from 'Office House' in Rangoon, the view from my verandah was a lively tapestry. A brief foreground of stony soil and cactus led to the cliff edge, which gave on to a wide vista up and down and across the Irrawaddy, the seasonal aspects of which provided a continuing programme of change. The oil derricks of Chauk were visible down-river and, immediately opposite, the distant contours of Mount Popa, an extinct but unmistakable volcano, rose sharply from the flatness of the surrounding countryside. Popa dominated the scene, sometimes broodingly, sometimes invitingly. Its oft-contemplated outlines are among the clearest memories I carry with me, as also is the silent though sterile menace of the crater which confronted me with startling abruptness when first I climbed the mountain.

Popa, by its isolation, had acquired much mystic significance for a Buddhist countryside. Pagodas and carved figures of the Buddha studded its flanks. The mountain was the dwelling-place of *nats* of contrasting dispositions. Here only was to be found the crystalline stone which, when fractured and smooth-polished, reflected symmetrically a white pagoda as its core. The crater was the home of the hamadryad, with its reputation for aggression without provocation.

These massive and deadly 'king cobras' were a familiar sight on club lawns and at public entertainments for their performance of a ritualistic dance, with a Burmese girl as partner, which reached its climax when the girl kissed the snake full on its deadly mouth. Infrequently tragedy resulted —the price paid by the girl, according to one local belief, for breaking her contract with the *nats* of the mountain by failing to return the snake to the crater within a prescribed period. There was so much superstition surrounding the mountain that even the most sceptical of climbers could not but be conscious of its aura.

The river, as a traffic lane, was a never-ending pageant. The Irrawaddy Flotilla Company ran a frequent service of sizeable paddle steamers between Rangoon and Bhamo, while Lanywa's production of crude oil was loaded into flats which carried it down to I.B.P's refinery at Seikkyi on the Rangoon River.

From time to time a government or private launch fussed against the current or ran down with it. In the high-water season, when freshets in the upper reaches of Irrawaddy and Chindwin were bundling the open season's harvest of teak logs down the swollen *chaungs* to the rivers, enormous log rafts, with what amounted to small villages mounted on

51

them, would come drifting down with the current, the smoke from the evening cooking fires sometimes creating an impression of motive power.

For sheer leisure such a mode of travel would be hard to beat. Indeed, a story is told of a government officer, with private means adequate to protect him against the worst that the 'Raj' could do, who spent three months in this manner implementing an order of transfer from Bhamo to Rangoon. The inevitably required explanation for his disappearance rested on the printed provision that 'Officers on transfer will travel by the cheapest means available'. The words 'and quickest' were subsequently inserted!

Trading craft, fishing boats and dug-out canoes swelled the water-borne concourse, and there was almost always something to speculate upon. With it all the flashing wings of gulls, terns and pratincoles provided a constant diversion to the eye.

Storms of great violence would sometimes rage across the flat swirl of the waters, rousing them to a fury that was hardly credible so far from the sea. In such conditions I was caught once in *Cicala* on a run across from Chauk. Even with the canvas storm dodgers lashed down, the three of us aboard were bailing like men possessed.

Although the longest motorable run at Lanywa, from the end of the guide wall to our water pumping station on the Yaw River, was only about six miles, I soon found myself handicapped by not having my own car. There was no restriction here on ownership by junior Assistants such as there had been in Rangoon. Indeed, incentive was held out to would-be owner-drivers in the form of a monthly allowance of eighty rupees plus twenty gallons of free petrol and servicing.

Taking advantage, therefore, of a visit to Rangoon by the Chief Engineer, I had a friend down there line up for his inspection a well-travelled 1928 Morris Cowley coupé. The C.E. approved, the friend closed the deal for five hundred and fifty rupees (about £40 sterling!) and shipped the car up to Lanywa on an Irrawaddy Flotilla flat. On arrival it was promptly christened 'the Mousetrap' and people gave me a wide berth while I learnt to drive the thing—with no worse damage to property than a large dent in the corrugated sheeting wall of a stores godown into which I drove in the belief that I was set to reverse. The independence conferred on me by possession of 'the Mousetrap' was welcomed by all from whom, hitherto, I had been wont to cadge a ride to the launch jetty or to the golf course whenever Company transport was not available.

My letters home made much impatient reference to the air mail service, which was then in its infancy. It is surprising now to read of the extent to which it was subject to delays and disruptions. One aircraft, for example, arrived at Mingaladon airport with no Rangoon mail on board; and it took four days to find that it had been off-loaded at Cawnpore. Of interest now, in the light of my ultimate but then undreamt-of retirement in Australia, is mention of the fact that the inaugural delivery of air mail from England to Australia was swelled at Rangoon by the addition of a letter from myself to relatives in Victoria.

I wrote of cricket and hockey matches, my playing introduction to hockey being made on the oilfields. I enthused over the delights of the cold weather and railed against a shade temperature of a hundred and twenty on the sand-fill in April. I described in detail a rip-roaring children's Christmas party at Lanywa, for which we brought a launch-load of youngsters over from Chauk.

Underlying all that I wrote was my conviction that I was living the best of all lives, and I rejoiced frequently at my divorcement from Rangoon. The weeks slipped by and I recorded the completion of six months as one-eleventh of my first chukka gone!

Rapidly approaching was my transfer to the distant and dreaded Indaw. My departure was deferred for a week or two to permit me to go down to Rangoon to sit for the Burmese exam. My programme provided for a complete packing of my kit at Lanywa, the river-cum-train journey to Rangoon, forty-eight hours in the capital and then return to Lanywa to collect my belongings and leave for the Chindwin.

In acceptance of a long-standing invitation, I stayed in Rangoon with my judicial kinsman, Ben. He was a most accommodating host and, after he had been dropped at the High Court in the morning, his car was mine until it was time to collect him in the afternoon. It was an imposing vehicle by any standards, and when you add a liveried chauffeur, and a *durwan* resplendent in the uniform of the High Court staff to open and close the door for me, it will be seen that I roamed Rangoon at will and in style.

The exam was held on the morning after my arrival. We were crowded, at diminutive desks, into a room in which the only punkah failed to function—and it was a fiendishly hot day. The papers included translations, in Burmese script, from Burmese into English and vice versa, readings from Burmese manuscripts, and a general conversation in Burmese. I left the room limp and exhausted, utterly unable to predict the outcome of my efforts and of the many hours of wearying labour that underlay them.

After the exam virtually the entire House of Steel assembled at 'the Gin Palace' to watch the final of their annual singles tennis tournament. It gave me an excellent opportunity to meet London Office friends who had arrived in Rangoon after I had gone up-country.

When the tennis was over, eight or ten of us assembled in 'the Gin Palace' for drinks that led up to a powerful sing-song. Ten minutes before my train for Prome was due to leave, the party was transferred unabated to the railway station platform, where the singing was still in full swing as I was borne beyond earshot. My return journey by river to Lanywa was strictly recuperative.

I had two days to kill at Lanywa before catching the Chindwin ferry. As I was fully packed, 'Mac' was kind enough to put me up.

On visiting my bungalow to supervise the removal of my kit, I was maddened to find that it had been broken into in my absence, and mystified on ascertaining that the only items missing were two gramophones—my own and an older model that an earlier occupant had bequeathed to the bungalow. I wired to District Headquarters at Pakokku for the police and instructed the Lanywa village headman to detain the servants I had recently paid off. These did not include my *lugalay* whom I was inclined to exonerate on the grounds that he had no roots in Lanywa, had been with me in Rangoon at the time of the theft and was leaving with me for Indaw the following day. The police came down from Pakokku while I was en route to Indaw and, after going through the usual motions, declared themselves baffled. I had not expected otherwise.

Virtually the last thing I did before sailing was to take over a young fox terrier bitch. Her previous owner had named her Mary, a somewhat prosaic name for a dog, but I let it go at that.

So I sailed for Indaw, a little worried perhaps by the universal commiseration offered to me by friends in Rangoon; a little bit apprehensive at the prospect of taking charge of even a minor oilfield before I had been a year in Burma; but curious rather than fearful, I think, at the malarial prospect which a study of statistics had shown to be not exaggerated. I certainly felt that I was on the threshold of adventure of one sort or another.

4 The Road to Indaw

May 1935 to February 1936

My first trip up the Chindwin, despite its undertone of questing excitement, is one chiefly to be remembered for its sheer discomfort. I was the only saloon passenger, and conditions were the product of a hot following breeze that had lost all power to temper the air by the time it had percolated the foetid length of the ship.

The skipper, after half an hour's relaxation on a xylophone, used to join me for a drink and the evening meal, that being the only opportunity I had of asking the many questions that thronged my mind at the end of the day's run. The heat of my cabin was intolerable and I used to dump my bedding on the deck for'ard in the hope that sleep would find me there. It seldom did because, apart from the temperature, we would be moored, virtually a floating bazaar, in close proximity to a riverside village. The hot night bred short tempers, and a cacophony of noisy bargaining, social bickering, brawls and expectorations was the result.

The initiation, our first night's stop, came at Pakokku. At least there was enough daylight left for me to take Mary for a run ashore. Later, as I sought to reconcile myself to the night's uproar, I reflected that depression could well be the only emotion left to me at the end of the week's journey. Already Indaw was assuming an evil countenance that had not plagued me hitherto.

I brooded over the outcome of the Burmese exam. To pass it sooner or later was mandatory, success within two years of arrival in the country being rewarded with a bonus of five hundred rupees—a sum that would hardly cover the cost of tuition, notwithstanding that it would be very welcome.

I had only been out nine months but at Indaw, with its regional dialect and unacademic way of life, I would be hard put to it to retain, let alone add to, the sum of my learning thus far. It was vital that I had passed, but I had no conviction of it.

The second day's run carried us out of the Irrawaddy and into the Chindwin; but they are both major rivers even at this distance from the sea, and the substitution was virtually indistinguishable. Our next port of call was Monywa, where our loading and unloading commitments involved us in a stop of thirty-six hours. At least here was some diversion.

Monywa was the administrative base for the Lower Chindwin District, as well as being a forest headquarters for the Bombay-Burmah Trading Corporation, hereafter to be referred to, Burmese-style, as the *Bombine*. Here I posted my letters and found my way along to the club and the hospitality that was endemic to such outposts. I watched tennis, drank afterwards with the players and the one or two others who were around, and was then taken off to dinner by the *Bombine* Manager and his wife. I spent a very enjoyable evening with them and their other guests, summoned only because there would be a strange face at the board.

The *Bombine* was the pioneer trading company in Burma and enjoyed a colourful place in British Burma's history. Its staff were recruited mainly from the universities, with the accent perhaps more heavily on the athletic than the academic qualification. Nowhere East of Suez would you find a greater assemblage of 'Blues' than among their ranks. The philosophy behind the policy was sound, as I came to learn for myself. It is that the art of living for long periods in solitude, in jungle conditions that are frequently uncomfortable and sometimes hazardous, is best learnt and mastered by the completely educated man. The *Bombine*'s 'casualty' rate was comparatively small.

After leaving Monywa we were seldom without a reminder that we were travelling in the low-water season. Though the paddle steamer's draft was only two feet, we were constantly running aground on sandbanks. Sometimes we would get free in a matter of minutes, at others it would take up to six or eight hours. The river was staked to show what had been the deep water channel when the stakes were planted; but shifts of sand, by hundreds of feet, could occur between the upward and downward runs of the same survey launch. In these conditions a scheduled stop could be reached hours late, and no one with a ferry to catch would dream of heading for the river bank until the siren could be heard miles up or down the river.

Our slow progress continued, with stops for the night at Okma, Maukkadaw and Kalewa (which last, one day, was to become a focal point in my wartime Intelligence network). The countryside, passing slowly astern, was mostly heavily jungled: a world of teak. If there was some sameness in the vista, we were always rounding a bend in the river, speculating mildly upon what might lie beyond.

At Kalewa I nearly drowned. Despite the sandbanks and the shallows behind us, the river here, as I was to learn, ran much deeper and more strongly. In escape from the heat I had dived over the side after we moored in the late afternoon. Having taken only a few strokes, I turned over to view my floating prison and was shaken to find it already far up-river. It took me a mile or two to reach the shore, and I lay there retching for some time before I could attempt a dazed and exhausting trek back to the ship where, badly frightened, I collapsed on my bunk, heedless of the heat.

Our next night's halt, and my last, was at Mawlaik. Here I found a second Monywa in that Mawlaik is the administrative headquarters for the Upper Chindwin District and likewise a *Bombine* forest base. Additionally, under a British officer, there was a platoon-strength outpost of the Chin Hills Battalion of the Burma Frontier Force. By not the wildest of romancing could I have foreseen that one day I was to be commissioned into that very regiment!

Once again I found my way to the club and, for the rest of the evening, was taken under the wing of the Divisional Forest Officer and his wife. They paired me for dinner with the attractive wife of a *Bombine* Assistant absent on a spell of logging.

After dinner the entire station assembled at the polo

ground for a fireworks display. The Royal Jubilee, for which the fireworks had been ordered, was past by some weeks; but, in the way of the East, the fireworks had only just arrived; so it was to be a case of better late than never. The proceedings moved at an incredibly slow pace, mainly because the master of ceremonies, that is the man with the box of matches, was a Sikh. Such was his concern for the safety of his beard that, after the application of each match, he would go like the wind for the other end of the field. Usually he would be about a hundred yards away before it became evident that an inherent dampness among the fireworks had come out on top. Ultimately he got results, but how far he ran that night defies calculation. The Sikhs keep themselves fit!

After we dispersed from the polo ground I escorted my partner back to her bungalow and then, by prior arrangement, found my way to the *Bombine* chummery where I was regaled until two o'clock in the morning, when I returned to the ferry. Where in all the world now, I wonder, can one find the special quality of hospitality that used to radiate from these small up-country stations?

Next morning's sailing was for me the last lap of this wearying journey. At eleven o'clock we moored at Pantha, the riverine jumping-off point for Indaw. Here I.B.P. operated a small refinery, supervised, one man at a time, by petroleum engineers on rotation from Seikkyi in the same way as the rest of us were rostered from the down-river oilfields to Indaw.

At this time the man in charge was Alex Wilson, but there was no sign of him when I arrived, and it was left to his clerk, who helped me to off-load, to explain that he was away escorting to and from Indaw the Deputy Superintendent of Police from Mawlaik on an official visit, together with the skipper of an Irrawaddy Flotilla Company survey launch who had gone along 'for the ride'. In due course the three of them, plus 'Hutch', arrived and we all lunched aboard the survey launch.

After beer and curry 'Hutch' and I took leave of the others and headed for Indaw. As we travelled, there was much that

I had to tell 'Hutch' of minor gossip from the world of men, and of comings and goings that could not be expected to echo this far. It is strange now to reflect on the inadequacy of communication in those days, little more than thirty-five years ago.

The first eighteen miles of our course were motorable by a truck specially fitted with a lower than bottom gear. The going was fairly level but pitted with shallow, stony *chaung* crossings into and out of which the truck wallowed and heaved. During the rains this means of transport was impossible, the choice lying then between ponies if the *chaungs* were not too swollen, and elephants if they were.

In the late afternoon we reached Lawtha, nine miles short of Indaw, where the Company maintained a semi-furnished bungalow for the benefit of any prevented by conditions from progressing further. From this point on, the truck was 'out' anyway. Carved out ahead of us was a cliff-sided valley through the jungle-covered hills, the worn-down bed of the Khodaung *chaung*, presently a sluggish stream broken by sandbanks, with an average width of two to three hundred feet, but in the rains, for hours or days on end, a vicious torrent.

In the remaining nine miles to Indaw this same stream had to be forded twenty-seven times and, in swollen conditions, elephant transport was the only means of getting in or out of the Field. For our present journey 'Hutch' had a couple of ponies waiting for us at Lawtha and we made the trip in this fashion. It was the first time I had ever been in a saddle!

The evidence on the way through of activity ahead was the telephone line from Indaw to Pantha, barbed to discourage monkeys from swinging on it; and the oil pipeline, buried wherever possible, and suitably protected or diverted at *chaung* crossings, so as to deprive wild elephants of the pleasure of breaking it with their trunks. Periodically we would pass stacks of casing or other oilwell equipment awaiting further shuttling forward to the Field. At times we would overtake sweating bullocks dragging through the fords cartloads of similar material.

By the light of a setting sun we rounded a bend in the

track that, with startling suddenness and complete incongruity, revealed Indaw's main crude oil storage tank and a football field, the two occupying the only relatively flat bit of ground in Indaw. Riding between them, we made the penultimate crossing of the Khodaung underneath the first of the gossamer suspension bridges that laced the cliff banks together for the five or six miles along which the Field straddled the *chaung*. The final crossing followed a few minutes later at a point where the Khodaung was revealed as the issue of two equally large *chaungs*, the Wettin and the Mawton, flowing down from north and south respectively. Further suspension bridges across both were visible as we forded the crossing at the confluence.

There remained the long, steep, twilit climb to the Agent's bungalow. Occasionally a jungle clearing revealed an oilwell derrick: pipelines spilled out of jungle, crossed our path and vanished into jungle again; transfer tanks were glimpsed in inconsequential settings. We passed the oil pumping station and the hospital in their individual clearings: then came the office at the head of a near-precipitous haulage way leading down to the saw mill at *chaung* level: next we were threading our way through a semi-cleared area known somewhat flatteringly as the 'farm', though it did at least provide the camp with fresh vegetables, fruit and milk. Finally, at the end of a week's journey, we halted at the bungalow atop the ultimate climb.

I had not lacked for priming before I headed for Indaw. From those who had been there, from reports and weekly mail copies, I had been building up my picture for months. Nothing, I could now see, had really conveyed the rugged desolation that introduction now revealed. As I separated myself from my saddle I knew that I had come a long way in more senses than one. Would I ever have left home, I wondered, had I truly known that such isolation, deprivation and responsibility were to be mine within the span of a year? Round me, as I stood at the bottom of the bungalow steps, the jungle brooded, but not in silence; the sounds of insect and animal life were incessant and varied. My musing was broken by 'Hutch'.

'Get upstairs, Harold, and have a bath. Keep on the move, especially while you are stripped. Then get into your 'skito boots, slacks and long sleeves and you'll find a drink waiting for you in the front room.'

I did not need to ask what 'Hutch' meant. I had done my 'homework' on *Anophelinae Minimus* and *Maculatus* and would be able to tell both from harmless old *Culex*!

To a minimum comprehension of this outlandish place some description is necessary, and I cannot do better than quote from a report by Colonel Strickland, of whom further mention will follow:

These three large streams are all similar in character. They are from 100 to 400 feet in width and about 1½ to 2 feet in greatest depth in the low water season. During the rains they are liable to sudden flood rises but except for occasional flood periods they are fordable by carts throughout the year. The stream beds are flat and sandy and the stream margins are either bare rock under cliffs or shelving sandbanks. There are some weedy stretches but marshes and marsh vegetation are for the most part absent. These streams flow in an unbroken series of wide meanders in the bottom of wide gorge-shaped valleys . . .

The larger tributary streams are exactly similar in character (though smaller in size) to the main streams . . .

In addition . . . there are smaller streams flowing in steep rocky beds quite different from the larger tributaries described above. All these smaller streams run in deep narrow gorges.

In every part of the area the slopes are precipitous. In the 1,600 feet from the junction of the Wettin and Mawton *chaungs* to the crest of the hill to the East there is a rise of some 700 feet or so at a gradient of almost 1 in 2 and the cliffs frequently rise sheer to 300 feet from the stream beds. The level of the main stream junction is about 700 feet above sea level.

Except for small cleared areas round bungalows, lines and wells the whole region is covered with thick evergreen jungle composed of large trees with thick undergrowth. There are no villages other than the settlement on the field itself within about 7 miles of Indaw.

The oil wells spanned about seven miles of the Wettin/Mawton 'artery', from which, scattered between the 'veins' represented by the plunging tributaries, they were seldom more than a quarter of a mile distant. The 'artery', as already described, was criss-crossed by suspension bridges for foot traffic only. In the low-water season these were supplemented by flimsy foot bridges across the *chaung* beds.

A rough road ran parallel to the 'artery' to its east, and this crossed the 'veins' by wooden bridges strong enough to carry an elephant and its hauled load. There was no wheeled transport on the Field, though we had a few tractors for work at *chaung* level, usually in co-operation with the elephants. Ponies were the one alternative to walking, and then only in the dry season. Where wells were drilled on very steep slopes, access to them was by railed haulageway.

This, the furthest-flung of Burma's oilfields, had been discovered without the aid of scientific methods, on seepage evidence alone. The total production when I was up there was little more than two hundred barrels daily from about thirty working wells. The oil was raised by gas lift, the gas 'shots' being injected electrically from a centrally-located 'clock' device, the invention of an I.B.P. engineer.

Up to the time when the Field was denied to the Japanese, no well had penetrated as deep as the horizon that was the source of the seepages. The shallow, apparently migrated oil which we produced was obtained by percussion, or cable tool, drilling from between fifteen hundred and thirty-five hundred feet. Below this was high pressure gas and two attempts to drill through it with rotary equipment had failed.

The justification for such remote, small-scale production was that in quality it provided an excellent lubricant base, which was a valuable complement to the petroliferous crudes obtained from the down-river Fields. The small refinery at Pantha did no more than extract petrol and kerosene to supply the Upper Burma market. The residue was 'flatted' down to Seikkyi in the high-water season.

The staff on my arrival comprised 'Hutch', as Agent, Dave Warden, a Scottish Field engineer (due for relief in a matter of weeks by another Scot, Pete Fraser) and an American driller, Jimmie McMurtrie, who had preceded me from Lanywa by a week or two. Jimmie was in his mid-forties and doubts had been expressed about sending him up at his age. However, a thorough medical going-over had satisfied everybody, and Jimmie, exceptionally, was keen to go. He was a real roughneck, and when I asked him how he had fared at the doctor's hands he replied:

Jeez! That goddam sonofabitch says to me—Jimmie, he says, you're fit enough; but at your age you'd better start slowin' down on the wine, women and song: so ah'm quittin' singin'.

Indaw boasted a club in which the normal senior staff of three, plus an Anglo-Burman power house engineer on rotational transfer from Lanywa, foregathered on Wednesday and Saturday evenings. The amenities comprised a bar, a small library, a billiards table and a tennis court. I used to speculate upon the ingenuity that must have attended the conveyance of the billiards table from Pantha. Two dedicated elephants in tandem was as near as I could get to a solution!

The 'streets' in the residential area were lit by gas flares, and the bungalows were heated in the cold weather by gas piped in to open fireplaces banked up with logs of petrified wood. These were procured from the beds of some of the rocky *chaungs* and, as they heated, they glowed with all the semblance of the real thing. Gas was a commodity of which we had an otherwise wasted surplus.

A typical Indaw day, at the time of my arrival, started with a cold, heavy mist which gave way to a shade temperature of over a hundred by mid-day. This in its turn fell away to a cool evening and the need for at least one blanket at night. The routine involved a brief, early morning call at the office, followed by five or six hours doing the rounds of the Field in one context or another. The afternoon was spent mainly in the office where, with afternoon tea, the *lugalay* delivered the soon familiar mosquito boots, long trousers and long-sleeved shirt into which one promptly changed. The only meaning assignable to a.m. and p.m. in that place was ante and post mosquito.

The anti-malarial work, for which the Agent was personally responsible, became one of the most fascinating sides to my life at Indaw. Some years previously, when the mortality rate had assumed proportions that made it difficult to get staff to accept a posting to Indaw, the Company had commissioned the School of Tropical Diseases in Calcutta to run a survey over the place and lay down a programme of preventive action. The School's Principal,

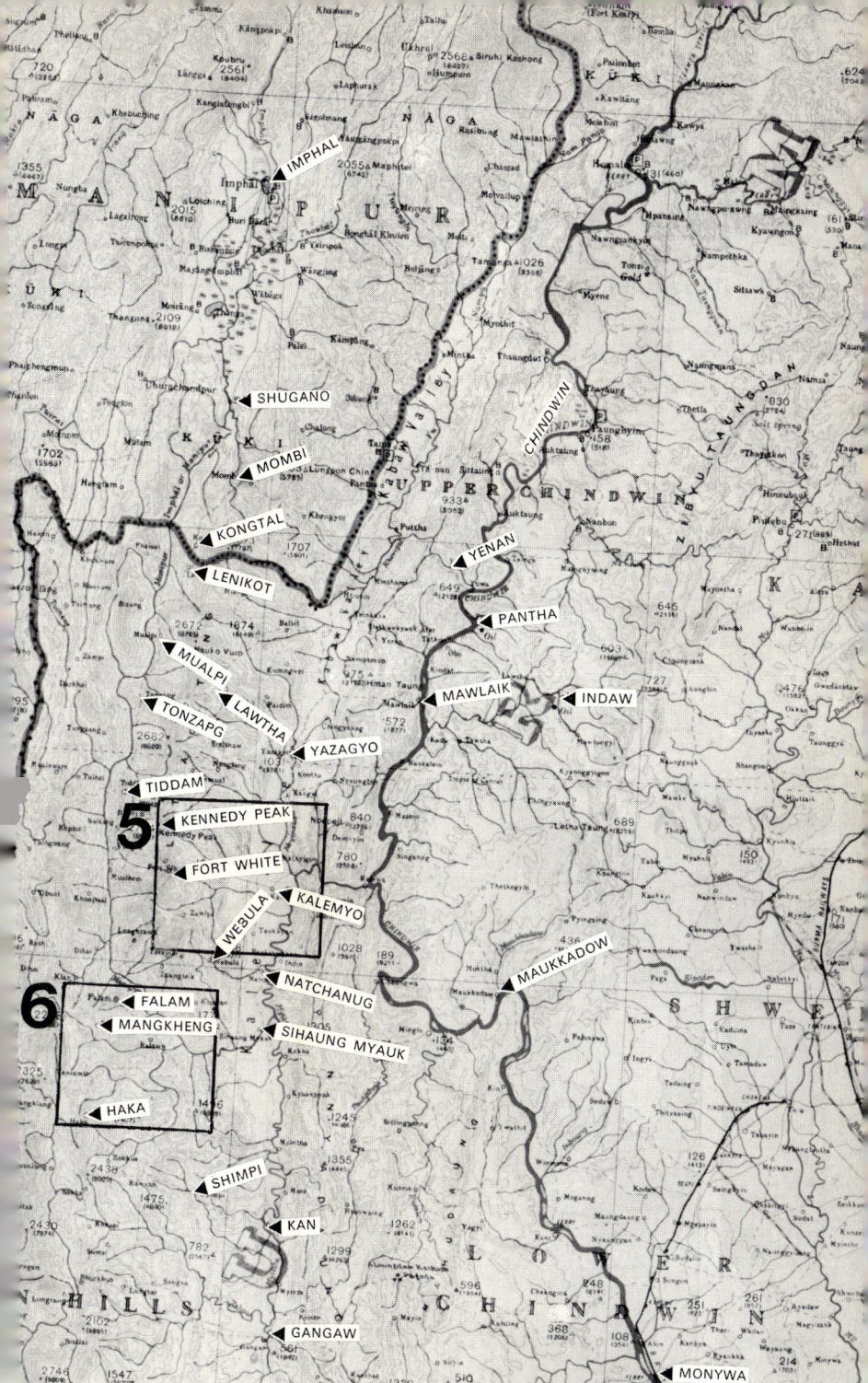

CHINDWIN RIVER and CHIN HILLS
and showing location of maps numbers 5 & 6

Indaw—The Author with the office staff
Chindwin River—Teak raft

Colonel C. Strickland, of the Indian Medical Service, personally conducted the survey, and his report, from which I have already quoted, included a comment to the effect that such serious malarial potential was outside his experience.

Accordingly the Company accepted his recommendations, which were based on the recruitment by himself of two suitable Indians to be trained for the particular problem and then sent to Indaw, as members of the Company's staff, to carry out his programme. These two men were still at Indaw during my time there and I did a lot of work with them.

The core of the problem, at least under Burma conditions, was that at each of two widely separated places, 'A' and 'B', there might be found twelve species of the Anopheline mosquito. At 'A' three of them might be carriers and the remaining nine harmless. At 'B', likewise, three might be carriers; but it did not follow that they would be the same three as at 'A'. Accordingly the situation had to be determined separately for each area.

At Indaw we did in fact have three carriers among thirteen Anophelines represented. The first stage of the anti-malarial work, therefore, had lain in determining which species were carriers; the second in ascertaining the favourite breeding grounds and habits of the carriers; and the third in concentrating the preventive measures accordingly.

The standing routine involved approaches from opposite directions. From the one we were required to catch two hundred Anophelines every evening. These were dissected and microscopically examined in the laboratory the next day. Not only did this keep a check on the possibility of deviations as between carriers and non-carriers (there were, in fact, none); it also made it possible regularly to graph the seasonal variations in the incidence of the disease.

From the other pole we were required daily to collect live larvae in quantity. These, on hatching out, whether they were from carrying or non-carrying varieties, were obviously untarnished at this stage. They were then encouraged to drink their fill of the blood of malarial patients in the hospital via the human arm inserted into the hatching tray through a mosquito netting sleeve. All would then be dissected and put through the microscope, the results providing complementary data to that derived from the opposite approach already described.

The method employed to catch two hundred live Anophelines every evening is worth a brief description since, in the interests of easy supervision, most of them came from the Agent's bungalow. My living room was enclosed on three sides by a wide verandah from which it was separated by mosquito screening. When night fell a member of the mosquito squad would arrive on the verandah, armed with a rack of test tubes and a wad of cotton wool. As mosquitoes, attracted by the light from within, settled on the screen, a test tube would be popped over them and partitions of cotton wool pushed down after them, to leave about half an inch of freedom to each mosquito. A completed tube, thus, would house about a dozen segregated insects. The time taken to collect two hundred in this fashion had progressively lengthened to several hours as the preventive measures began to make themselves felt.

Having established by laboratory processes the identity of the killers, and by larval collection their favourite breeding grounds, it was then a case of applying the clearing and oiling programme to best effect. Clearing involved whatever was necessary to induce standing water to flow, where this was possible: oiling called for the installation and regular replenishment of drip pots over running water to promote a film of oil widely over the surface of the hostile *chaungs*. Additionally, men of the mosquito squad, with oil cylinders on their backs, would be hand-spraying such locations as did not lend themselves to drip-oiling.

Over a period of years it had been established, firstly, that the worst time of year for malarial infection was the interval of a few weeks between the 'mango showers' and the monsoon. This was because newly fallen water at this season stood free of the flushing effect of the heavy and regular rains that were to follow; secondly, that the more you exposed sunless water by jungle clearance, the more you encouraged larval breeding (which shattered a popular misconception); and thirdly, that water collected in fallen teak leaves and elephant foot marks provided popular breeding locations for the killers. This last, of course, militated against the complete success of any clearing and oiling programme, since both of these reservoirs were numerous, haphazard and transient. Nevertheless, by patient pursuit and rigorous stamping on any tendency to let up, the campaign steadily improved the health record of Indaw and more than justified its adoption and cost.

Such a fascinating activity made an instant appeal. I had major responsibilities to attend to but, even so, many were the hours spent walking the *chaungs*, white enamelled collecting spoon in hand.

'Hutch' and Dave Warden left, but not before a celebratory occasion on my receiving from Rangoon a letter of congratulation on my success in the Burmese exam! The relief I felt cannot be described.

Pete Fraser had made it in just ahead of the monsoon and almost simultaneously with an assault by a tigress on a bullock which was hauling casing. There were similar attacks within the following few days and two of our local hunters went off in pursuit armed only with shotguns, but not to be dissuaded. They wounded the animal from a *machan* (platform) and, in following up, were surprised by it at close quarters. They must have kept their heads because they dispatched it in a virtual free-for-all, with no worse injury than slight mauling to the arm of one of the pursuers. The tigress was brought into Indaw for skinning, fragments of its bones then being widely distributed for medicinal (*sic*) purposes.

A week or two later we had a similar threat to our line of communication from a rogue elephant. This time it was two bullock cart drivers who were pulverized, so the animal had to be hunted down and shot. As was usual, the occasion brought from Jimmie McMurtrie *le mot juste*. We were beering and lunching with him on a Sunday and postulating, each of us, our own individual reactions to an encounter with the rogue.

'For my money,' I kicked off, 'I'd head for where the

trees seemed thickest in hopes that the brute would not be able to follow me through.'

'Well,' said Pete, 'knowing how slow an elephant is in getting down a steep slope, I'd drop into the nearest *chaung* and run for it.'

'Jeez,' said Jimmie, his hand caressing his bald pate as a characteristic aid to thought, 'no elephant would catch me for slippin' in the shit'!

As the monsoon closed in on us, our evening tennis became a diminishing activity, and life an increasing affair of changing out of wet clothes and testing the depth of our own resources. The Mawton and the Wettin swelled from rivulets threading among the sand to roaring torrents that could be heard from the top of bungalow hill. I was glad that my mastery of the swing bridges—three planks wide and up to four hundred feet in length—was already well established.

McGilvray was the man to talk of one of the greatest days in Indaw's waterlogged history. It fell in 1926 when he was Field Agent. At that time only the driller's bungalow was east of the Mawton/Wettin divide. The Agent's and the Field Engineer's were on the other side about fifteen feet above the highest known water level. A cloudburst in the upper reaches of the Mawton produced a flash flood that raised the *chaung* level by thirty feet in less than a third that number of minutes. 'Mac' got enough warning to run out of his back door, and he had to keep running to the top of the slope. From there he watched his bungalow wrenched from its stilts, swirl out into mid-stream, roll over and sink. The Field Engineer also survived, but likewise with the loss of his bungalow.

Cut off from the commissariat store and all other facilities by a raging torrent that promised no abatement for days, and with the swing bridges gone, they inspected their resources. The engineer could contribute nothing, but 'Mac' had his tail and dinner jacket suits, which his *lugalay* had taken up to his own quarters for an airing over a *sigri* before the disaster. Thus attired ('Mac' by right of office in the tails!), they made the sodden thirty-mile trek to Pantha until such time as it became possible for them to make the hundred yards crossing of the Mawton to the east bank at Indaw!

Eight years later, when I was up there, the shifting sands were still yielding up equipment lost on that dramatic occasion, but a locomotive-type oilfield boiler, a workshop lathe and the office safe still had not come to light.

In order to give ourselves an interest, Pete Fraser and I organized an inter-departmental soccer tournament to be played during the rains. Considerable enthusiasm was aroused and the final was fixed for a Burmese festival holiday that dawned fine and clear. Jimmie had been in a bad way with malaria for a week and, worried about him, Pete and I went along to his bungalow after lunch to see how he was and to decide whether either or both of us should stay back from the match. Jimmie seemed to be in better shape than he had been since going sick, and he scoffed at the idea of either of us missing the game, in which we were both due to be playing; so we went off and enjoyed ourselves.

Great was our distress, on return, to find his bungalow in confusion and Jimmie himself alternating between raving and unconsciousness, with his Burmese 'wife', who had been with him for years, vainly trying to cope. We cleared the bungalow of 'flapping' servants and others and got our Indian doctor along. There was little he or we could do, however, beyond keeping Jimmie held down in bed and sponging his face. He died late that night.

Pete and I took swift counsel together. We considered the precedent offered by the grave of Adam Bowman on high ground overlooking the confluence of the *chaungs*. However, he alone of overseas staff who had died in Indaw was buried on the Field, because weather conditions had ruled out any other course. Now the *chaungs* were down, and at Mawlaik there was a Mission and consecrated ground. Our decision was unanimous, though I think we might have decided otherwise had we been dealing with a stranger, for the task was formidable.

By telephone I roused Alex Wilson at Pantha, dictated telegrams to be sent to Rangoon and Mawlaik, and arranged that he send through forthwith a supply of tinplate for lining the coffin, which Pete, by this time, was having made. The job took us most of the next day because the tinplate was not malleable enough for the purpose.

After a few hours sleep I left by pony for Pantha in the small hours of the following morning, having sent the coffin on ahead with thirty-six coolies to operate, twelve to a gang, for only a few hundred yards at a stretch. This, I felt, would ensure an average rate of travel sufficient to connect with the downward ferry, though Alex was confident that the skipper would defer his sailing for as long as was necessary.

That lone ride through the darkness of the living jungle and the twenty-seven *chaung* crossings was a frightening experience. It was a vile journey for the coolies also, for the Khodaung was still pretty turbulent and progress was slower than I had estimated. Nevertheless they were on the river side of Lawtha by the time I caught up with them. We reached Pantha late, but only to find the river in the grip of a thick mist and the ferry still unheard of. Alex arranged food and shelter for the coolies before they returned to Indaw, and there was still time for me to change out of my wet clothing and get some sleep.

The ferry arrived at about mid-day. Alex saw me off with my dolorous freight, which was already betraying the fact that our attempts at lining it had been less than adequate. By the time we approached Mawlaik in mid-afternoon the last of the mist had lifted. The skipper was making an unscheduled stop at a private ghat near the Civil Lines, some miles upstream from the town moorings. As we drifted alongside I was confronted with an astonishing spectacle. All the senior residents, with their ladies, government and *Bombine*, were present, formally attired and wreaths in hand. Drawn up at the top of the bank, with a flower-decorated bullock cart behind them, was the Frontier Force platoon, while their officer, in full ceremonial rig, was on the ghat. I could almost hear Jimmie say 'Jeez!'.

From that point on, mercifully, for I was young, exhausted and somewhat overcome, matters were taken out of my hands. A few whispered words of sympathy from those who had entertained me five (only five!) months previously, a

'Present Arms' as the coffin was carried ashore and placed on the bullock cart, and we were off in measured procession to the cemetery. The burial service, in the absence from the station of both the missionary and the Deputy Commissioner, was read, as authorized, by the Deputy Superintendent of Police, the senior government officer present. Jimmie was laid to rest alongside 'Kep' Brown, the preceding victim of an Indaw posting. This alone, for some reason or other, made me feel justified in bringing Jimmie out.

The service over, I started to inquire about means of getting back to Pantha without delay. Immediately I was called to order by Colchester ('M.T.'), the *Bombine* Manager, who told me that he had a foursome of golf arranged for me forthwith and a dinner party for later in the evening; and furthermore that he would take responsibility for restraining me, forcibly if necessary, should I make any move to attempt to return to Indaw before the following day. I suppose I felt, or professed to feel, shocked; but the psychology was wonderful and I shall always remember with gratitude the kindnesses that were shown to me from then on.

'M.T.', who had known Jimmie as a ferry companion, had himself travelled fast and far in order to attend the funeral. He was a bachelor and a hilarious character with some reputation for absent-mindedness. It was told to me that, on a rare occasion calling for a dinner jacket, he was ready with fifteen minutes to spare and so had reclined in a long-sleever with a book and a drink. His *lugalay* interrupted him with the startled observation that a vital fly button was missing. 'M.T.' peeled off his trousers, which the *lugalay* then bore away to repair. Before the lad returned, 'M.T.' finished a chapter, drained his glass, scrambled to his feet and strode out into the night. He was half-way across the polo-field before his shouting, trouser-waving *lugalay* arrested his progress.

After my social fling I found that my return to Pantha had been provided for by speed boat, the property of a local Sikh trader. We did the journey within an hour—an unheard-of performance. I lost no time in going through to Indaw. The Khodaung was still uncomfortably high for passage by pony but I pressed on and made the camp before nightfall.

I greeted Pete Fraser almost with embarrassment: he had been living with problems while I had been up for air. Apart from helping Jimmie's 'widow' to pack up, Pete had been trying to free stuck casing in Well No. 66, which Jimmie had been drilling up to the time of his death: so far he had had no success. Jimmie had also been bailing out from Well No. 28 an accumulation of sludge that covered the producing zone. This seemed a straightforward job, so I got a drilling gang on to it and resumed operations. Within no time we'd left the bailer in the hole so, before worse befell, I closed down until a driller should again be available.

Rangoon lost no time in sending up a relief and Jock Scott arrived within two weeks. He had a fearsome time getting through. There had been more rain, and five crossings out from Lawtha he got washed off his pony and could not regain it. He achieved the considerable feat of swimming the five crossings back, only to find that his kit was held up by a landslide on the other side of Lawtha! Fortunately I was able to tell him over the phone that on a verandah in Lawtha village I had noticed a mosquito net. This he managed to borrow and he made do with it as a blanket for the night. In the morning I sent an elephant out to bring him in and he was a pretty weary man when he arrived! I had not previously met Jock. He proved to be a tough, twinkle-eyed Scot of genial nature—a very good man to dispel the gloom that had descended on us with Jimmie's death.

Jock succeeded with the 'fishing' job at Well No. 66 and completed it as planned. Unfortunately it proved to be a poor performer and, with disappointments in other directions, it began to look as though the drilling programme projected for the open season would be inadequate to maintain production at the required level.

Current operations were concentrated in the south end of the Field, but Rangoon now decided to drill an exploratory well to the north as an addition to the programme. The location was seven miles distant from the site for Well No. 67, which Jock was already rigging up. This raised an obvious problem of supervision, so Sandy Webster, a junior driller, was sent up from Lanywa to swell our ranks. His was the only journey through from Pantha on which my letters are silent, so presumably, and exceptionally, it was uneventful!

We were now well into November, and the cold weather was moving in on us. I was hearing regularly from 'Hutch', who had graduated to the Rangoon office. He had been having quite a bit of malaria, despite the fact that he had kept very fit while he was at Indaw. This was a familiar pattern: it seemed that the let-down gave the infection the chance it had been waiting for.

'Hutch' told me that I could expect to be relieved within a matter of weeks by John Lindsay, the Assistant Agent at Yenangyaung and my senior by about seven years. My posting was to be back to Lanywa. Frankly I received the news without enthusiasm as I was so enjoying the weather and the work that I was in no hurry to get out. It was no holiday posting, however. I was fully occupied one way or another for about ten hours daily from Monday to Saturday and until noon or near it on Sunday: but there was infinite variety.

Beyond passing references to wild elephants and tigers, I have said nothing of the fantastic fauna and flora of this untamed corner of the world. Disposed as I am towards ornithology, I was seldom to be seen without binoculars round my neck, and few were my circuits of the Field from which I did not drop out for at least a few minutes to watch some new, and often improbable bird. The most amazing single specimen, readily observable, was the Great Hornbill. This immense creature, over four feet in length, was a major spectacle in flight. You could hear it become airborne at a distance of about a mile and, if it were coming your way, you would see it thrashing a noisy course through the teak like some grotesque ship of the air in full sail.

Monkeys abounded, and at all times of the day troops of them were liable to strike up in a concerted howling that was banshee to some, though I always found it oddly companionable.

Snakes there were a-plenty, and local superstition attributed Jimmie McMurtrie's death to the fact that he had killed a twelve-foot python lying gorged near Well No. 66 a week or two earlier. I had a request from the curator of the reptile house of the Rangoon Zoo to collect snakes on his behalf. I turned it aside, however, when I found from his instructions that the preliminary move required of me was to steer the snakes into large paper bags, the implausible assurance being generally to the effect that where the head led the tail was bound to follow! I was also asked by a society in England to undertake the collection of orchids, of which I'm sure I could have produced some rare varieties; but there was no suggestion that I would be reimbursed for the considerable expense manifestly to be incurred in packing and dispatching them by air to England.

At a certain time of the year, unrecorded in my notes, we would be invaded at night by swarms of the Atlas moth, one of the most startlingly beautiful creatures of all. The biggest specimen that I caught measured ten and a half inches across the wings.

In a present-day world, where technical skills dedicated to the feeding of man tend to achieve the extermination of wild life in all its forms, I hope that Indaw will live on, remote, malarious and antagonistic to the human intruder.

The domestic elephants merit more mention than they have so far received. I remember them all—Phalomay-gyi, Phalomay-galay, Pubaw, Pubay and Moksohaing, all bulls, and Jenny, the cow.

Jenny was the most remarkable. The working years of an elephant approximate fairly closely to those of the physically active human, say eighteen to sixty. Jenny, reputedly seventy, was theoretically therefore a pensioner; but such was her nature that we kept her on light duty: she was unhappy without it. Physical attributes apart, Jenny flaunted her sex. She was the only member of the herd that never crossed a bridge: her refusal invariably was flat, and it was ever the long way round for her.

When it came to the annual innoculation against anthrax, Jenny alone had to be tethered fore and aft to trees. The bulls submitted meekly to the process of scrubbing, soaping, washing and iodining, and did little more than wince when the needle of the enormous syringe was plunged home. Jenny was quite otherwise, and the maximum of precaution was necessary when putting her through the procedure.

Each elephant was 'crewed' by two men, the *oozie* who sat astride the animal's neck, conveying orders by pressure of his knees or heels, and the *pejeik* on foot, threatening any recalcitrance with a sharpened spear with which, nevertheless, he never touched the beast. Understanding between the three was complete, and they had probably been brought up together.

At any given time the working elephants assuredly knew not only what they were doing but why. Their intelligence was marvellous to watch, and frequently one would see them resolve their own problems of route or detour. I remember once watching an elephant taking an 'easy' after racking oilwell casing. Swinging his trunk and swishing his tail, he was eyeing his completed task. Slowly, without prompting and unattended, he moved forward and *ounged* (headed) into place a joint that was protruding abnormally.

In some respects, however, the elephants were 'tender vines'. Six working hours ending at noon was the regulation day's shift. They were susceptible to harness sores and to boils, which were nauseous things to lance, and they often had to be 'physicked' with Epsom salts concealed in balls of jaggery (crude sugar), which latter they relished. They fed at night on bamboo and other vegetation strictly of their own prospecting, for which reason they had to be shackled at the fore feet and liberated to go their own way. In the grey dawn the *oozies* and *pejeiks* might have some miles to walk before 'recapturing' their charges, though there was never any doubt about which way they had gone or that it was his own beast that each was following.

I recall a night when Evangelista, our Anglo-Burman power house engineer, left his bed and bungalow at high speed in an apparent earthquake. At the bottom of his garden *terra* seemed to be *firma* even though the bungalow maintained a violent vibration. Reconnoitring an explanation of this phenomenon, he came upon a foraging elephant —one of our herd—scratching its flank against the corner of his stilt-borne dwelling!

Over thirty-five years later, technology has yet to produce a working device that could displace the elephant in such conditions as were to be found at Indaw. Though the knowledge I personally gained of elephant husbandry was rudimentary when compared with what was required of a teak wallah, it was yet enough to be of great value in wartime to come.

The elephant and the mosquito! How great, come to think of it, was their impact on our lives; and the mosquito was the more to be feared.

Next—the dogs. Mary was my constant companion whenever I was walking or climbing about the Field. There was also Jess, 'Hutch's' pi-dog, which he had felt unable to take with him to Rangoon; and finally Jack, the nondescript, innocent cause of 'Kep' Brown's death.

'Kep' had been working down a *chaung* on anti-malarial routine when Jack got stuck on the edge of a waterfall. It looked like a dry and flat approach to effect a rescue, but damp moss and an imperceptible slope brought 'Kep' down and there was nothing to stop him sliding until he went over the edge. He fell sixty feet on to rocks and burst his malaria-swollen spleen. Even so he managed a one in two climb of about five hundred feet back to the bungalow, where he died some hours later.

The ponies were stabled on the 'farm' near my bungalow and I used to take an interest in them. Unfortunately, two of them, including my favourite, the docile Clarence, fell victims to an outbreak of surra that swept the Upper Chindwin District while I was up there.

We ran a commissariat store which, at one time, had catered for the senior staff as well as the labour. Progressively, however, there developed among the former a preference for direct ordering from Barnett Brothers in Rangoon. The sole reminder of old habits was a large stack of plum puddings, the result of a bulk order inadvertently expressed in gross instead of dozens!

I have mentioned the saw mill. The Indaw oilfield was located within a *Bombine* forest lease, so the teak trees were not ours to extract. However, some years previously, we had made an arrangement with the *Bombine* whereby they had allotted to us two hundred and fifty of the trees which Government had girdled in their leased area. These we were then free to fell and log as required.

The oil derricks at Indaw were wooden and the foundation sills at least had to be of teak as protection against white ants. The superstructure would be made of other and less valuable timber, so our consumption of teak was not great. Haulage of logs to the saw mill, I suppose, was the one occasion when the elephants were employed on the task to which they were born, as they were all on loan from Steels' Forest Department.

Once a year, in the open season, it was the Agent's duty to walk the pipeline from Indaw to Pantha on inspection. Though in distance it was only twenty-seven miles, that tells you nothing. It was an unending alternation of footslogging, hand-over-hand climbing and slithering down steep *chaung* banks—laced with occasions, where the line was buried, when you lost your way altogether. Thank heaven I was fit!

Mails (the ferry service, *chaung* level and God permitting) were delivered weekly on Sunday evenings. My letters over this period are one long paean of enthusiasm for the climate. On Christmas Day we dined in my bungalow in evening dress: it was the first time for eight months that I had had a tie round my neck. Pete Fraser played host on New Year's Eve, for which occasion we were a party of six, since Pete's relief, Jim Mitchelson, had arrived. He reported that John Lindsay was still waiting to be relieved in Yenangyaung.

John finally arrived towards the end of January, but went down to disaster a few days later. We were riding back to the bungalow for lunch when Jack, the dog, panicked the ponies by getting among their feet. Both bolted, in the bungalow direction, but we had a right-hand turn to make across a narrow wooden bridge in the 'farm'. John was a horseman but I was the one who made it. John took a fearful toss, and when I got down to him he was in agony, with his shoulder severely misshapen. With assistance I got him up to the bungalow and into bed.

I wired Mawlaik for the Civil Surgeon and, by the greatest good fortune—for in the open season most of his time was spent on tour—got a reply to the effect that he was on his way up. Thanks to various misfortunes *en route*, it took him twenty-nine hours to get through, during which time John was in agony and I was helpless except for keeping him as drugged as I could and maintaining a constant programme of gramophone music. When Kyee Lwin the surgeon arrived (he was a Sino-Burman) he was in need of a brandy before he could start work, having come face to face with a tiger only just short of Indaw!

Kyee Lwin found that John's shoulder was dislocated, and pretty rigidly so by this time. He fashioned a mask of wire and cotton wool, ordered me to sit astride John's chest, handed me a bottle of chloroform and told me to keep dripping it on to the mask until told to stop. As soon as John went under Kyee Lwin launched into a sweating fight on the shoulder, levering himself against the bed with his foot and pulling on the arm as if to tear it out of its socket. At intervals that became briefer and more apprehensive, I kept reminding him that I was still dispensing chloroform, but each time he told me to keep going until, with astonishing suddenness, John's arm jumped back into place and Kyee Lwin collapsed into a chair, gasping for breath and with the perspiration pouring down his face. It must have made a ludicrous scene.

Kyee Lwin stayed a couple of days with us in order to satisfy himself that John would now make normal progress, and a very pleasant guest he was.

With Kyee Lwin barely gone, and John still convalescent, I was roused from sleep in the very early morning by the fire siren, the terror of an oilfield. It was a well burning, and one on which I knew a gang of coolies was working. I pulled trousers and sweater over my pyjamas and blundered down the cold darkness of the hillside to a scene of pandemonium. Three of the men were burnt and being carried to the hospital. We got hoses on to the blaze, but it was not until we rigged up steam jets that, over an hour later, we killed the fire. Fortunately all three casualties survived, but I had a wealth of reporting to do under the provisions of the various Oilfields Regulations to which we were subject.

This completed my 'blooding' at Indaw. John made a good recovery and, with no more than a week's deferment of my departure, I headed for Pantha with mixed feelings. A nine months spell I knew was long enough, and I was the youngest ever to have been sent to Indaw; but basically I felt that I had measured up to the challenge of the place and a part of me was sorry to go.

I boarded the ferry at Pantha, and as I disposed my kit in my cabin I peered into the dressing table mirror. It was the first time, I felt, that the reflection of a man returned my gaze.

5 Irrawaddy Occasions

February 1936 to June 1937

I think the Chindwin, for all its latent hostility, comes near to being my spiritual home. Pre-war it was remarkably little travelled by Europeans. The tourist route followed the more glamorous Irrawaddy. The turnover at Mawlaik and Indaw was small and largely repetitive, and when you talked of the Chindwin down-country there was little in the way of informed response. The world at large had not heard of it.

One day, alas, this beautiful river was to acquire notoriety as a baleful, bloody destroyer of fugitive hopes; but now, as I was borne southward by it, the only saloon passenger once more, it was mine. The skipper, Hammersley, was a remarkably well-read man for such backwoods employ, and his floating library was a delight.

Though we ran with the current, the shallows were still obstructive and the needs of river trade demanded much the same in the way of stops for the night. All was peace and leisure, though I continued to prime myself—as I had resolved to do for some weeks yet—with the Italian Esanophele which, at that time, was considered to be the best available anti-malarial prophylaxis, and which all at Indaw were required to take regularly.

My return to Lanywa was the prelude for a while to a somewhat gipsy existence. Among the junior Assistants on the Fields I was something of an odd man out and found myself used for plugging gaps. To start with, I was required to undergo a thorough medical examination. My blood, apparently, showed possible signs of suppressed malarial infection and I was switched from Esanophele on to a heavy dosage of Atebrin. This affected me to some extent, but basically I felt fit.

Tin Dredge on the Yamone River
The Managers Bungalow at Yamone

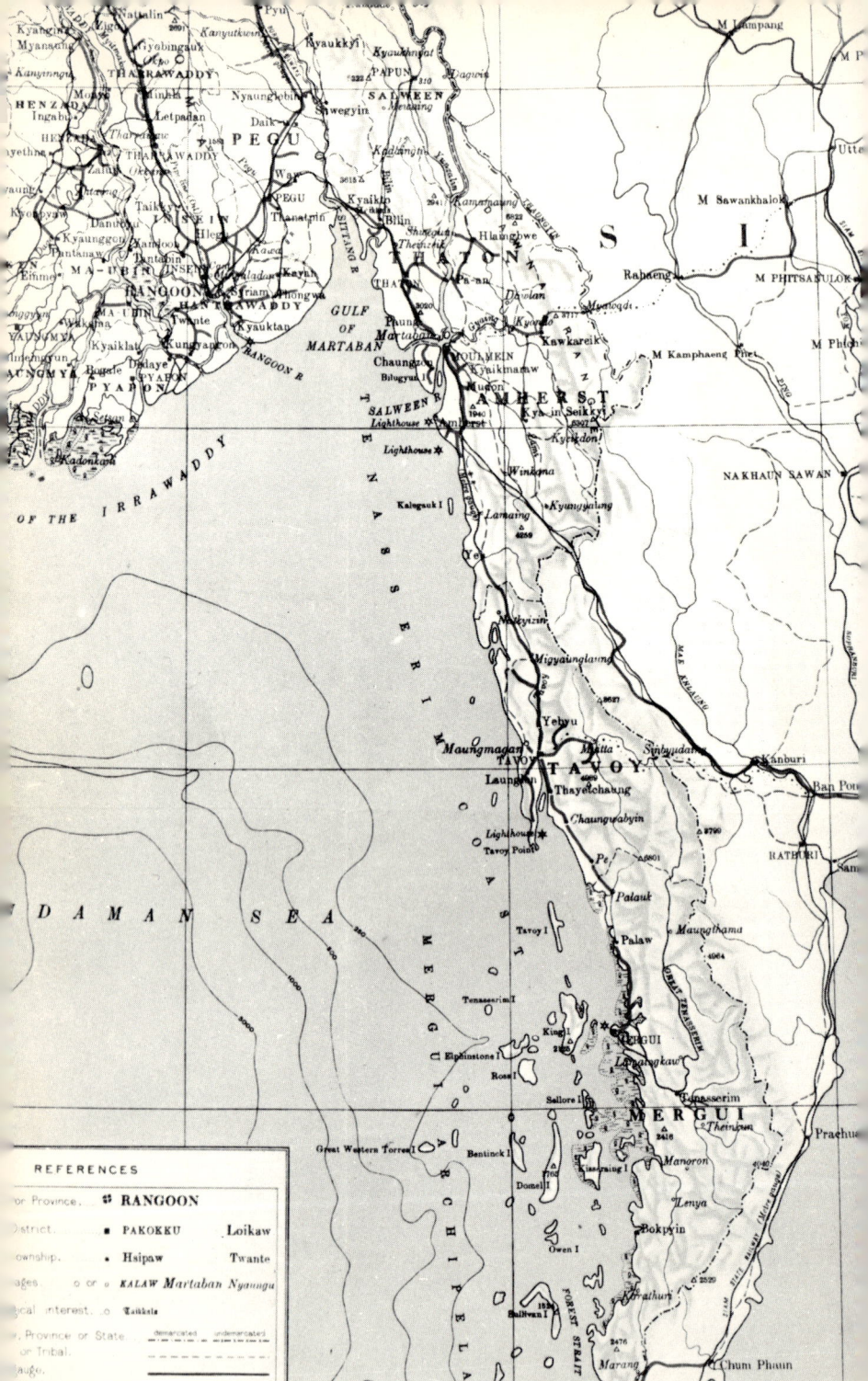

TENASSERIM ARCHIPELAGO

There were ludicrous comparisons to be drawn between my first and my present posting to Lanywa. On the earlier occasion I was a young man leaving the city lights for the hazards and the imponderables of the unknown. Now I was the seasoned campaigner returning to the fleshpots. Here were cars for elephants, roads for waterways and feminine company instead of the jokes, the quirks and the peevishness of men you had come to know to the core.

'The Mousetrap' had been put onto the road by the time I arrived and I was soon back into my old routine. With the money so easily saved at Indaw, I branched out into such luxuries as a radio set and some bungalow furnishings over and above the standard issue.

'Mac' had been transferred to Rangoon in my absence. In his place was Duncan McKenzie, a Scot of some twenty years service, all of which had been spent with The Attock Oil Company, another associate of Steels, located in the Punjab in that part of Western India that has since separated as Pakistan. Duncan was a widower with a son at school in Scotland, a rather shy, nervy character, at his best in a small group rather than a large party. On the job he had the happy knack of leaving you alone, so long as results were coming, to work out your own routine and methods. I got on well with him but on less than intimate terms, which he did not seek. Bill Grant had been joined by his wife, Ursula, whom I liked a lot and who proved to be about my 'weight' at golf. Otherwise little at Lanywa had changed.

My first transfer came after only a few weeks and was merely across the river to Chauk, where, at the time I went up the Chindwin, I.B.P. had had no stake. Now, in equal partnership with the British-Burmah Petroleum Company (B.B.P.), the two companies having contiguous leases some seven miles from the Chauk Field proper, there had been floated a joint venture with the object of reducing competitive drilling, of which there was to be an inescapable minimum anyway since a B.O.C. lease flanked both of ours.

In these conditions it would happen that a company on one side of the lease line brought in a good producer at the statutory minimum distance of three hundred feet from the line. Inevitably the drainage area of such a well would extend across the line, so the rival company would then drill an offset well to secure its own oil. Thus would develop a 'line fight', with wells being sited tactically instead of economically. These matters are better ordered now, but at one time 'line fighting' could be recognized from afar by the parallel march of rows of largely superfluous derricks.

My immediate job at Chauk was the short-term one of setting up the stores godown and organizing the receiving and issuing procedures—pedestrian stuff, but it was experience that I needed. I lived with Geoff Grindle, B.B.P's Chief Engineer at Chauk, moving in on him very apologetically because I am against shared accommodation in small communities. Fortunately, however, we knew each other already through common membership of Toc H and settled down in amity.

I found no little novelty in having access to the amenities of Chauk without the preliminary of a launch trip. I took the opportunity of climbing Popa and of visiting the ancient Burmese capital of Pagan, with its myriad pagodas. 'Hutch' recently had been transferred from Rangoon to Yenangyaung and I visited him there on several occasions. Unfortunately he was having recurrent spells in hospital with malaria, in which respect my luck continued to hold.

Poor old Geoff arrived home one evening with the news that his leave had been postponed for a year. On the last occasion he had met a French girl on his way back to Burma and had kept in touch with her ever since. He now took off for Colombo on three weeks compensatory local leave, having arranged for Madeleine to meet him there for another look at each other. He brought her back as his bride, it being fortunate that their arrival coincided with my own return to Lanywa, whence it was to be possible to oversee the job at Chauk on the basis of periodical visits.

My immediate task on reopening my bungalow was to throw a party for the newly-weds on their first Saturday together in Burma. At this time I traded in 'the Mousetrap' for a no less recognizably second-hand but vastly superior Ford V8 coupé. It was well above earning a derogatory nickname! Jock Scott arrived in Lanywa after being relieved at Indaw; but he too was having bouts of malaria.

There came a spell when I found myself acting for Duncan McKenzie, who had gone into hospital in Yenangyaung with an appalling carbuncle on his face. One evening, on my own in my bungalow, I was assailed by the most awful stomach pain. After writhing for an hour or so on my bed, I got myself to the telephone and called for help. The B.O.C. doctor at Chauk arrived in the small hours, pronounced acute appendicitis and hurried me down to Yenangyaung. On arrival in hospital next day (to the astonishment of McKenzie and 'Hutch', who was visiting him), I was operated on immediately. The doctor told me later that I was only just in time, and I remembered with horror what I now knew to have been a previous attack while I was at Indaw. What a haven in which to progress through peritonitis into Eternity! McKenzie was in no state yet to return to Lanywa, so 'Hutch', who was number two to David Thom in Yenangyaung, packed a bag and took off to hold the fort.

As I neared the end of my stay in hospital, the question of where to go for two or three weeks sick leave bulked as a problem. *Faute de mieux* I had almost decided to lie low in Rangoon, when Billy (my cousin) and Judy Rivers walked into my room. They were spending the hot weather in Maymyo and, good golfers both, were down in Yenangyaung for a match against the oilfields. They were insistent that I should go up to Maymyo and stay with them. This was a gift from Heaven that I could not possibly spurn, and as soon as I was fit to travel I was on my way up-river.

As travelling companions I had Edward d'Abo, an A.D.C. to the G.O.C., Burma, and himself a returning golfer; and an extraordinary character whom I only remember as 'Uncle Arthur'. He was a major on secondment to the command of the Upper Burma Battalion of the Burma Auxiliary Force and was returning to Maymyo after inspecting the Yenangyaung detachment. Having announced that he was hurrying back to take part in a ceremonial parade on the occasion of the King's birthday, he then proceeded to get very drunk. During the course of the evening he insisted on giving us a wholly unsolicited demonstration of the use of the sword.

As 'Uncle Arthur' flashed and lunged and swung his blade, I, from a cowering position of safety behind the dining table, noticed the tip make contact with an iron stanchion and become alarmingly distorted. I further saw that it took the strength that belongs to inebriation to restore the sword to its scabbard. As I lay abed I saw the potential scene on the Maymyo parade ground when the order was given to present arms.

'Uncle Arthur,' I piped up at breakfast, 'I'd like to have a look at that sword of yours again.'

'Not likely, my boy. And if I overdid it last night, you can put it down to the behaviour of an old man who's been out here too long.'

'Uncle Arthur, I would still like to see your reaction to the order "Present Arms".'

Bleary-eyed, the old boy peered at me from across the table. He said not a word, but I could see the maggot of doubt beginning to gnaw. Suddenly he groped to his feet and made for his cabin. His absence was long enough to tell us that he was establishing the hideous truth for himself.

He reappeared, pallid and muttering,

'You're quite right, old boy, the damn thing's stuck!'

It took the three of us an hour or more to unsheathe the sword: and then, having beaten the tip of it flat, almost as long again to rehearse 'Uncle Arthur' repeatedly in the drill for which it was soon to be required.

I did not witness the parade, but I am quite sure that 'Uncle Arthur' must have been dripping the sweat of apprehension until the 'Present' was behind him.

Arrived at Mandalay, I found that Billy Rivers had laid on the town's most comfortable taxi for me. I was glad to have d'Abo for company, particularly since he asked to be allowed to split the cost. Just when I thought we should be moving off, I noticed that Edward's restraining hand was on the driver's shoulder and that he was gazing down the road with an expression of rage on his face. There, as my eyes followed, I saw a *gharry*-wallah trying to flog into activity his pony, so sore and bloodied from ill-attended harness as to proclaim the agony of its dumbness.

Edward leapt out of the taxi, his tall frame covered the distance in seconds and, against the expostulations of the *gharry*-wallah, his skilled hands liberated the pony from the shafts. Woe to the man who had stayed to argue instead of making a run for it! Edward proceeded to lambaste him into senselessness. By the time he returned to the taxi, dusting off his hands with studied aplomb, a vocal crowd had gathered. Where the balance of sympathy lay was difficult to determine, and I was glad when we took off!

The road out of town ran alongside the moat and the wall of Mandalay's historic fort, so tragically to be obliterated before my connection with Burma was ended. Soon we were climbing the twisting, wooded road that led up and out of the plain and I could feel the freshening air blowing cool on my face. Though Maymyo is only three and a half thousand feet above sea level, it has all that is needed to make a delectable hill station. Most of the timber-extracting companies maintained comfortable houses up there as refuges for their staff after long spells in the jungle. It was Army Headquarters for the Upper Burma Area, and had I been challenged to romanticize a set of circumstances that would account for my next visit to Maymyo being as a private soldier in a Yorkshire Regiment, I would certainly have been hard put to it to achieve plausibility! As we drove through jungle tamed into parkland, skirting English-style houses in English-style gardens, my spirits rose at the prospect of total idleness in such a setting.

Billy and Judy Rivers looked after me marvellously. I was free always to choose between joining them or wandering off on my own. I played with their infant, Christopher; and I met and was entertained by their friends—even by my own, for I ran into some who had made me welcome at Mawlaik on my way to Indaw, including the attractive young grass widow who had been my partner on that occasion. This time she needed no squiring for her husband had been transferred to Maymyo!

Armed with bird book and binoculars, I used to wander

round the lake and down the rides and across the golf course until convalescent weariness drove me to bed, where, through my open window, I would lie taking in the sights and sounds of this so different, so nearly English Burma. Or else I would explore the bazaar, or drift along to the club and find myself a shaded table on the lawn where I could read or write to the lubrication of long glasses of iced lemon squash. Here was far more than bodily recuperation: it was balm to senses and emotions that too rapidly had been deployed over the past year. I slowed down to the walk that is my natural pace.

I returned to Lanywa wonderfully refreshed, but barely had I picked up the threads again before 'Hutch' in Yenangyaung followed my lead and went into hospital to have his appendix removed. So I was moved down in his stead.

The Yenangyaung oilfield was remarkable enough to merit some description, as it had been worked since before the British annexation of Burma in 1886. During geological ages the reservoir rocks had fractured, leaving the oil free to migrate upwards to wherever it could find lodgement. Thus the structure held oil at all levels, in accumulations of varying volume and, in the main, with the pressure that had provided the motive drive dissipated. Oil seeping to the surface (the translation of *ye-nan-chaung* is water-smelly-creek) had proclaimed the presence of a remarkable substance, with lubricant and flammable properties, long before the European arrived with his drilling equipment.

For years the Burmese had produced oil from hand-dug wells from depths of down to about a hundred feet, and their right to continue to do so was preserved when applications for oil prospecting leases started to come in. It was a remarkable sight to see a hand-dug well, about four feet in diameter, being worked against a background of wells pumping on the beam from perhaps three or four thousand feet. As often as not it would be a husband at the bottom of the hole, hand-filling a four-gallon kerosene tin, while his wife at the surface pumped air down to him through a pipe linked to a mask covering his nose and mouth.

The owners of these small well sites, the *Twin-zas*, had the option of leasing them to the drilling companies on a royalty basis; and it was not uncommon for three rival companies to be producing from three individual wells located within an area equal to that of a tennis court. There were no clearly defined lease lines here! The wells, as may be imagined, were numbered in thousands; and the Field as a whole looked like some impressionist artist's conception of a leafless forest of trees.

Yenangyaung provided the largest Anglo-American community I had seen since leaving Rangoon—about six hundred. Even card-dropping was still in vogue! The Americans were in sufficient strength to run their own club, but it was by mutual arrangement with the Yenangyaung Club that one or other, by rotation, was closed on Saturday night. This ensured a crowded dance floor as a weekly feature.

I stayed at Yenangyaung some weeks longer than was required by 'Hutch's' incapacity, as he was posted to Chauk after his return from sick leave. I was due to go back to Lanywa for another extension of the guide wall but, as a preliminary, was given a week's 'dental leave' to Rangoon.

This was a time-honoured device that enabled Steels to field their strongest possible fifteen for the annual rugby football tournament for the Public Schools Cup, which provided the basis for something of a 'Rangoon Week'. I had been given enough notice of this dispensation to get myself fit, despite that I had been back in hospital since my appendicectomy with a severe go of dengue. In my case the excuse for going down to Rangoon was not too much of a facade as I was badly in need of the ministrations of both a dentist and an oculist.

That week in Rangoon had a strange quality to it. Life, on my first arrival there, had had an exotic flavour that a spell up-country seemed to have erased. Now, hands on hips and gasping for breath as I waited in a line-out for the ball to be returned to play, my eyes ranged along the ranks of spectators. For the majority of them, the bankers, the shippers, the insurance wallahs, a lifetime in Burma would be bounded by Mingaladon golf course to the north and the Strand Hotel on the south. For them Burma, and a retirement of talking about it, would always and only be Rangoon.

For me, now, Rangoon had no claim to be Burma. I was aware of the lofty conceit of it, but I knew also that I had crossed the line that separates the port dweller from the jungle wallah. In came the ball: my weary frame leapt for it and the train of thought was broken.

The Cup eluded us when we succumbed to the Gym in a good game. I was still playing well enough for an abortive application to be made for my inclusion in the Burma side for the 'All-India'. Nightly I beat it up in the Gym or the Silver Grill. By day I was expected to be in the office whenever the dentist and the oculist required me not. I had a good time without enjoying myself, and was glad to go.

On my return to Lanywa I was absorbed in the pleasurable task of preparing my bungalow for a cold-weather visit from my parents and my sister, Vivian. My father had been a tea taster and, in retirement, he had a seat on the Board of a group of South Indian Tea companies. In the familiar manner, the Board was sending him out on a tour of inspection of the gardens and factories, and he had decided to combine business with pleasure by bringing my mother and sister with him in order to visit my brother, Jim, who was now in Calcutta, and myself in Burma.

The family duly arrived in time for Christmas and shared a few very enjoyable weeks with me. Apart from my own entertainment of them, the camp as a whole appreciated the novelty of cold-weather visitors who had by-passed Rangoon, and they were considerably regaled. My father, who had been a keen climber as a young man, made the ascent of Popa with Alfred Day and Charles Moore, two of the I.B.P. geologists. Vivian was a welcome new partner at the Chauk Club dances.

Soon after my people were gone I was again on the move in a stop-gap role. Down river at Thayetmyo, and since my first posting up-country, Steels had launched into a cement-making project, using as fuel natural gas from a sizeable reservoir they had drilled into at a place called Pyaye nine miles from the river. The first Agent of the new company, Bill Morrison, was having a run of bad health, to which Indaw malaria was a contributor, and he had been ordered into hospital at Yenangyaung. On his being declared a case for overseas convalescence, I was sent down to stand in for him.

I could not have arrived at a more interesting time as the factory was just about to come 'on stream': in fact Burma's first cement was produced while I was there. The factory stood on the bank of the Irrawaddy. The limestone 'feed' was quarried from the top of a hill some miles distant, whence it was carried in large buckets down a very long aerial rope-way to where a locomotive and open trucks took over and conveyed it to a crushing plant alongside the kiln. Everything was very new and up-to-date except for the senior staff's living accommodation, which had not yet been built. I inhabited a rented house in the bazaar without power or water. This made for somewhat primitive domestic arrangements but I found the game to be worth the candle.

The highlight of my stay was the initial firing of the kiln. It was only the second occasion on which a cement kiln had been fired on natural gas, and the operation was considered tricky enough to warrant the flying out from Europe of a couple of expert Danes. It was an occasion of tenseness and recourse to much in the way of precautionary devices, but everything went off as planned and great was the relief and the beer drinking that followed.

Within a few days we were making cement and, for the official opening ceremony, the guests of honour were General Sir Aylmer Hunter-Weston and his Lady. She, the daughter of the founding Steel, performed the 'launching' ceremony. Her husband, a colourful veteran of the Gallipoli and Western Front campaigns, insisted, jacketless but with brilliant braces, on climbing through, under or over everything in his pursuit of comprehension.

Of 'Hunter-Bunter' is told a well-known story of the First World War. At a time when the Allied trenches virtually linked the English Channel with the Mediterranean he was inspecting the northernmost unit of all. Addressing himself to a sentry, whose immediate concern it was to keep his feet dry from the rising tide by a periodic shuffle to his right, Sir Aylmer said:

'My man. Do you realize the special importance of your responsibility?'

'No Sir,' replied the unimaginative peasant from the Shires.

'Well,' said Sir Aylmer, 'if the Allied Armies were given the order to "left form" you'd be marking time for two years!'

The senior staff of the cement company, in due course to be reduced to three, numbered about a dozen at this time. The permanent residents of Thayetmyo added up to rather less than this, so life for them took on something of a new dimension. I got to know the brothers Fortescue and their wives who, as a family, operated at Yenanma, Burma's smallest oilfield, shipping their crude from riverside tankage by oil flats to the B.O.C.'s Refinery at Syriam on the Rangoon River. Their young sister, Gwen, was staying with them and I sought her company often. Then there was 'Hercules' Flint, the Divisional Forest Officer, and his immense, terrifying hound; and Reynolds, the Anglo-Burman Civil Surgeon and his wife and daughter, Lucy. (Two attractive young unmarrieds in such a small station was something!)

Riding one day with Lucy, my horse bolted on a rough road flanking the barbed wire entanglement-protected lines of the Military Police outpost. A stirrup leather broke. The saddle went one way and I the other, plunging, as I tried to keep my footing, into the wire. By the time the tearful Lucy had assisted me to final extrication, I was covered in blood and clad only in a jock strap and a wrist watch: the rest of my clothing was on the barbs. 'Doc' Reynolds dealt with his daughter by sedation and myself with what surely must have been a bucketful of iodine. The station had much to say!

Bill Morrison returned from sick leave before life became too complicated, and I returned to Lanywa for the few weeks that remained before my name came again to the top of the current Indaw roster. This time, however, I was due for only a three-month spell as I was sharing the open, drilling season with Duncan McKenzie whom I would be relieving. Duncan, normally, was of an age and seniority that put him beyond a stint at Indaw; but, newly arrived on the Burma scene as he was, he had not had the experience and I suspect that it was at his own request that he was sent up there.

For my second journey up the Chindwin (during the course of which, incidentally, the political separation of Burma from India became effective) I was accompanied by two robust Burmese drilling headmen from Lanywa. To meet a fortuitous shortage in this cadre, a substantial financial inducement had been offered and they had volunteered for a few months service. Nothing illustrates better than their fate the endemic nature of the malaria at Indaw and the resistance acquired against it by the permanent residents of the place. Though they were a sickly-looking lot, deaths specifically from malaria were not numerous. Yet, of the two men I took in with me, one was dead within a couple of months and the other I shipped out an unrecognizable wreck.

I played no part in the first man's burial but, though my letters do not record it, Buddhist convention would have required that I sign a documentary release for his spirit before interment.

From Monywa to Kalewa I had the delightful company of Major Bill and Sally Brown and their infant son. They were *en route* to Falam, the Headquarters of the Chin Hills Battalion of the Burma Frontier Force. As travelling companions they could not have been bettered. One evening I was walking with Bill along the caked flats of the low-water Chindwin. We were out of step and suddenly I saw that our inside feet were poised simultaneously to descend on a Russell's viper asleep on a mud cake. Urgently I gave Bill a mighty shove at precisely the same instant as he did likewise for me. The timing was perfect and each of us measured his length.

I dined with the Browns in the Kalewa rest house before saying my regretful 'good-bye'. Ahead of them was a remote eight days march through the foothills and up and over the shoulder of Kennedy Peak's near nine thousand feet onto the spinal ridge that would take them to Falam. One day I was to know, and alternately to dominate and to fear, every mile of that route!

I was denied an evening ashore at Mawlaik by a stranding of many hours duration some miles short of the town; and the same thing occurred next morning between Mawlaik and Pantha, where I did not get ashore until early afternoon.

Since my last visit the refinery had been closed down permanently, all the Indaw crude now being sent down-river by flats to Seikkyi. Under the conditions of yesteryear I would probably have stayed the night, but now, even though the bungalow was being maintained in habitable condition, its last occupant, Alex Wilson, had died in a road accident and the refinery had a dismantled and derelict look about it. I pushed on, contemplating as I travelled that, with the Pantha link gone, Indaw's isolation had increased by one more notch.

Conditions favoured my passage and I was drinking beer with Duncan McKenzie before nightfall—in slacks, long-sleeved shirt and mosquito boots once again!

After Duncan's departure we yet numbered five. Charles Moore, the geologist, was up for several weeks of field work and was sharing the Agent's bungalow with me. The driller was an American, and there were two young Scottish engineers. Collectively our biggest excitement during the present chukka was the bringing in of a well worth over a hundred barrels a day. Only a few of the existing wells were worth better than ten barrels, so this achievement made it possible to call a halt to drilling before the rains made it a miserable task. It had been a different story on my first spell!

All my old interests reclaimed my enthusiastic attention—the mosquitoes, the elephants and the bird life; but a three-months spell was soon ended, and it seemed no time at all before I was handing over to the senior engineer who, combining my duties with his in the absence of drilling, would be running the Field on a care-and-maintenance basis during the wet season. I went out with the driller and was soon headed down-river.

At Monywa I was required to break my journey. Some nine miles up-river from the town, I.B.P. had a tank farm into which the Indaw crude was decanted from the Chindwin flats for repumping into the Irrawaddy flats. With the closing down of Pantha Refinery it had become necessary to increase the tankage, and this required the purchase of more land. Optimistically I had bargained for this being a two or three days 'chore'. In the event I found that seven different landholders were involved, that collectively they spoke for about forty family and other partners, and that each and every one of these insisted on being present at all negotiations. I nearly went crazy. It was like getting thirty-nine sheep through a gate and then having half of them escape while rounding up the fortieth; and it went on for nearly three weeks.

During this paralyzing performance I was living in the town's rest house, which was hot, filthy and without passable amenities; added to which my *lugalay* was going down with bouts of malaria nearly every day. My only escape was to the club where I enjoyed a few games of tennis and the invariable up-country hospitality.

At last, near to defeat, I achieved the collective signing of the deeds of sale and left for Mandalay and the journey to Rangoon by train—permission to travel down-river via Lanywa having been revoked when it was found how long I was taking over the job at Monywa!

After nearly three years up-country I was in fact headed for a Rangoon posting. My feelings were very mixed. I had had a wonderful time of it, living the life of a large frog in small puddles, running my own bungalow, entertaining on behalf of the Company and subject to entirely adult treatment. Now I was to become a cog in a wheel, a minion instead of a master, an executor instead of an architect of programmes and decisions. As the train rumbled through the night I felt rebellious. All of which added up, doubtless, to the loss of a sense of proportion and the need for a change of diet!

6 City Lights

June 1937 to December 1938

Arrived in Rangoon, I suppose my elevation to a suite in 'the Gin Palace' should have cheered me with the reflection that the years were starting to line up behind me. However, I went straight to bed with an odious plague of boils, the legacy I was sure of that ghastly rest house at Monywa. At the same time my *lugalay* was persisting in his malaria and it was largely thanks to his teenage son, who came daily to lend a hand, that I got unpacked and more or less established. The rugger season had started and, though obviously far from fit, I was rarin' to go.

The enforced delay in my reporting for duty meant that the man from whom I was taking over had left on transfer to Lanywa by the time I got to his desk. It was the same stores purchasing job as I had been put onto when I first arrived in the country; but with what a difference! Then I had been flying blind: now I was buying for I.B.P. and the Burma Cement Company, with both of which I had served at the receiving end. Decisions at which I once might have quailed now came easily off the bat, and I was able to regiment my time and my routine to suit my convenience to a very fair extent.

I swung into rugger; my car had been shipped down from the Fields; gone was the restriction on membership of clubs; a sizeable minority of friends I had made up-country were now themselves in Rangoon, while others were to be met with on their way to or from leave. Among these were 'Hutch', with matrimony as his goal, and Geoff and Madeleine Grindle returning from their first home leave together.

Despite another bad attack of dengue, I gradually got

myself to the state of fitness where I added soccer to my twice-weekly diet of rugger. I started as something like fourth reserve to the Gymkhana Club's eleven but before long was a twice-weekly regular. I even extended to a fifth exertion by playing soccer for the I.B.P. once a week. Apparently this was not enough—or maybe it was that subconsciously I felt the need to exorcise three years of the jungle from my system, despite my enjoyment of it—for I found myself reviving a dormant interest in amateur dramatics.

I started modestly enough in the role of a policeman, with the principal function of catching a corpse as large as myself as it fell from a cupboard that I had curiously opened. This I followed by playing the male lead in Ivor Novello's *Fresh Fields*. The part is that of a middle-aged Australian and our staging of the play is memorable for its last night—the 'society' one. The leading lady had fallen ill and disaster stared us in the face. However, a Bibby liner had docked the previous Saturday, and from somewhere the word got around that a passenger, a mother visiting her son in Rangoon, had acting experience and had played this particular part many years ago. She rose to the occasion, retired for some hours with the script, and came on stage, far from word perfect but with the course of the action clear in her mind. I should never have believed that I myself could get through on the extemporaneous basis that was inevitable, but she was marvellous and I never had a moment's anxiety.

The Press report on my own performance calls for some explanation. It read:

Mr Harold Braund would have found it easier to portray a bluff Australian fifty years of age if he had had one or two more chukkas behind him, but he played the part excellently and his love scenes (attempted and actual) with Lady Lilian were among the best bits of the play. In short I have no criticism of him except that if he continues with the 'outside in' swing at golf he will never get anywhere.

The final, intemperate comment was aimed, I admit, at Rangoon's worst golfer. The action required that, while practising my swing in Lady Lilian's drawing room, I accidentally hit the ball and shattered a statuette of Love poised on a pedestal across the room. The achievement, in my case, was rightly regarded as impossible; so Love carried round her dainty neck a length of wire which, when pulled from off-stage at the critical moment, was supposed to confer on fiction a semblance of fact. In the event, on almost every occasion, my smite never remotely approached the status of a near-miss. Love collapsed, as was her role, presumably from fright or some other emotion; and the house rocked with unbridled hilarity at a point where Novello clearly envisaged nothing more than restrained laughter.

Having some small talent for tap dancing, I was soon swept up in Rangoon's world of amateur cabaret. I joined a classically-oriented male voice octet that used to contribute to concerts on various charitable and other occasions. I resumed my worship at the Anglican Cathedral and accepted an invitation to join the Council. I held (without violent advocacy of them) pacifist views that stayed me from service in the Armoured Car section of the Rangoon Battalion of the Burma Auxiliary Force, of which most of my 'Gin Palace' colleagues were staunch members. I maintained an active association with Toc H and became chairman of the Rangoon branch.

But rugger it was that was the breath of life, and I got myself back to the state of fitness where Steels were asked if again they would release me for the All-India Tournament at Calcutta. I was most anxious to go because I could see from the draw that I would almost certainly find myself playing against my brother Jim. 'Mac', now my Rangoon Manager, was a keen rugger man and all looked to be set fair. Alas, it was not to be. I.B.P. at the time were agitating for another Assistant to be sent out from London, and the view prevailed that to release for a football tour a member of what was being represented as an attenuated staff was to invite a rebuff. Accordingly I found myself ill-humouredly captaining the 'Possibles' against the 'Probables' in the final trial before the Burma side sailed. The Sports Correspondent of the *Rangoon Gazette* made a final throw on my behalf when he wrote of this match:

... and Braund, who led their forwards, played a magnificent game. In my opinion he is the best forward in Rangoon at the present time and his inclusion in the Burma team would make a vast difference.

That didn't work either, but I.B.P. got their new recruit!

When the Burma side returned from Calcutta we all got down to the serious business of our year, the tournament for the Public Schools Cup. As had been my lot in the past, 'dental leave' was granted to two or three good players who were stationed up-country and we fielded a strong side. Nevertheless we went down in the semi-finals to the Kings Own Yorkshire Light Infantry, who later drew with the Gym in the final to share the cup with them.

There followed the cold weather with its constant round of fun and frivolity. My principal partner-in-crime on many of these occasions was Derek Lewton-Brain, another denizen of 'the Gin Palace', and, like myself, the occupant of a top floor suite. The hangovers we nursed on high it boots not to recall!

There were occasions, however, when even Derek had to be disposed of, for I had fallen under the spell of a girl who had come out to stay with relatives for the cold weather. She was two or three years older than me and since, in order to preserve the mobility of their junior staff, Steels operated a ten-year ban on matrimony, it was an empty pursuit from the start. Within the limits of this tacit understanding we had some wonderful times together, but it was my first experience of serious heartache.

The absurd occasion of 'bazaar bargaining' in which I had been ensnared at Monywa on my way down the Chindwin erupted into fresh argument and I was sent up to resolve matters. Even the shortcomings of the rest house were softened this time by the magnificence of the Upper Burma cold weather. Between disputes in the court-house I played golf and tennis with *Bombine* friends, and one evening I entertained John Lindsay and Jim Mitchelson who were on passage to their second spells at Indaw. It was a needed break from artificial living and I returned to Rangoon with my mission successfully accomplished.

Back I came to rehearse shanties for the Blind School

concert and carols for a Christmas presentation at the Gym; to the tumult of Steels annual rugger tiffin and the pagan exuberance of the Caledonian Ball; to wrestling with the pros and cons of resigning from Steels and taking another job that I had been offered; and to coping in an inexperienced way with the running of the Rangoon Boys Home, the brainchild of John Hedley who was to be away from Rangoon for some weeks. My chief contribution hitherto had been teaching the boys to box, though I lacked any qualification to do so.

Ben Braund's wife and daughter were now in Rangoon and I was included in a number of parties at the High Court level. I weekended once with Billy and Judy Rivers on their property at Kyauktaga and collided with a water buffalo on my way back to Rangoon, the damage to my car being not inconsiderable. And, of course, I dined and danced at every possible opportunity with the girl of the moment.

As an end to what was fast becoming a crescendo of living, it was no bad thing when Gordon Nicoll called me in one day to tell me that a revision of the staff programme required John Lindsay's recall from Indaw and that I was to go up and complete the open season. The girl friend sailed for home just before I left, so I was able to turn my back on Rangoon with more of anticipation than regret. There was a state of severe financial malaise to be corrected apart from anything else!

Rangoon was the most distant starting-point for Indaw from which I had hitherto taken off, and the long river journey was restful and relaxing. I achieved much in the way of arrears of letter writing and had transient company for most of the journey. At Monywa I received the customary *Bombine* hospitality: at Mawlaik there had been a change of *Bombine* Manager. 'M.T.' Colchester had gone and I dined with the newcomer, Kenneth Bloxam and his wife. I reached Pantha at eleven o'clock of a morning and, since the truck was on the road, I made it to Lawtha the easy way. I completed the journey to Indaw by pony, arriving drenched from a raw, chilling rain against which a hot bath, whisky, aspirin and three blankets made up the prescribed treatment.

John Lindsay departed within a few days: I stood in need of no lengthy handover by this time. I was left with Jim Mitchelson as field engineer and two British drillers. The drilling programme was going smoothly, although the two wells drilling were at long distances from the office and I was promptly in need of walking legs. Rugger does not provide the right training for this kind of life.

Jim and I were foolish enough to undertake the annual walk of the oil pipeline in the heat of April. We did the Indaw to Lawtha stretch one day, trucking it thence to Pantha. The following day we walked from Pantha to Lawtha to complete the journey thence by pony. I wrote home of this trip:

We started back for Lawtha along the pipeline sharp at six on Monday morning. Although the road from Pantha to Lawtha is nearly twenty miles the pipeline measures rather less than thirteen, so you can realize that it is no respecter of hills and dales. 'As the pipeline runs' might well supersede for me 'as the crow flies'. When we were not climbing steep slopes by our eyebrows or sliding down them on the seats of our pants, we were wading through swamps or crossing *chaungs* on rickety bridges. We came across elephant tracks in plenty and also a tiger's: monkeys were plentiful and we also saw a barking deer. I must have picked up a touch of the sun the day before because when crossing a bit of swampy ground I had a complete 'black-out' and came to flat on my back with Mitchelson sprinkling water over me. However, I got over that and survived the worse that was to follow because when we finally made Lawtha at about 12.30 the sun was terrific and we were burnt to cinders, particularly under foot. After some beer and breakfast we tried to sleep till the cool of the evening but it was quite impossible. We started off for Indaw by pony at about 4.30 and arrived at 7.30 after a very leisurely ride through. Mitchelson bathed and changed in my bungalow and had dinner with me: it was his birthday and I don't suppose he— or I—will forget it in a hurry.

I had indeed collected a touch of the sun for I suffered from occasional passing-out for over a year afterwards.

To add to my experiences at Indaw we had an earthquake a few days after the pipeline walk. It was not a very serious affair and did little material damage on the Field: however it cracked our cement tennis court and stopped the pendulum clock in my bungalow.

That pre-monsoon season in Indaw was a succession of

violent storms. Watching the elements one evening through the mosquito screening of my bungalow, I saw a tree struck by lightning and burst into flames in most spectacular fashion. I wrote:

The weather over this last week has been changeable to an amazing degree and has included heat, rain, fog and gales. To give a picture of it, I have padded round the Field with the sandy roads almost burning through the soles of my shoes, I've sat after a bath with the perspiration making the clothes as wet as the ones I'd taken off, I've leapt out of bed in order to get the windows shut before a gale hit the bungalow, I've sat in front of a fire in the evening and slept with two blankets on my bed, I've worn a woollen cardigan and a scarf to the office and I've stood on a hillside with a perfect view of the Manipur Hills away in India and yet been unable to see the office a hundred feet below me. The only thing I don't seem to have done is to skate on the water reservoir.

In these conditions I received that rare happening at Indaw, an invasion of visitors. They were the Bloxams and the Sutherlands from Mawlaik. With the former I had dined on my way up the Chindwin: Steve Sutherland was the Divisional Forest Officer. Kenneth Bloxam was coming 'officially' on what he had intended as the last leg of a pre-rains tour. I described their arrival.

The relieving engineer from Lanywa just made it, but my visitors were marooned at Pantha until Tuesday evening when they arrived in half dead—the menfolk anyway—as, having started out from Lawtha on ponies, they were washed off them two or three crossings out and had to wade, and in some cases swim, the remaining ones. The memsahibs were not so badly off as they got through on an elephant.

Bloxam's work in the teak context was completed within a day, but it was several days before the party could attempt the return journey to Pantha. This suited me admirably! Every evening we played Mah-Jong; they were excellent company and I was sorry to see them go.

At this time I heard the first rumour of an entirely novel posting awaiting me soon after my return to Rangoon. Away down south of Mergui, in the Tenasserim Archipelago that forms Burma's long 'kite tail', Steels had ventured on a tin dredging enterprise that was soon to require the posting of an Assistant to take administrative charge. My name, apparently, was being bandied about in the connection. It all seemed too improbable and I tried not to think about it.

My departure for Rangoon coincided with Jim Mitchelson's return to Lanywa. The occasion set the seal on my connection with Indaw and, though it is engraved indelibly on my memory, I revert again to my letters for a contemporary description of it.

Well I'm out of Indaw—as also Mitchelson—but only just. All through the last week the rain continued to pour and we were shipping the kit out as and when we could on the elephants (I can see my wireless set has been under water even so). Finally, with all the fit elephants out of the camp, we set off on a raft at 3.00 p.m. on Friday for Lawtha. It's about fourteen or fifteen miles following the *chaung*, and at 8.30, with only half a mile to go, we struck a submerged teak log and wrecked the whole show. We grabbed everything we could, but not before our suitcases had disappeared under water, and in pitch darkness with the water swirling round us and our arms full of kit we waited while the coolies tried to get us off. It was no use, however, and we had to start off for Lawtha on foot across sand and mud flats into which, for quite long stretches, we were sinking to the knees at each step. As you can imagine, we were soaked, muddy and tired when we reached Lawtha, where we had nothing but wet clothes to change into. There was nothing for it but to hang up our wet mosquito nets, knock back some beer and curry and climb into bed: not forgetting a double dose of Esanophele.

A sense of filial propriety doubtless omitted the explanation that the beer came from a full case that we had managed to salvage from the wreck; and that we consumed it in such quantities as to ensure that stupor would compensate for certain loss of natural sleep!

When I rose in the morning and sloshed *chaung* water over my throbbing head, I paused nevertheless to gaze back up the surging Khodaung before heading for Pantha. I knew, somehow, that I would not be coming back. During my three spells at Indaw I had known fear and frustration, I had walked with contentment and distress; I was much better aware of my capabilities and of my shortcomings, and I was schooled for unsuspected tougher demands to come. I raised my hand—it was both a salute and a farewell—and was gone.

I suppose it can be said that I did visit Indaw once more vicariously. It was as a signature on ten thousand leaflets that were dropped on the Field and at Lawtha and Pantha during the Japanese occupation; but the opportunity I had hoped for of following them up in person never came, and now it never will.

At Pantha, by prior arrangement, Jim and I boarded a B.O.C. launch for Mawlaik. The B.O.C. by this time was hanging onto I.B.P's coat-tails by drilling up-river at Yenan on the strength of the Indaw seepages. At Mawlaik all was carnival. Their popular Anglo-Burman Deputy Commissioner, Porter, was being transferred, and from logging camp and outpost every Mawlaik-based individual who could make it in had done so. The club was bedecked as 'Porter's Pub', and we numbered about two dozen that evening. In a world that has now gone colour-mad, it was a wonderful demonstration of unstudied inter-racial harmony.

In the small hours of the morning, Jim and I were escorted aboard the ferry and soon we were sleeping our way down the Chindwin. When I finally got to my feet I stood pyjama-clad in the prow, watching the divide of the waters and the river craft and the birds and the endless background of teak. Consciously I tried to memorize it all, to absorb and make it a part of me; for I knew that I must.

I parted company with Jim at Monywa and, on reaching Rangoon by train, found that Rumour had only partly opened her wings. Not only was I destined for transfer to the novelty of the Tenasserim project: the planned start of operations required that I be sent home on leave a year before I was due—or less than six months hence!

This news was as good as a new mainspring and I flung myself with zest into all my old pre-Indaw activities. However, I was having bad trouble with my tonsils and the doctor said that they would have to come out while I was in England. I was still having the black-outs that I inherited from the line walk between Indaw and Pantha: and finally, just when I was ready to congratulate myself on having got off scot-free, I went down with the first of many bouts of malaria. *Minimus*, or maybe it was *Maculatus*, had got me!

The fever followed a curious pattern of short, sharp jabs at intervals of a week or ten days. Typically, at three o'clock of an office afternoon, I would feel the shivers mounting; I would be driven straight to 'the Gin Palace' and put to bed, by five I would be delirious with a temperature of a hundred and five; by seven, rational, limp and exhausted, I would be lying on my back listening to the perspiration dripping on to the floor through the thickness of the mattress; at nine, I would get up, have a bath and weigh myself on my bathroom scales—and be from five to seven pounds lighter than I had been that morning; and then, if it was important to me, I would be at the Gym or elsewhere by ten or ten-thirty. Others with the same complaint might be having spells in hospital. I got away with it on this somewhat nerve-eroding basis.

Meanwhile I was unravelling the story behind my future posting. A certain James Ingram Milne, a mining engineer, had under lease in the Tenasserim Archipelago two alluvial tin-bearing areas. They were dredging propositions and he lacked the finance to go it alone. He had approached Steels with a proposal for a joint venture and Steels had arranged for an independent survey of what he had to offer. The recommendations had been favourable, and Milne came out of it with cash, shares, and a seat on the Board of the new Company. He came up to Rangoon for a top-level meeting and I was asked to sit in. I watched him with curiosity, a hard-bitten, hatchet-faced Scot with a monocle, bad teeth, a ready smile and an affected enunciation that did a poor job of overlaying his Aberdonian accent. He looked tough, and in due course I was to learn that he was.

Rangoon at this time became involved in a frenzy of communal rioting between Hindus and Burmans. A letter home gives a fair picture, I think, of what these affairs meant.

The riots here are having a rather dislocating effect on business and the services generally. The office is virtually closed because the clerks of both creeds are not prepared to run the gauntlet of getting there, and most of the junior Assistants are out serving with the Armoured Cars or on patrol duty down at the mills. The whole trouble started over a book which, though it has been on sale for seven years, has been found to contain something offensive to the Buddhist creed. The situation appears to be well in hand now, but the death roll must be considerably bigger than the newspapers and wireless bulletins would have you believe. So long as the trouble was localized in the East end of the town there was no trouble in having a sufficient concentration of police and military to keep things within bounds, but when the trouble became widespread and the forces had to be scattered in twos and threes over the whole town, looting and incendiarism started on a big scale and people of both creeds were being picked up dead or badly battered in all districts. In my opinion the calling out of the military and the order to open fire in order to disperse crowds and stop looting should not be two separate events in cases like this. It should be made clear that as soon as the military are called out there is not going to be two or three days of standing around looking ornamental with fixed bayonets before the shooting starts. I admit that to fire down crowded streets, no matter how much the crowds have been warned to disperse, is a drastic measure, but when people have been worked up to the point of fanaticism over religious issues, gunfire is the only thing they will listen to and I think it involves less bloodshed in the long run.

Both military and police are now firing where necessary: the Armoured Cars and Auxiliary Force were called out on Thursday and the rest of us in the Chummery and mills have since been organized into two parties in conjunction with the Bombay-Burmah for the defence of our respective mills which are alongside each other and which, in view of their lakhs worth of teak stocks are a golden object for incendiaries. We all mustered down there yesterday with camp beds, stores etc. Steels party consisted of nine of us—six from the Chummery and three from the mill—and we spent the night watching strategic points on the basis of two hours on duty one off. A barbed wire barricade had been put up round both mills and our job was to patrol the strip of ground between the barricade and the mill fence. We were armed with revolvers, sticks and torches, and our instructions from the police were that if anybody tried to get through the wire we were to shoot first and inquire into their business later . . .

This letter, in retrospect, stresses the defence of property rather than the protection of life. In fact we had the entire Indian population of the mills on the inside of the wire with us. None would have survived for long beyond it.

A clear memory is of the infinite good humour that went with the uncompromising firmness of individual British soldiers in this crisis; and it often tipped the scales the right way.

Soon after this my brother, Jim, arrived in Rangoon from Calcutta on a business trip that kept him three weeks. The social life of Rangoon had revived after the riots and we pursued a lively course after our respective days' work was done.

There followed the Munich crisis and all the fear and apprehension that this promoted. My own letters home expressed views that I was soon to renounce. Loudly did we all acclaim Neville Chamberlain's 'piece of paper' and stoutly, with whatever lack of conviction, ridicule the prognostications of those Jeremiahs who regarded the whole affair as a Hitlerian manoeuvre. Selfishly I rejoiced in the removal of the threat to my leave.

My departure, indeed, was now at hand. I would again be travelling out of season and had no difficulty in booking for myself one of the best two-berth staterooms in *Derbyshire*— particularly as Steels were Rangoon agents for the Bibby Line.

Saturday, 26 November, was my twenty-fifth birthday and I was sailing two days later. I had a dinner party for eighteen at 'the Gin Palace' and we then all went on to a Ball at the Gym. It was a cabaret occasion and I was the only male in the cast. The Master of *Derbyshire* was among the guests: there and then he appointed me to organize his shipboard entertainment for the homeward run!

Somehow I made the gangway on Monday, and we sailed.

The passengers were few in number from Rangoon, but at Colombo we picked up, among others, three nursing sisters, who livened things up a lot. At Port Sudan we added some of the actors and the technicians of a company that had been filming *The Four Feathers* in the Sudan Desert. In the main we avoided them because they seemed only to want to talk 'shop'.

We reached Marseilles on 23 December. I was resolved on getting home for Christmas and left the ship there with a suitcase. Europe was having an appalling winter. On what was my first flight we took off from Marseilles in blinding snow and were back within half an hour with engine trouble. We got away at the second attempt but landed at Paris with an engine on fire and the airport in pandemonium on that account.

The weather had worsened and all cross-Channel flights had been cancelled. I found a train leaving for Dieppe, with no guarantee of a packet connection. Luck was with me as a boat was just leaving, but I could hear the seas thundering beyond the breakwater. I borrowed the bunk of an officer on watch, drank two large bottles of stout in quick succession and knew no more until we were alongside at Newhaven. Still in heavy snow I caught a train, and I knocked on the front door of my old home at eight o'clock on Christmas morning.

When I unpacked my suitcase, in the presence of my mother, I found it thickly ballasted with confetti—a parting gesture, as I guessed, from the nursing sisters. It took me some time to assure my mother that the worst had not happened!

7 Beachcombers' Coast

December 1938 to November 1940

I lay on my bunk in *Staffordshire*, sweating my way out of the delirium of a particularly rough attack of fever. Gradually my senses took in the white-gleaming, jacketed pipes clamped to the cabin ceiling and pondered their abrupt emergence from one bulkhead and their total plunge into the other. Then my eyes found the circular porthole and the gently heaving sky beyond, and I remembered where I was.

With my mind at slack, my thoughts wandered back over the events of my leave, extended by nearly a month to compensate for illness: the three weeks ski-ing in Switzerland, the visits to scattered friends and to my old schools, the spells in hospital with malaria and for the removal of my tonsils, my introduction to the marvel of TV, and the 'where do I go from here' in the matter of an *affaire de coeur* (my second in little more than a year!).

Occasionally the aged ship's doctor bumbled in. I suspect that he was a retired GP taking a working holiday, and I'm sure that he knew less about malaria than I did. However, I did not have to worry as I had struck up a friendship with a young doctor returning to Singapore after leave. He knew his stuff and, in an unofficial way, used to look in occasionally just to make sure that I was not being done to death.

In my stricken condition I underwent something of a traumatic experience. The war clouds over Europe had not thinned during my leave, but I had persisted in the effort to convince myself that the worst would not happen. Now, somehow, I knew beyond a peradventure that it would; and I cursed myself for being on an east-bound course. Clearly it had been my duty to resign from Steels and try for a commission in the R.A.F. I had dodged the issue and I was a coward.

A few days later, fit again and in company, I curbed my mood of self-censure but resolved nevertheless that, on arrival in Rangoon, I would cast around for at least some preliminary participation in events.

We sailed up the Rangoon River on 1 July and the usual welcoming contingent swarmed aboard as soon as we were berthed. Among them was Derek Lewton-Brain, who had been up-country when I went on leave. It was good to see him and we were soon doing the rounds together. However, I was due to sail for Mergui on the twelfth, and there was much in the way of preliminary education awaiting me in the office; so we fairly had to cram the lighter side in.

True to my shipboard resolve, I found my way, by dint of devious inquiry, to the office of a senior police official whose staff, under cover, were concerned with Intelligence. I explained the reason for my call and the nature of my coming posting. After quite a catechism I was briefed in the need for obtaining information on the accelerated activities of Germans extracting wolfram over the Siamese border east of Mergui. I was told how to send back information, that there were others involved, but that I should learn who they were only if it became necessary. Apparently it never did, which leaves me to suppose that I didn't notably make my mark as a spy. On this present occasion, however, I left the rendezvous with a high sense of mission, furtively looking back over my shoulder to make sure I was not being followed!

I sailed from Rangoon in *Sir Harvey Adamson*, the oldest ship in the B.I.S.N. fleet. She came out before the First World War and was known locally as the *Scurvy Harvey*. She survived the Second World War but then, restored to the run I was now making, was lost in a hurricane with over two hundred people on board and never a piece of wreckage found. On her present trip she rolled monstrously and, true to form, I spent most of the time on my bunk being violently sick.

Jim Milne came aboard the morning after we berthed and took me ashore. As a *pied-a-terre* in Mergui he had rented a new but crudely built house on the waterfront, that served both as a residence and as a transit stores godown. I was impatient to make my first inspection of Mergen, to give the town its ancient name (though the present-day Burman knows it as Beik-myo). Maurice Collis had only recently published his fascinating *Siamese White*, which I had read with anticipatory thoroughness. I quote his brief description of the place.

It is a town of some 20,000 inhabitants, situated on an island of the utmost fertility at the edge of a great archipelago. The inhabitants in general are dressed in Burmese clothes and use the language of that country, though they are of the mixed blood of Burma, Siam, Malaya, China and India, with strains of Portuguese and Arab. It is a place overshadowed by a various past.

Jim took me round the town introducing me to Government officials, some of them British and some Burmese. We toured the residential area as well as having a look at the incredibly motley bazaar. None of it was quite the Burma that I knew and I recognized that something of the atmosphere of the Straits lay upon it. Certainly in the club—and in no other in Burma—one used the Malayan words when ordering a drink—*stengah* for a whisky and *pahit* for a gin.

We left Mergui for the Mine next morning in the Company's cabin cruiser *Island Queen*. (We were, by the way, 'The Lenya Mining Company Limited'.) For a number of miles our route lay in the open sea, so it was well that the turbulence of *Sir Harvey Adamson*'s passage had totally subsided. Freed from the bondage of seasickness, I was able to take in something of the splendour of this most glamorous of all coasts, with its hundreds of islands, all jungle-covered and some of them rising to about three thousand feet; its many leagues of mangrove swamp simulating a shore line, and the variety of craft that moved up and down on business that often was as questionable as legitimate. Here were pirates, smugglers and poachers (who by this time had virtually extinguished the rhinoceros, so highly prized for its 'medical' components).

Mergui's principal 'cottage' industry was the preparation of *nga-pi* (rotted fish), a prized delicacy throughout the length of Burma. When the wind was off-shore, as I was later to learn, Mergui proclaimed its approach by this fact alone at a distance of five sea miles. You either came to terms with the aroma or were eternally repulsed by it. If you had occasion to send home a wedding present from this part of the world it would be something in mother-of-pearl: a powder bowl, plates, or knives and forks.

Maurice Collis has described Mergui as the place where the South Seas begin. The definition was soon credible.

We had ahead of us a normal run of three to four hours, but soon after entering the mouth of the Yamone River, via the larger Tenasserim, we were halted for an hour or two by engine trouble. The delay proved critical because some miles short of the Mine the river narrowed to a rapid when the tide was ebbing, and the strength of the bore was such that no craft could get through. The tide had in fact turned by the time we arrived, so we had to anchor for several hours before we could proceed.

My introduction to Yamone (Jim had appropriated the river's name for the camp) was therefore in pitch darkness, and as we struggled up the hill to our bungalow, somewhere about the ninetieth of the two hundred and thirty inches of rain that we could expect was teeming down. I was chilled and fearful of a bout of malaria, but fortunately I was spared.

Next morning I was up early to explore my new domain, and within a day or two I was sending home a first impression that still serves better than unaided memory.

The camp is situated on about seventeen acres of relatively dry ground bordered on three sides by mangrove swamp and on the fourth by the Yamone *chaung*. The bungalow is a teak-wood affair—as yet unpainted—without lights, fans, long baths or sanitation. It is at about the highest point of the 'island' and commands a very fine view. From the verandah you look down onto the camp and the Dredge—a most ungainly monster—beyond it in the river. There is as yet no office, so I use partly the stores godown and partly the bungalow for work purposes. The clerks are about as ignorant as I am at the moment, and on top of everything else I have to do most of my own typing!

There was nothing here of the creature comforts of the oilfields, and I soon found that I had to combat an odd quirk in Jim Milne's make-up. Put him among the lights of civilization and he would settle for nothing less than the best; but in the jungle he took an almost masochistic pleasure in doing without even the simplest amenities: and on a job where we were some months distant at least from profitable working, it was somewhere near to mania. He took an extremely poor view of my having persuaded the Rangoon Office before I sailed to send down a kerosene-operated refrigerator.

'You young fellahs don't know what it is to live in this country. I was out here the thick end of twenty years before I had a cold drink.'

(The 'thick end' was a favourite expression: and Jim was a man to be stood up to if you were not to find yourself being pushed around eternally.)

'Yes, Jim—and look at you now! Now listen—you took me away from a life I was enjoying when you shanghaied me into coming down to this bloody place; and I'm damned if I see why I should have to put up with warm sodas and tepid beer into the bargain. You'll be lucky if I stay!'

Later in the evening, when I caught him in the act of helping himself to a cold soda, there was a twinkle in his eye. The fact remains that we would never have got the refrigerator had I needed his approval for the purchase.

I had by no means been misled in what to expect and was equipped with a good, battery-operated radio, a gramophone with a wide selection of classical records, and even a guitar which I was resolved to teach myself to play, though in this I certainly failed.

Company was sparse. The Dredgemaster was a diminutive Australian, Danny Higgins. He had his virtues, but he spoke only the language of blasphemy, and I could see that a small island was not going to afford much room for escape from the tedium of it. The Dredge Engineer was a Scotsman, a parsimonious young man with nothing to contribute. And, with Jim, that was the lot!

I found my salvation on a neighbouring lease a mile or two up-river where the Yamone *chaung*, as a navigable waterway, petered out against the foothills of the mountain range that furnishes this lengthy isthmus with its spine.

111

Here, on a gravel-sluicing proposition and on his own, was George Wilson, a man after my own heart. He was a tough, stocky Yorkshireman who had known no parents but had a public school education behind him. He had once held a regular commission in the Kings Own Yorkshire Light Infantry, but had left the Army when the 'Geddes axe' had dimmed promotional prospects. He had then spent some years in Malaya alternating between mining and rubber planting—and he was a man who did all things well.

George never allowed himself to become too deeply involved in anything, however, and he returned to England after a few years of this. There—and I think it was for no other reason than to satisfy a very distinctive sense of humour—he removed his moustache and enlisted in the ranks of his former regiment under an assumed name. He bought or otherwise found his way out after a year or two and returned to Malaya. In his present employment he had charge of the only footing in Burma maintained by the Osborne and Chappell Group of Malayan Mining Companies.

George had a very well-informed appreciation of classical music, and as a military historian he was almost in the Liddell Hart or Cyril Falls category. On his job he was extremely efficient. He maintained the most sparsely furnished bungalow, bar one, that I ever saw (the other story will follow) and indulged in it a passion for cleanliness: everything was highly polished and gleaming. I slipped and fell on his teak-wood flooring on several occasions: George never did. In such an out-of-the-way spot as this I was indeed fortunate to find such stimulating company.

Yamone Chaung was the northernmost of the two alluvial tin areas that Jim Milne had ceded to Steels. It had a potential dredging life of only four or five years, after which a move would be made to the more extensive Khe Chaung far to the south. The Japs forestalled my ever getting a sight of this place, which perhaps was just as well as it was the ultimate in isolation.

The Dredge, a diesel-powered bucket unit of the most modern design, had been constructed and erected in the

Netherlands. It had then been dismantled, shipped out to Burma, re-erected in Mergui and towed to its present site. The project involved dredging the bed of the Yamone and the mangrove swamp to the south of it for a distance of some hundreds of yards from the river. There was about thirty feet of overburden to be removed before the tin-bearing stratum was reached. The Dredge was not yet ready to start digging. With memories of the *Margaret* at Lanywa, I suggested to Jim that we should name our craft. He would not hear of it and, understanding his unsentimental nature, I let it go at that.

The Dredge was fuelled on charcoal gas, the charcoal being burnt locally from mangrove. Before the start of digging we carried out wide-ranging experiments with all manner of techniques and kilns. We finally settled for a formula that seemed to give charcoal of an optimum quality, but what we could produce at the Mine itself was nothing like enough for our needs. We were faced with the necessity of creating a new village industry and, in so sparsely popu-lated an area, this involved spreading the 'gospel' along hundreds of miles of waterway.

Accordingly I set off for a week of 'selling' in the *Island Queen*. We criss-crossed a fantastic network of major and minor rivers, stopping at sizeable villages, summoning through the headman a concourse of villagers, and then demonstrating, with much sweat, the digging and loading of charcoal pits. In many cases we seemed to be regarded as no more than a troupe of entertainers, and on completion of our labours the villagers would disperse laughingly before the hat went round. Increasingly, however, we made headway, and by dint of 'after sales service' we got what we wanted, with the added pleasure of seeing impoverished villages gradually becoming income-earning beyond their experience or their dreams.

There was much hard work in all this, but the evenings at anchor contemplating an impossible sunset or a sky run riot with stars were a never-staling relaxation. Sometimes, when my thoughts dwelt on Rangoon and of my enthusiasm for social involvement during my spells there, I used to wonder at my ready acceptance of the life of solitude that had become my more usual lot.

One evening, before sunset, I dived off the launch for a swim. I trudgened my way for fifty yards or so before pausing for a look round. Not far from me, on a mud bank, was a large crocodile eyeing me with the utmost malevolence. My time back to the launch is not to be found in the record books. But after hauling myself aboard and recovering my wind, I gave old Barkat Ali, the Chittagonian serang, absolute hell for not warning me that we were in crocodile waters. The old man laughed and tried to assure me that the local crocs never took more than monkeys drinking at the water's edge and that I had been perfectly safe. In the long run I learnt that he was right, with the rare exception of an occasional village woman being taken in similar circumstances, but on the present occasion I was not easily mollified.

On another evening, and for the second time in this story, I faced death by drowning. We had berthed for the night in Auckland Bay in the open sea. With *Island Queen* riding quietly at anchor, I had dived over the side and swum a short distance before turning on to my back. When I heaved myself into position for the return journey, the launch was a long way off straining against an ebbing tide, and Barkat Ali and his engine-room hand were below preparing the evening meal. I was beyond shouting range and could do nothing but pray for someone's re-emergence: I knew I would achieve nothing but exhaustion by attempting to swim shorewards.

After a few minutes that seemed an age, Barkat Ali appeared on deck with a pail of slops. He flung these over the side and seemed to be about to go below again when he paused to look around for me. I could sense his agitation at not finding me and I started to wave as he scanned the sea. Mercifully he spotted me and dived below: within a minute or so I heard the engine start up and rescue was on its way. I was badly scared, but I think the old man was even more so and I knew him often to shake his head over repetition of the story.

When we returned to the Mine it struck me that this

week's cruise had been my longest spell so far without speaking English. However, there were much longer spells to come.

At least once a month I used to go down to Mergui to collect cash and stores. George Wilson nearly always came with me, and we usually took my Company's second launch, the *Yamone*. Although nothing more than a country boat fitted with an engine, she had the legs of *Island Queen* and of most other boats on the river, for which reason she was better suited to cash carrying, even though we travelled armed. Our weekends in Mergui were always memorable for something or other because this coast was Somerset Maugham country, a haunt of beachcombers.

Pride of place among these characters belonged to Benjamin Jubb, an unscrupulous reprobate who feared neither God nor man: he had tremendous personality and influence, the latter illicitly acquired, and a large indigenous family, likewise. The stories about Ben are legion, and any brief attempt to portray him must fail. Suffice to say that he was the soul of hospitality and good fellowship unless and until you crossed him. Then you were wise to leave the archipelago—for good.

There was one whom we will call Bob Wood, an errant member of the aristocracy with a seat in the House of Lords coming to him on the death of his father. He was a genuine remittance man, his monthly payment being conditional on his not leaving Mergui—a course which I don't imagine he ever contemplated. He managed a locally owned rubber plantation, whereon he lived in an *atap* hut with his Burmese 'wife' and children. His ability to offer you a drink depended entirely on the state of the pecuniary moon.

Next we might mention Ross Blackie, an Australian with an income tax problem of sufficient complexity that the Department agreed to send an inspector down from Rangoon to try to sort matters out on the spot. Ross knew as well as the next man how much cash he would need in his pocket to convince an Income Tax Inspector that all was well, but he made the mistake of coming into Mergui overnight and betaking himself to the club. Came the dawn and *Sir Harvey Adamson*'s arrival in the harbour. Through his alcoholic haze

Ross saw the Inspector only as an arch-enemy, and he knocked him out cold on the deck of that case-hardened vessel.

I should not forget, perhaps, poor old Maxton Latour, worthy citizen to the point that he really qualified for the classification of 'distressed gentleman' rather than 'beach-comber'. Despite his lack of vices he became the thoroughly disreputable hero of a novelist's pen. Sad, because if you acquire a Mergui label there is no redress: everything sticks.

There was another member of this colourful crowd called Moisey, who was known to George Wilson and myself. One weekend when we were in Mergui, the Assistant Commissioner got hold of us to say that reports had come in that Moisey had apparently gone off his head and was resisting with rifle fire any attempt to approach his bungalow, which was in an isolated locality some miles from the town. Would we be prepared to do something about it?

We duly set off. The bungalow, the usual high-stilted affair, stood at the centre of a cleared circle of about a hundred yards radius. Our reconnaissance revealed no sign of Moisey and, armed with revolvers, we made the bungalow by short, covering bounds. There was still no sound and we rushed the stairs, to find Moisey well and truly in the grip of the grog. He was inert but we brought him round and made him eat a meal. He was incredulous of his alleged behaviour over the past day or two, was most apologetic for the trouble he had given us, and we parted on such affable terms that we never cast an identifiable backward glance over our shoulders as we made for the trees.

I shall always remember Moisey's bungalow. It was immense. The furnishings comprised a bed, a table and a chair, a small arsenal of rifles and shotguns and, hanging on the wall, a large family tree tracing his own descent from Sir Richarde de Maisey, who invaded England in the entourage of William the Conqueror!

Mergui boasted a church, but the archipelago chaplain visited the place only once a quarter. I increasingly found the shuttered building a reproach, so I applied to the Bishop of Rangoon for a Lay Reader's licence. This was duly granted and I used to conduct a service of Evensong whenever I was down from the Mine. The congregation numbered about a dozen on average: enough, I felt, to justify the effort.

One occasion of a visit by the chaplain is particularly memorable. His name was Molyneux and I had known him briefly as oilfields chaplain at Yenangyaung. I had invited him out for a weekend at the Mine and he was occupying Milne's bedroom, the latter being away at the time.

Molyneux was a creature of habit and, after cleaning his teeth before getting into bed, it was his practice to get everything ready for a repetition of this performance in the morning. To this end he filled the tooth tumbler with water, placed it on the corner of his dressing table nearest to the open window, and laid his toothbrush across the top of it.

In the morning, before our ablutions and still in pyjamas and dressing gowns, we met in the living room for a cup of tea.

'What kind of animal' asked the padre, 'would it have been that was circling round the bungalow last night?'

I hadn't a clue. I had slept like a log.

'Maybe' I hazarded, 'one of our milk cows was having a sleepless night and went a-wandering.'

'It couldn't have been a cow,' protested Molyneux, 'the footfalls were far too regular and it took the same time each time to go round the house.'

I had no further suggestion to offer and let it go at that— for the moment.

A few minutes later, as I was dressing, I heard Molyneux calling to me to come into his room. White-faced, he was pointing to his tooth glass. It was still erect and the toothbrush still lay across the top of it: but there was no water in the glass for the reason that about the largest fragment of the tumbler that could be subtracted from the whole without upsetting the balance of the remainder was lying on the floor in a pool of water.

I went to the window and took a look at the ground outside. It was trodden flat by pug marks which, where you could see them in isolation, were clearly those of a tiger. At some stage in its perambulation the animal must have jumped up so that its fore-paws rested on the window sill;

and it must have struck out blindly into the darkness, leaving for solution the phenomenon which met the gaze of the already apprehensive cleric.

Without regard for sequence, I should pass now perhaps to another story that sometimes arouses incredulity in the listener.

An evening's run from Mergui to the Mine, when the moon was riding high, was ever bewitching for the added brilliance of the phosphorescence that creamed from *Yamone*'s prow, and for the further illumination provided by the millions of fireflies that crowded the mangrove banks of the *chaung*. It all made for a veritable fairyland.

Constituting probably less than one per cent of the mangrove jungle was one particular species of the tree: it would occur, perhaps, at an average interval of a mile or more. Its effect on the fireflies was dramatic beyond belief. Not only were they attracted multitudinous to its shade, but, once there, every insect present would synchronize its blinking—the effect being of a massive lantern lighting and dimming at intervals of about a second. This is a most imperfect description of a truly fantastic spectacle, the explanation for which, I have read, is to be sought in the love life of the firefly.

Before leaving the not-so-easily swallowed, I must risk straining credulity further yet by an incursion into the occult of Indian medical methods.

Many of George Wilson's labour force were Tamils from Southern India. On an occasion when I was staying a weekend with him, we were invited to attend by night a mass curing of back troubles by a celebrated practitioner—witch doctor—medicine man—call him what you will.

The procedure required that two minions, travelling with the healer, stood facing each other about five feet apart, each holding—one in each hand—the ends of two long slivers of bamboo. The general effect was of a set of thin parallel bars with four closed fists as the end supports.

From a dirty cloth receptacle the healer then proceeded to sprinkle back and forth across the centre point of the bamboos a fine dust; whereupon the bamboos started to bow inwards until they met at a point.

When they met, the healer deftly tied the bamboos together at the meeting point and severed both at distances of half an inch on either side of the string. The resultant pair of conjoined, inch-long slivers he then bound to the back of a waiting patient, who, in each case, appeared to go on his way rejoicing, no matter how crippled he might have been at the outset.

Obviously, I thought, the bamboos bowed inwards because their holders imperceptibly leant towards each other.

'May I' I asked of the man who had invited us, 'take the place of one of those two men?'

The practitioner was consulted and he readily accepted my participation.

In the light of the flickering torches I grasped my ends of the two bamboos, resolved to watch my opposite number like a hawk—and, if necessary, to lean over backwards to frustrate any *chalaki* work on his part.

As the scattering of the dust proceeded, some of it lodging on each bamboo, the bowing started and I knew it was not occasioned by any such facile subterfuge as I had suspected. I was in the control of the uncontrollable, and that's all there was to it. I can offer no explanation for what happened.

Now, in later life, plagued as I am with sacro-iliac trouble, I would have no hesitation in accepting the ministrations of that midnight medico could I but meet him on his own terms!

The dweller in the Tenasserim Archipelago almost invariably had as a house-mate the Tuktoo lizard, a large creature of clean habits and startling vocal talent. Without his companionable presence on the wall, bad luck threatened your abode. The cry of the Tuktoo, described by its name, was uttered uniformly as to tone, but at a declining intensity and tempo: seven successive cries were necessary as an assurance that all was well. It is one of life's impossibilities not to count the Tuktoo's cries. As four slows down to five and then lingeringly spills over into six, the agony of waiting for seven wholly destroys the last vestige of concentration on whatever it is you are reading.

As the crow flies, George Wilson's bungalow was about a

mile distant from mine. On a still night I could hear the Tuktoo calling from his walls and, inevitably, I would be counting with him. It was a peculiar bond.

One strange evening my hillside became the deathbed for many hundreds of Blue-winged Pitta, a ground-living bird about the size of a quail. Apparently they had been driven off course by some unimaginable hazard of migration. Some dozens of the birds flopped down exhausted in my living room, open to the night via its wide verandah. With blankets, and saucers of milk tinged with brandy, I threw myself into the fruitless task of succouring them. All were dead within a few hours, by which time the pitiful cheeping of the many more within earshot was also stilled. There was nothing apparent in the local weather conditions to account for such a catastrophe.

One of the problems of living on a small island, as we were for all practical purposes, was that of exercise. Whenever possible at weekends I took the launch up-river to George Wilson's place, as from there we could walk for miles on dry ground. One of our favourite routes took us to a secluded village of Christian Karens tucked away in the hills. Free of proximity to mineral deposits, agriculture was all their life, and they were the most gracious and untainted community I think I have ever known.

On Christmas Eve, of their own volition, about fifty of these Karens of both sexes trekked and boated down to my bungalow and gave a recital of carols on my verandah. Even with their giggling and shyness, it was all so obviously a natural gesture of praise to God as to be deeply moving. The timing of their visit was such that, after their singing, I was able to sit them all down with hastily concocted lemon squashes to hear the broadcast of the King's Christmas message to the Commonwealth. They listened, with polite lack of comprehension in most cases, and then set off in the darkness on their long plod home. I wonder how near to Heaven they are permitted to live now.

I needed exercise nearer home and managed to obtain from the Rangoon Boat Club a pair of oars and a sliding seat and out-riggers. These the Mine carpenters fitted for me into a local dug-out canoe, which was 'tailored' appreciably beyond local requirements and design. Thenceforward I spent many hours sculling up and down the river.

By the end of two months I had an office built and commissioned. The rainfall was something quite outside my experience. I had thought Indaw wet at ninety inches a year, but what I now had to get used to went far beyond this. I soon found that to seek protection in a raincoat or under an umbrella was sheer waste of time. I adopted the practice of having four sets of clothing sent down to the office early in the morning. Then, with emptied pockets, I made my several rounds of scattered operations, towelling down and changing at each return to the office. There was virtually no malaria in the place, presumably because there was no standing water! Occasionally I had bouts of fever, but there was never any reason to doubt that it had its origins in Indaw.

Though at Mergui there was the usual Civil Surgeon and hospital that went with a District Headquarters, we had no doctor at the Mine. Entranced by that classic tome, *Moore's Family Medicine*, I established a small dispensary where I used to treat the sick and sorry along the rule-of-thumb lines laid down by that imaginative physician. My patients, for the most part, were sufficiently ignorant to place unbounded confidence in me; and, since nothing works like faith, I acquired something of a reputation as a man of medicine.

There came a night, however, when I was called out to deliver a baby. After a quick examination of the expectant mother, I risked the decision that her groans were but 'the music of a distant drum' and bundled her into a hastily manned launch for Mergui. Fortune was with me, and mother and baby had the benefit of skilled delivery: but I think my reputation was slightly tarnished from then on.

Of my pre-leave dogs, Mary had been run over by a car in my absence, and for Jack I had found a good home whence I felt that he should not be uprooted. I now acquired from a breeder in Rangoon two pedigree Labrador pups, Paddy and Tessa. Their house training was added to my other activities. They were the wettest pair I have ever encountered, but they certainly developed into wonderful company.

The long-awaited day came when the Dredge started digging, but we promptly ran into teething troubles of a formidable nature. Though the mangrove provided charcoal of excellent calorific property, the latter, when burnt, exuded a thick, tarry residue that played havoc with the vertical pistons of the diesel engines that powered the Dredge: everything ground to a halt within twenty-four hours. After two or three strippings and cleanings it was evident that no solution lay within our immediate resources.

Jim Milne set off in *Island Queen* on a tour of other dredges along the coast to seek the experience of their operators. He visited Rangoon to pick the brains of experts there, but it was of no avail. The evil lay in the choice of vertically rather than horizontally pistoned power units: the latter might have ejected the tar that clogged the former. Back we had to go to Holland for specially designed tar extractors, which took many weeks to reach us. Poor old Jim, whom I had come to like a lot, was barely acceptable as company; and when the extractors finally arrived, nobody worked harder physically than himself—and he was fifty-seven—at getting them installed: but he had been given the answer.

The Dredge started up again, and soon the racket of the top tumbler became part of our life. I spent as much time on board as I could, watching the play of the cables as they tracked the Dredge back and forth across the river and into the cleared swamp and, after each such run, a little further forward up-river. I used to watch the black tin sand being bounced into separation on the jigs, while the tailings poured off the stern chutes into the river.

Soon there were bags of unwashed tin being brought ashore to the cleaning sheds. Here a skilled team of Straits Chinese hand-operated a sluicing and straining procedure that yielded tin of about seventy per cent purity at time of dispatch. With ill-concealed excitement we stacked our first launch-load of tin of our own digging, and a few days later M.V. *Pahang* conveyed it from Mergui to Penang for smelting. A week or two later I had the infinite pleasure of entering proceeds in our books of account at the Mine. Simple stuff if you like, but it was the climax to months of frustration, and of acrimony in our mail exchanges with Rangoon.

We were out of the wood, but now were threatened by a far graver intervention in our affairs. In Europe the heavily banked war clouds broke into storm, and during a never-to-be-forgotten weekend that George Wilson and I were spending with rubber planting friends beyond Mergui, we listened to Neville Chamberlain's words to the British people and learnt that we were at war with Germany.

On our homeward run in *Yamone*, my agonized mind ranged over the possible perils that might even now be threatening my family; but soon I found myself forced to listen to George. He was a man with no family that he ever spoke of: I suspect that he had been born an orphan.

With the phosphorescence dancing at the prow, and the fireflies scintillating among the mangrove, he wandered into an exposition on the probable course of the war that, to look back on, was pure prophecy. Everything that was to happen was there—the German *blitzkrieg* on France, the jackal role of Italy, the turning on Russia, Japan's lightning attack on an American base. One could wish now that such informed, clear thinking—by a man immured in a distant archipelago —could have been available on tape to the Councils of War in England. One knows by the course of events, alas, that it would have gone unheeded. By futile comparison, a letter of mine written when the war was about six weeks old made the prophecy that 'Hitler will be the late Herr Hitler within six months'.

Except for some deterioration in the regularity with which air mails came through from England, the war made no impact on life at the Mine. Things were otherwise in Mergui where the unimportant airfield was expanded to receive bomber squadrons flying through to Singapore, while a Sunderland flying boat, based in the harbour, was making regular reconnaissance flights up and down the coast.

From Derek Lewton-Brain in Rangoon I heard of friends being called up for military service. I had already sent to

Steels my resignation on the grounds that I wished to enlist, but the refusal of it had been backed by a copy of a Government order laying it down that civilian companies were to release none of their staff other than to, and at the behest of, Burma Command. It made sense all right, but life became a very galling procession of days. I sought to salve my conscience by donating ten per cent of my salary to the war effort, but it did nothing for my soul. My mood was not improved by hearing of the engagement to a man in uniform of the girl I had fallen for in Switzerland, and with whom I had been corresponding regularly. Honesty makes me add that she was committed to me in no way at all. My diversions, according to one letter were simple: 'I took a sampan up the river and spent the night with Wilson: the evening's programme was Beethoven.'

The same letter records that I had heard of the torpedoing of *Yorkshire*.

The advent of the cold weather, combined with our elevation to profitable dredging, had quite an effect on Jim Milne. Soon the bungalow was being painted and wired, and a sofa suite and other furniture were being ordered down from Rangoon. On my initiative *Island Queen* was wearing Steels house flag for'ard and the Red Ensign aft! We had quite a spate of visitors, the Deputy Commissioner, the Conservator of Forests, planter friends, and finally—for a week—my old chief, McGilvray, who was now Fields Manager in Rangoon, and whose portfolio included The Lenya Mining Company. He put in a lot of work familiarizing himself with our problems, but on my twenty-sixth birthday we pushed off for a day-long picnic in *Island Queen*, not entirely spoilt by our stranding on a sand bank for some hours only a mile or two short of a secluded bay of the sea which had been our objective.

Even with the major dredging problem solved, we continued to have our occasional irritations, one of which I described in a letter.

On Monday morning the cargo launch bringing the week's stores received from Rangoon (about five tons of stuff valued at five or six thousand rupees) sank on the way up to the Mine. No two versions of what happened seem to agree. I spent nearly all of Monday supervising salvage operations, but even in the spell of slack water which you get at low tide there is still five feet of very muddy water above the roof of the launch and the current makes it very difficult for men to dive down and try to get grapples fixed under the roof in order to lug it off. We've given up trying to lighten the launch by this means and have now got a steel cable fixed to her and to a ten ton block ashore. The latest news is that she's been moved about thirty feet. Among other things the mail bag with any letters it may have for me is at the bottom: if we recover them at all they'll probably be illegible. The only cheering side to the whole story is that a case of whisky which I had ordered for the bungalow mess and which I assumed to be on board arrived the next day, having been short-shipped!

We did recover the launch, but the condition of the mails was as predicted.

Law enforcement in a jungled archipelago that held a magnetic attraction for law breakers and fugitives from justice was rather a nebulous term at the best of times. In war it tended to empty itself of any residual meaning. George and I were being plagued by a Chinese tin stealer who had established himself on a tongue of dry land between our respective leases and was operating on familiar lines. There was no tin there: that was certain. However, this *soi-disant* miner had 'salted' a number of test bores in order to obtain a lease, and was now in business. Whether his production came from George's lease or mine is immaterial: it did not come from his. Late one evening we raided him and drove him and his party out and down the river. We burnt his buildings and wrecked what we could of his 'workings', and he did not return.

I imagine the Deputy Superintendent of Police in Mergui got wind of the affair, but he never alluded to it in our presence. My only reprimand came from 'Mac', to whom I unwisely related the incident while he was staying with us. He certainly considered that I had exceeded my mandate and, under normal conditions, I imagine that I would have been relieved of my posting. The reference to the occasion in my letters is diluted almost beyond recognition. I must have judged that my mother would not have approved either! There was a possible repercussion some weeks later in an act of attempted sabotage on the Dredge, which fortunately failed of its well-informed purpose. We had a mainly Chinese crew, most of whom were trustworthy: but there must have been a nigger in the woodpile, and he doubtless was the supplier of the stolen tin.

In Mergui one weekend, while relaxing in the club, I found myself idly listening to an elderly member reading extracts from a letter he had received from a crony in Siam. Suddenly I became alert at the mention of Germans paying high prices for wolfram, and of steps being taken to speed up production. I remembered my commission and instantly I was the crafty spy! I found no means that day of getting my hands on the letter, but on the next I casually wandered into the man's bungalow when I knew that he himself was again at the club. I had to be ready with a plausible story should a servant emerge to ask my business, and I had no means of knowing that the letter was not still on the recipient's person. Luck was entirely with me: not a soul stirred, and the letter was visible on an open desk. A copy of it went to Rangoon by the next sailing of *Sir Harvey Adamson*.

The cold weather receded and the change of season was marked by violent storms, in one of which our camp power house was struck by lightning and put out of action for two or three weeks. The same storm felled my wireless aerial.

On return from a visit to Rangoon, Jim Milne announced that at a Steels Managers' conference it had been decided that he should hand over charge of the Mine to me and leave. Jim had irons in other fires which were claiming his attention, and it was only the troubles with the Dredge that had tied him to Yamone for so long. In particular he was in partnership with a Chinese on a gold-mining project on Russel Island some way down the coast, and the time had come when his technical knowledge was required there. He continued to base himself at Mergui, so I saw him from time to time; and he was always willing to visit the Mine with a helping hand whenever we ran into unfamiliar problems.

Mails from England reached me in erratic batches. My brother and sister were both in the Services. My father was an air raid warden and my mother on part-time hospital work. In the newspapers the casualty lists were getting longer and more depressing. In one batch I read of the award of the D.F.C. to a school friend of mine: in the next was the report of his death. Derek Lewton-Brain was keeping me posted from Rangoon on how call-ups were depleting the Rangoon office staff: quite a number now had commissions in either the Burma Rifles or the Burma Frontier Force, while two were in the Burma Navy. Me? I was eating my heart out in over two hundred inches of rain, and in pretty sterile company at that. On 14 July I completed a year at the Mine—my longest spell in any one posting yet.

The last straw was when George Wilson received his marching orders. Frankly I could not understand why he had not gone long before this as he was outstandingly a ready-made officer. I went down to Mergui with him to see him off in the *Pahang* bound for Singapore. I travelled back to the Mine with his relief, a man in his mid-fifties. He was a nice enough fellow but could not possibly fill the void.

As the German *blitzkrieg* swept westwards, engulfing Belgium and the Netherlands and eclipsing France, the prospect for the British Army falling back on Dunkirk, contemplated from afar in rain-sodden solitude, seemed hopeless in the extreme. Life for me became a back and forth procession between office and bungalow to listen to wireless news bulletins.

Jim Milne came up from Mergui one day to ask me to join him in a plan for getting away from Burma if the worst befell at home and the Government of Burma came under German orders. For his frequent passages between Mergui and Russel Island he had built a small schooner, the *Island Gold*. I had sailed in her and knew her as a very well-found craft, and she was fitted out for much longer voyaging than Jim's inter-island run called for.

'From now on,' said Jim, 'I'm keeping her fully provisioned and in a constant state of readiness for a run down to Australia. I suggest that you put aboard now your basic requirements in the way of kit and be ready for word from me to come down to Mergui and sail.'

In retrospect my faith in the rock whence I was hewn

must have been at very low ebb but, in conditions of depressed inertia, it was at least an invitation to do something. I jumped at the offer and stowed my gear accordingly.

Britain was not invaded. The monsoon dripped to its close, and I prepared to make the best I could of another cold weather at the Mine. The Dredge was now producing better than a ton of tin a day, and I had established eleven tons a month as the minimum required to cover all outgoings.

The Mine engineer had been transferred. His relief had spent two days with us and had then decided that the life was not for him. I had received in his stead Andy Armit, a Scot of much tougher fibre. Danny Higgins was still repeating his oft-told stories of a real or imaginary 'cobber' who was so invariably unlucky that 'if the sea were to turn to soup he'd be the only bastard there with a fork'.

Elsewhere men were dying bloodily, and women and children, with bundles on their backs and little in their bellies, were on the trudge. It was obviously now going to be a long war, and if I were to be doomed to see it through in abandoned isolation I would probably end up by 'going native' and becoming one with the beachcombers.

One day the *Rangoon Gazette* carried an announcement of the formation of a Burma Air Force and invited applications for pilot training from men under the age of twenty-seven. Without expectation I wrote to Gordon Nicoll, and asked to be allowed to apply. I pointed out that the age limitation made it a case of now or never for me. To my delight, I received a favourable reply, with the added comment that, since there was no Steels Assistant to relieve me, arrangements were being made for me to hand over to C. V. Thornton, an itinerant geologist in his fifties who was periodically employed by Steels on prospecting work. Nicoll's letter went on to say that, since Thornton had no experience of office procedures, he would be sent down as soon as possible to ensure an adequate handing over. I seemed to be getting somewhere at last!

Then, without benefit of interview, I received a list of the successful applicants for flying training. My name was not included.

How drunk I might have got, and for how long, are fortunately academic questions. Hard on the heels of the rejection came a Burma Command order instructing me to report at Alexandra Barracks, Maymyo, on 21 November 1940 to join the Militia Company of the 2nd Battalion The Kings Own Yorkshire Light Infantry.

As *Sir Harvey Adamson* bore me away from Mergui after handing over to Cyril Thornton, I reflected that I was leaving behind me an ideal peacetime posting. In the circumstances, however, frustration had ruled my days and I was more than glad to be on my way. Administratively I alone of Steels staff now had practical experience of the tin dredging business, and I reasonably hoped to be back again in happier days: but events were to decree otherwise.

Paddy was piddling against a bollard. He and Tessa were travelling with me, though I had no idea what I was going to do with them once I became a Soldier of the Line.

8 A Private of the Line

November 1940 to May 1941

With a number of other recruits, I was entrained for Mandalay *en route* to Maymyo. I was travelling second class on an Army travel warrant. Behind this democratic facade, however, was a somewhat ludicrous but wholly acceptable reality. Steels had laid it down for their staff that those called up for military service would suffer neither by loss of seniority nor pay vis-a-vis those who were left to keep the wheels turning. My basic salary from Steels at this time was five hundred and fifty rupees a month: my pay as a soldier of the King was to be one and a half rupees a day. The difference was to be paid into my bank account monthly.

Coming from what was classified as a priority occupation, I had been warned that failure to be selected for officer training at the end of three months in the ranks would mean my return to Mergui, but I had no fears on this score. Having got into the act, I was going to stay.

On arrival at Maymyo I had a couple of days to spare before reporting to barracks. By the kindness of Steels Forest Department, the five of us from the Company who had been called up for militia training were made free of 'Ingleston', the spacious residence that the Department maintained in Maymyo for the benefit of their staff on local leave—the stipulation being that we did not dig ourselves in to the exclusion of bona fide sojourners. On this basis George Astell, of the Rice Department, and I shared a room in which we stored dinner jackets, tennis rackets, golf clubs and such other impedimenta as might be expected to scandalize an Orderly Corporal.

By a stroke of good luck I made the acquaintance of a

British N.C.O. living in married accommodation in the cantonment, who was delighted at the suggestion that for a reasonable consideration he should look after Paddy and Tessa for me.

While we were yet civilians, George and I established our membership of the Maymyo Club, within the holy precincts of which no private soldier normally could hope to seek a drink. There had in fact been no little discussion at the committee level with regard to the continuing eligibility or otherwise of privates of the Militia Company who might already be members. Fortunately reason, as we saw it, had prevailed.

George and I reported together at the Militia Company's guard room on what we soon found was to be no empty formality. I was impressed from the start by the complete indifference shown by the Warrant Officers and N.C.O.s at an intake so far removed from what must have been their normal experience. Managers, chartered accountants, engineers, civil servants—we were just one more bunch of 'bleedin recruits' to be made men of as quickly and as irrevocably as possible. Any show of familiarity or hint of patronage was rounded on with stentorian bellows of 'jump to it' or 'stand to attention when talking to me'—and God help the fool who assumed that this treatment was just an act and invited a second dose!

Soon we were blundering around with arms full of equipment and bedding; and with rifles, and anything else that could be suspended, hanging round our necks; and with Company Sergeant-Major Guest colourfully reminding us that we weren't in a 'carpeted bloody office' now.

Having found our way to 'A' Platoon's barrack, we received from Corporal Butcher a quick-fire demonstration of how to make up a bed, un-make a bed and then make up a bed again; next we learnt how to stow our equipment in cubic capacity half of what was required; then we received instruction on how to clean rifles and equipment; and finally on how to spring-clean the barrack daily. (Down at Yamone by this hour Cyril Thornton would be reclining with his feet on the verandah rail and a whisky in his hand!).

We retired exhausted on beds that discountenanced sleep, and at six were routed out for chilling, barbaric ablutions and a resumption of bed-making. Then, at the double, we moved off to a three quarters of an hour session of PT that uncovered every physical disability to which each of us was subject. Back we came to a breakfast mocked by the challenging inquiry of 'any complaints?' Then, cursing as we tangled with each other in the narrow corridor between the lines of beds, we fought our way into our jungles of equipment and tumbled onto parade against a background of Benny Guest's 'jump to it!' Then, as we stood dumbly at attention, came his crowning derision—'Call that attention! Lock your legs together! You won't drop nothing!'

Four hours of shambling around, with or without packs, gas masks, bayonets or other scaffolding, and we were back for lunch—a nameless stew off chipped enamel plates. Then for an hour and a half we went on a route march at light infantry pace just to ensure that we did not lack for exercise. At last we were free to do whatever we liked provided it involved cleaning something.

'Can anyone tell me', pleaded George Astell through a smog of polish fumes, 'why I bothered to bring my golf clubs to Maymyo?'

The odd thing was, however, that we mastered all this after little more than a brief introduction. There were those, of course, who surreptitiously 'contracted out' their cleaning and polishing to some cash-hungry regular. These, for the most part, were men who had no taste for soldiering and were prepared to invite return to civilian employment at the end of the course. Alternatively they were those who had wives or lady friends in Maymyo, chafing at the inadequacy of the social company the Army made it possible for them to provide.

Gradually we all fell into one or other of three distinct categories—the keen, the resigned and the antipathetic. Even though I claimed membership of the first of these, it was not long before I was finding time of an evening to slip into Maymyo, having acquired a bicycle, for long enough at least to collect Paddy and Tessa and take them for a walk. A few weeks later I had progressed as far as nine holes of golf with George Astell and the occasional set or two of tennis.

Before long I was bumping into friends from other parts of Burma up for local leave: among them, to my delight, were Geoff and Madeleine Grindle who, with home leave barred to them by the war, were staying two months.

In *The Times* I read of the death of my friend John Ball during a bomber raid on Gibraltar, where he was serving as a medical officer. Sadly my mind went back to our day with the Stone Curlew on Swincombe Down, and with a sense of shame I contemplated my present sheltered existence.

On the business side of the barrack gates we were progressively getting away from our blundering peregrinations back and forth across the square into activities that smacked more recognizably of preparation for legalized murder. On one occasion, in gas mask and with fixed bayonet, I was put to demonstrating how to slaughter about a dozen remarkably passive 'enemy' in sixty seconds.

'Watch him,' roared Corporal Butcher (and my pounding heart yet found the means to rise at the obvious pride in his voice) 'There he goes—a trained killer!'

A week or two later, with oaths and imprecations, we were battling our way through the acres of lantana scrub that proliferated round Maymyo in pursuit of an enemy called 'Redland'. The obliging characteristic of this particular foe was that he invariably withdrew before our assault, no matter how ragged or uncoordinated it might be. By night, of course, these operations were attended by complications such as might lead you to cast yourself down for the purpose of consuming a leaden sausage roll and a flask of greasy tea, then to discover that inadvertently you had a 'Redland' platoon for company!

More and more people were coming up to Maymyo on local leave. At 'Ingleston' we had the company of several attractive Forest grass widows: tennis parties became increasingly intimate affairs, and pairings-off were more and more the pattern on the dance floor of the club. Of a typical Sabbath I wrote,

'We went to Holy Communion at 8.00 a.m. and then played 18 holes of golf and 5 sets of tennis, sandwiching a tiffin with the Grindles in between.'

As near neighbours at 'Ingleston' we had the delightful Jack and Mary Mustill. Jack was Game Warden, Burma, and, though not so young as most of us, had got himself included on the militia course. Also nearby were Billy and Susan Williams of the *Bombine*. Billy, who later was to achieve fame as 'Elephant Bill', did me the service of ending a prolonged search for an errant Paddy, whom he found astray and brought back to his bungalow without knowing he was mine.

Staying with the Grindles for a few days was Maxine Strong, an American girl on an extended visit to her father, who was a driller on the oilfields. She was heavily squired by chaps on the militia course who knew her already, being themselves from the oilfields. For this reason I did not see much of her then, but I was more than attracted.

At times I would have a twinge of conscience with regard to my fellows in the Battalion, the sometimes Kiplingesque regulars of the other companies, to whom were denied the pleasures that so freely were mine. I got to know a bunch of them, characters all—notably the corpulent Bandsman Marriott—with whom I would get together in the canteen of an evening. The bawdy stories matched the beers we consumed. PT on mornings after nights like this was sheer hell. As your head went down between your knees, every internal component of it was mobile. Nevertheless I maintained a great state of fitness and was only rarely having malaria. One evening I set off on a cross-country run of five miles with the Battalion's champion. He held himself in of course, but I was with him in a sprint finish.

Over Christmas and the New Year we got an eight days break. George and I headed for Yenangyaung as members of a military cricket team that was to play two matches on the oilfields. The trip started disastrously. We were two of an open coupé-load of four, and as we were descending a steep, stony hill to Rocky Chaung at the foot of Mount Popa, the accelerator jammed, the brakes failed to hold, and inevitably we dived off the road. We came to rest upside down over a dry nullah just wide enough to provide support for each end of the car. We had been so wedged together that, absurdly, we were still all in our seats and had to drop, onto our hands, to the ground about twelve feet below. We were all shaken but, apart from cuts, none was hurt.

Not far behind us, also bound for Yenangyaung fortunately, was John Hedley, now a lieutenant in the Burma Rifles, and his wife. Somehow they accommodated all of us and our kit and we reached Yenangyaung just before midnight. George and I were staying with the I.B.P. Agent and his wife, and the food and drink they put before us was desperately needed after our early morning start.

The two-day match against Yenangyaung was memorable for a partnership in which George made 126 and I 13! Despite my parlous contribution, the winning hit was a desperate six off my bat!

After the second match at Chauk, George and I slipped across the river to Lanywa for a quick round-up of old friends there. It was the last time I saw the place. We returned to Maymyo in time to make up a party with the Grindles for the New Year's Eve dance at the Mandalay Club, whence we carried our hangovers back to Alexandra Barracks and resumed the mantle of 'brutal and licentious soldiery'.

The military grind proceeded apace, and so did the social life. For six weeks I had the use of a car belonging to an officer friend out on 'ops'. George and I challenged two fellow-privates, late of the B.O.C., to an 'entacathlon' comprising golf, tennis, billiards, bridge, table tennis, squash, badminton, swimming, darts, running and skittles, the losers to pay for the dinner—and a good one!

I used to drive the car out into the countryside with Paddy and Tessa. They slept in the sun while I watched birds.

As the militia course drew towards its close, it was decided that we throw a large-scale dance to celebrate our release from the ranks. It was one thing to find myself conscripted to the committee, but quite another to be deputed to organize a cabaret—particularly as I was already involved in arranging accommodation and hospitality for the Yenangyaung cricket team who were coming up for a return match over the same weekend. All this had to be done nightly after what can fairly be described as a pretty tough day's soldiering: but done it was, and the dance was a terrific occasion. George and I took the opportunity of repaying hospitality by having a dinner party for twelve at 'Ingleston' before going on to carouse. It wasn't easy to stay sober until my cabaret contribution was behind me; and not surprisingly we lost the match against Yenangyaung!

A week or two later the Militia Company held its passing out parade, and I was one of the majority selected for the O.C.T.U. (Officer Cadet Training Unit) course which was to start a week later.

By this time I was hearing the call of the wild again and, with Tony Symns of the B.O.C. (another successful militia-man), headed north for the old ruby-mining town of Mogok, our selection of which for our leave provoked a hilarious spasm of ribaldry from the militia staff responsible for the issue of travel warrants. The other ninety-eight budding officers, almost without exception, had applied for warrants for Rangoon.

'Mogok!' from Benny Guest, 'where the bleedin' hell's Mogok? What's the matter with you fellers anyway? Don't tell me that you can get it easier up there than in Rangoon!' And more in the same strain.

Mogok is east of the Irrawaddy about seventy miles north of Maymyo. Most of the world's best rubies have come from there, although, even at the time of our visit, the mines were worked out and flooded. The town most attractively semi-surrounds the deep blue waters of the lake that covers the old workings. From the less populous shore the hills rise to a peak of seven thousand feet at Bernardmyo which, in the early days of the British occupation, was a sanatorium and convalescent station for sick troops. We found little trace of this era beyond a few crumbling foundations. On these hills Tony and I spent our days, studying a wealth of bird life beyond our acquaintance.

The prime object of our trip had been to see if we could

get a sight at least of the rare and magnificent Argus Pheasant which inhabited those parts. Tony was an acknowledged authority on birds (he had also published a book on the snakes of Burma) and I could not have had a better opportunity to learn. One small passerine species, the Silver Eared Mesia, which neither of us had seen before, was particularly common and we came to know it well. A year or two later I had no difficulty in identifying a small flock of them in the Chin Hills, where they had never before been recorded.

Our evenings, since we had brought no servants with us, were spent 'peeling potatoes, shelling peas and wondering how much salt to put into this and that'; and with it we were being dazzled by the arrays of 'emeralds, lapis lazuli, topazes, spinels, peridots, agates, sapphires, moonstones and amethysts' which the locals sought to press upon us at fancy prices.

After supper we usually took a walk of half a mile that carried us, half a century back into history, to the bungalow of old Major Enriquez. This magnificent character, in his seventies or more, had been a professional soldier and, having married a Burmese girl, had settled at Mogok with his daughter. He was a remarkable man to regard—a roseate countenance with piercing blue eyes and great sweeps of white whisker, the whole crowned by a double terai hat.

He used to sit us down in comfortable chairs in his beautifully kept garden, see to it that we had full glasses and that the decanter was within reach, and then regale us with reminiscence that was never repetitious and always fascinating. There was only one interruption, and that was invariable. As the sun sank, he would rise to his feet, straighten himself up, march across the lawn and lower the Union Jack that hung from a staff beside the bungalow. Then he would return and carry on from where he had left off. Here was Empire going out with a bang!

I have made no further mention of the Argus Pheasant. We did not see one until we were leaving Mogok headed back for Maymyo. Then one ran across the road out of and into thick jungle a few yards in front of our car.

On return to Maymyo we found ourselves reporting as Officer Cadets at the selfsame guard room as had been the hub of the militia course. That, as a reminder of past horrors, was enough without being confronted by Benny Guest; but I really could have been knocked down with the proverbial feather when he advanced on me with outstretched hand, a broad smile on his face, and a greeting of—

'How are you *Mister* Braund. How nice to have you with us. Did you have a good holiday?'

This was something!

The O.C.T.U. was accommodated in the old familiar barracks, but with what a difference! Curtains on the windows, bedside rugs and a well-appointed lounge and mess. My pay, though academic for reasons already explained, had risen from forty-five to three hundred and seventy-five rupees a month.

The Officer Commanding the course was a somewhat Gilbertian colonel named Bertie Dawes. He got away to rather a bad start by being overheard at the bar of the Maymyo Club complaining about his unsought task of having to convert a hundred boxwallahs into gentlemen within two months. There was that in Bertie's nature, however, that stripped his fellows of the ability to take him seriously, and we were to have much fun at his expense. My Group Leader, to my delight, was Major Victor Morton of the 'Glosters', with whom and his wife I had become so friendly in Rangoon some years previously. The equipment to be drawn was distinctly less burdensome than for the militia course! I recorded it as 'mainly notebooks, pencils, protractors etc.' The curriculum was largely made up of 'Tewts' (Tactical Exercises without Troops) and lectures, and much was necessary in the way of homework and syndicate discussions after hours.

Bertie's lectures were always a highlight. He had the ludicrous habit of peppering his talks with the word 'gentlemen'. They would start somewhat on the lines of: 'And now, gentlemen, we are assembled here this morning, gentlemen, for the purpose, gentlemen, of . . .' Once the form had been established, the rest followed. We reserved seats at the back of the hall for the three bookmakers of the day and placed our bets according to our estimates of the frequency of the gentlemanly utterance. The last five minutes of any lecture were a well-concealed riot. Beneath the desks there would be knuckle-white fists gouging silently into the bruising palms of those whose interest it was to urge Bertie on to greater effort: others, open-handed in a sort of lateral dog paddle, would be trying to induce him to a halt.

Another lecturer who proved popular was Captain Jimmie Moore of the Burma Rifles. His normal forte was 'Regimental Accounts', a sphere of primitive inadequacy at the best of times; but Jimmie learnt his lesson early. At his first appearance, swinging the billiards cue that we came to accept as his normal accompaniment, he concluded his talk with the invitation 'any questions?' His listeners included no less than twelve chartered accountants and, without any semblance of affront to military discipline, Jimmie was slowly and painlessly taken apart until, red-faced and rattled, he called a halt to the proceedings and swept out.

Despite all this we learnt apace, although, in retrospect, I think that too much effort was devoted to fitting us to play our parts in the Boer War.

With the advent of the hot weather in the plains, Maymyo more and more became the refuge of those taking local in lieu of home leave. Steels General Manager, John Tait, and his wife and daughter were up; so was my old friend Bill Grant from Lanywa, and others from the Upper Chindwin and Mergui.

Maymyo, annually in April, held a 'Week' which this year obviously was assured of exceptionally wide support. Apart from the usual polo, cricket, golf, hockey and tennis tournaments, there was much being arranged for the benefit of war funds and charities. One of Steels wives at 'Ingleston', Kathleen Howe, had been a leading member of the Covent Garden Opera Company before her marriage. She asked me to be her 'publicity manager' in arranging for her a concert at the club. All the local youth and beauty were conscripted to sell tickets, programmes and corsages. We had a massive attendance, Kathleen gave a superb performance and we cleared over eight hundred rupees.

On my own account I was rehearsing hard for a tap dancing duet to be included in the cabaret programme at the April Ball. My partner was Mabel Clark who, with her husband Tommy, I had got to know when convalescing in Maymyo some years earlier. Mabel was a trained and accomplished dancer; I was self-taught and had never danced other than solo. Co-ordination took us several weeks of rehearsing three or four times a week. Mabel was Irish, an utterly delightful person, and she swore like a trooper. I can hear her now.

'Harold, ye bluidy fewl: if ye think it's me that'll be followin' ye thru that rigmarole, ye're bluidy well mistaken.'

With fear and trepidation we committed our names to the programme for the Ball and, when it came to the event, we never had a moment's anxiety.

Since all this was occurring in wartime, it may give proportion to some of what I have written if I quote from one of my letters home.

A perusal of this letter must inevitably leave you with the impression that the War leaves us untouched and that pleasure is unconfined. This is largely true, but I don't think there can be many who don't feel a hopeless sense of frustration at not being allowed to do anything useful. I wish they'd draft out people who have already 'done their stuff' to relieve us.

Behind all the fun and frolic there was a sorry undertow of hard drinking and broken marriages.

With the end of the O.C.T.U. in sight, I made a last throw at transferring to the Air Force. My bid ended at an interview with the G.O.C., Burma, General McLeod. After I had been asked to state my business, the conversation did not drag.

'Now, Braund, do you speak Burmese?'

'Yes Sir' (proudly).

'Well that's too bad, because in this war anybody who speaks Burmese stays on the ground.'

I had failed to learn a private soldier's first lesson—don't give the right answer if it's the wrong one!

There was nothing left for it but to go back to Bertie Dawes and accept an earlier invitation to express a preference in the matter of a posting. My reasoning was ultimately to look foolish, but I wrote home:

I have put myself down for the Frontier Force as likely to provide the more interesting life and, also, the more independent one. I don't much like the idea of living in a Mess.

At least I did avoid the latter!

Of a hundred cadets on the O.C.T.U. about eighty received commissions. I passed out second, so there was no difficulty about my being granted the posting of my choice. I was destined for the Northern Shan States Battalion of the Burma Frontier Force with Headquarters at Lashio on the Burma/China road. On my graduating from the militia course I had arranged for all my personal belongings crated and stored at Mergui to be shipped to Rangoon. I now asked Steels to rail the whole lot up to Lashio.

There were several days at my disposal before I had to leave for the north and, freed of all pre-occupation with military affairs, I flung myself zestfully back into the social whirl of Maymyo. My final contribution to the season was to captain an O.C.T.U. rugger fifteen against the club. The obvious place for the encounter was the polo ground in front of the club building but there was quite a bit of resistance to be overcome from some polo die-hards who considered it sacrilegious or bad for the turf or both. Finally we won our way, and the gate yielded over two hundred and fifty rupees for war charities.

9 Playing at Soldiers

May 1941 to January 1942

'Second Lieutenants Braund and Hutchinson reporting, Sir.'

This was not 'Hutch' of Steels, but 'T.C.', a Rangoon banker and a fellow-graduate from the O.C.T.U. The C.O. to whom we were presenting ourselves was Lieut.-Colonel 'Ted' Cartmel, with whom I had travelled in *Cheshire* all those years ago. It was 5 May 1941. The war was twenty months old and here we were, embarked upon something that differed scarcely at all from peacetime soldiering.

The motto of the Burma Frontier Force, *Civis sed Miles*, gives a clue to its role. It was a military force with battalions based at Bhamo, Myitkyina, Falam, Lashio, Taunggyi, Pyawbwe and Rangoon; but in normal times it was an instrument of the Civil Government, not of the Army, being exercised in keeping the peace on the frontiers of Burma, which included the lengthy and disputed border with China. The force, when I joined it, was commanded by Brigadier F. A. G. Roughton with the designation 'Inspector General'. For operational purposes the disposal of the force had been transferred to Burma Command since the outbreak of war.

The Northern Shan States Battalion maintained outposts eastward along the Upper Salween, and northward along the border with Yunnan. In Lashio itself there were only four King's commissioned officers, the C.O., the second-in-command and adjutant, Duncan Low, who also was a regular, 'T.C.' and myself. There were others commanding outposts distant by anything up to sixteen days marching. I soon found myself hankering after one of these.

'T.C.' and I were accommodated in one of the 'town

houses' of the Sawbwa of Tawngpeng, one of the princely Shans. It was a fair enough prospect except that it was only minimally furnished and badly in need of painting, and we had to share it with scorpions. We were both impoverished after five months of Maymyo living but had to pitch in to the extent of bare necessities at least. It was good to have my own possessions around me again.

Lashio normally mustered about a dozen British residents, but now it was leaping into prominence as the Burma/China road gained in strategic significance, and there was a growing number of short-term visitors in one cause or another. The ubiquitous Steels had opened an office there as they had transport interests; and transport, there and then, was the bloodstream of life. In charge of this office was an asset to any small community in the person of Jimmie Cook, an erstwhile rice mill engineer. I had known him but slightly pre-war. I cultivated him now, not only for his cheerful humour but also for the nostalgia of the link he represented with my peacetime way of life. An occasional 'Steels evening' was a pleasant release from the drabness of the headquarters round.

Echoes of my barely remembered success in the Burmese language exam were revived when I found that the Army valued it at fifty rupees a month on top of my pay. I was even more pleased when I found that Steels did not take this into account in the matter of 'make up'! It bestowed some merit, perhaps, on the G.O.C.'s leading question in Maymyo at the end of the O.C.T.U. course! I was appointed Battalion Sports Officer and, with rather less relish, Officer in charge of the Band. I was on shaky ground here!

Of my other duties I wrote:

Apart from the training programmes for which we are responsible there is a very tedious amount of office work of a most unbelligerent nature, and as with all Government Departments it could easily be halved if run by a commercial firm. Since, however, the machine does not provide for—in fact discourages—initiative in these matters, there is nothing for it but to plod along through a sea of references and counter-references till the War is over!

As at Mergui, there was a church at Lashio which only

opened its doors periodically for the visit of a wide-ranging chaplain. On learning that I had a Lay Reader's licence, he asked me to hold a service on the third Sunday of each month. These services were quite well attended and, since 'T.C.' was an accomplished performer on the harmonium, we were able to offer value even to those who came along for the novelty of the thing.

We could not pass up the excellent opportunity we had of learning to ride, and placed ourselves in the hands of a Sikh *Subahdar* in the battalion riding school, who included us in a squad of raw recruits. He saw to it that we started right from square one, and as I recorded,

'It's a very different business, when tackled properly, from bouncing into Indaw on a Chindwin pony.'

Soon we were learning to jump and finally summoned up the courage to ride onto parade in the mornings.

One evening at the Club I had a very interesting encounter. I was introduced to a Major Strickland, and my first question confirmed that he was the selfsame I.M.S. colonel as had conducted the anti-malarial survey at Indaw while he was Principal of the School of Tropical Diseases at Calcutta. During all my time at Indaw I had been required to copy to him my weekly reports on the progress of the anti-malarial work. It was more than interesting to meet the man in person. He was possibly the greatest authority on his subject in Asia at that time, and now was Senior Malariologist (or some such designation) to the Army in Burma.

Another man I met—and this is a measure of our isolation from events—was a young major who had won the D.S.O. at Namsos. This was my first encounter with a man who had seen action in the present war!

Through the kind of contact that one makes in an 'off beat' place such as Lashio then was, I started sending my letters home via the China National Airways planes that plied between Lashio and Hong Kong. It obviously was irregular because, by so doing, I was sidestepping Burma Command censorship at least, but it halved the time that it took to get my mails home. Soon after I adopted this procedure one of the C.N.A.C. planes was forced down by Japanese fighters; it was then that I started writing my letters in duplicate and sending the two copies by different routes or in succeeding weeks, and I kept this up until the end of the war.

It places these Lashio days in the context of time when I say that my comments on events elsewhere covered the loss of Crete and the German invasion of Russia. Of minor historical interest, perhaps, is this fragment:

I see references in the home papers to the desirability of turning in scrap paper. There must be a lot of books in my shelves that I shall never read again and I leave you to turn in obvious cases.

Sir Robert Brooke-Popham, Commander-in-Chief, Far East, paid a visit to Lashio and spent a few minutes watching 'T.C.' and myself pushing through some bogus manoeuvre or other. I had just had word of the deaths in action in Europe of two more friends and was feeling like an actor in a tragedy condemned to play it as a farce.

One of the N.S.S. Battalion's nearer outposts was at a place called Kutkai on the Burma Road between Lashio and the China border. In command at this time was Glen Gaudie of Steels, and I combined business with pleasure by going up to visit him. I never dreamt of finding what I did, and my next letter attempted a description.

The scenery . . . was absolutely unadulterated Sussex. It was unbelievable, and I was speechless for quite a while. There were the long, rolling downs and the short cropped turf, broken here and there by patches of cultivation. There were even skylarks singing overhead.

I was playing soccer for the Battalion regularly and included myself—I think on merit—for the annual 'needle' match against the Burma Corporation Mines at Namtu. These were reckoned to be among the richest silver and lead mines in the world at that time. I had often wanted to see the place but, off the beaten track as it was, the populace of all races was soccer-mad on the occasion of a match against a visiting side, and I wasn't given time to see all that I would have liked. The match was watched by an uproarious crowd of over three thousand and was played at a killing pace. I was the only European on the field. My next letter

home testifies to the state of my fitness if not of my good
sense:

> . . . an unexpected trip to Maymyo. . . . in addition to two visits to the
> dentist I found time in rather more than twenty-four hours for 27 holes
> of golf, a dinner and cinema party on Saturday night (after which I
> danced till 5.00 a.m.), a call on some friends on Sunday morning,
> followed by a tiffin party before returning to Lashio.

During these Lashio days Duncan Low, his wife Beryl and
their two children provided me with a welcome home from
home, and a delightful family they were. I was to be
sickened later by Duncan's death in action. Beside the Lows,
there was John Birt of the Asiatic Petroleum Company, who
was a fluent speaker of Mandarin Chinese. As an interpreter
he was frequently in demand for the lavish Chinese dinners
that followed meetings between Chiang Kai-shek's officials
and those of the British and American agencies pushing
equipment through to China along the Burma Road.

On obscure pretexts John often arranged my inclusion at
these occasions. The food invariably was out of this world
and would be followed by a heated session of the Chinese
finger game, for which purpose we hangers-on would be
seated as two sides behind the most accomplished exponents,
the losers to down a drink each time a winner was declared.
It was often rough going!

Then there were the Steels people, first Jimmie Cook
already mentioned, and then David and Marjorie Thom,
lately of the oilfields. If you wanted a really heavy evening
you went along to the Flying Tigers' Mess just up the road
and joined in a session of 'Beat that you bastard', a game I
have since met in dilution as 'Liar dice'.

Twice during the rains I was sent down to Maymyo on
courses. The leave population had thinned considerably, but
there was still plenty to go for and I managed several games
of rugger. On one occasion I slipped down to Mandalay to
visit Tony Symns, now of the Bhamo Battalion, Burma
Frontier Force, who was in hospital with sprue and hook
worm. We planned a Christmas bird-watching holiday at
Sinlumkaba in the Bhamo Hills, but events to follow
wrecked the idea.

One day, while changing in the Maymyo Club, I saw a squash racket leaning against the wall with the name Braund inked on the press. It was not mine, and I sought out this unknown namesake. I found him to be a member of an Australian contingent that had been sent out to Maymyo for training at 'Mad Mike' Calvert's Bush Warfare School. This name, contemptuously, or more usually enviously, plagiarized as the 'Bush Welfare School', was a cover to a project that had as its object the production of experts in demolition to be sent over the border to work with Chinese guerrillas. The cover was necessary because we were not yet at war with Japan. In the event, and thanks wholly to the sheer ineptitude of our Chinese Allies, it was to earn the dubious distinction of being the war's most abortive and frustrated mission.

Fenton Braund and I established that we were in fact distant cousins, and in recent years I have had the pleasure of visiting him and his family in New South Wales.

Soon after my return to Lashio from the second of the Maymyo courses, I put in for command of a column on either the Salween or the China frontier. I found, however, that the Inspector General had already requested my transfer to an unspecified project in the Southern Shan States, and that an outpost commander twelve marches distant had been sent orders to come in to relieve me. My new posting, I learnt, was to involve hutted accommodation, so I had to pack the bulk of my possessions for storage in the battalion quarter-guard at Lashio. I checked each piece in with the Q havildar, took his receipt for the lot, and never saw any of it again. After a round of farewell parties I headed south.

I was bound for Thamakan between Kalaw and Taunggyi. I travelled by train and it was an abysmal cross-country journey of thirty-six hours, which included an attempted night's sleep in the Ladies waitingroom at Thazi station. (It was the mosquitoes, not the Ladies, that bothered me.) There we took on a battalion of British troops, and since there was nothing like enough second class accommodation for them, I had to make room for as many as I could in my compartment. Paddy and Tessa also had to be squeezed in somewhere.

Compensation came with journey's end. Thamakan was a beautiful spot at an altitude of 4,200 feet in open, rolling downland studded with clumps of pine. For the dogs it was perfection after Lashio, where I had had to keep them pretty well confined from the unceasing traffic of China-bound trucks. The project was a newly formed Junior Leaders Training School under the command of a Major Jenney, whom I remembered from Rangoon rugger days. He was to command the senior wing, comprising Governor's Commissioned Officers (equivalent to Warrant Officer, peculiar to the Indian and Burma Armies though, in the former, they were known as Viceroy's Commissioned Officers), and I the junior wing made up of N.C.O.s. Our function was to devise and run courses in methods of fighting not hitherto taught in the Burma Army, but the need for which, based on experience gained elsewhere, was rapidly becoming obvious.

Jenney had preceded me to Thamakan by a week or two but unfortunately had been removed to hospital in Rangoon, sick with malaria, by the time I arrived.

The shape of the school-to-be was sufficiently discernible that I was able to carry on with construction and the planning of courses on my own. Life started pleasantly enough. The school was on the Taunggyi/Kalaw road and soon friends travelling from one to the other were dropping in for a drink or a meal, and one afternoon I slipped into Taunggyi to play rugger for the Army against the R.A.F.

I soon found, however, that an old and familiar enemy was at work. At over 4,000 feet, Thamakan theoretically was too elevated for malaria, but before long I had staff going down with it at the rate of two or three a day. With my Indaw experience to help me, I was soon casting around for the source of the trouble. I had not got very far before two senior R.A.M.C. officers came up from Rangoon to look the place over. Unanimously they condemned it as unsuitable for the establishment of the school. I suggested, having regard to the purpose of the school, that to conduct it in a malarious locality would at least give us the opportunity to include instruction in resistance to one predictable enemy, and I told them that I could lay claim to something approaching specialist experience of the subject. The proposal, as I knew, was too radical to command acceptance, and a day or two later I received orders to catch the next train to Rangoon for the purpose of discussing with the Inspector General the move of the school elsewhere.

The Brigadier's car was waiting for me when I reached Rangoon and the driver carried his invitation to stay with him. Jenney was still too sick to take part in discussions, so it was left to the two of us to decide to transfer the school to Kutkai in the Northern Shan States. I was to meet the Brigadier in Lashio in two days time so that we could travel to Kutkai together to reconnoitre an appropriate site. My foreknowledge of the beauty and suitability of Kutkai did much to soften the surrender of Thamakan.

While in Rangoon I paid a quick visit to Steels office, and I spent the evening with Derek Lewton-Brain, still chafing in a civilian role. We were drinking in the Silver Grill when suddenly I espied Maxine Strong in the company of a Flying Tiger. After a waved greeting we were invited to join them and I had a couple of dances with Maxine. She told me that she was spending a few days in Rangoon with friends with whom she would than be travelling to Kalaw. As I would still be demolishing the School at Thamakan we arranged to meet one night for dinner at the Kalaw Hotel.

We did so on what in fact was the last night of my stay in those parts. Maxine was somewhat subdued as she was getting over the shock of a broken engagement, and we dined quietly, *tete-a-tete*. She was wearing a most attractive multi-coloured panelled dress. After dinner, in bright moonlight, we strolled down a little-travelled road to a point where we were able to sit on the parapet of a bridge. Overhead a tree was shedding the white petals of its flowers until Maxine's dress was studded with them. Then and there I nicknamed her 'Petal'. I was in love, but there was nothing that I could do about it.

That night I drove as far as Taunggyi, where John Bowerman, the Commandant of the Southern Shan States Battalion, had a bed waiting for me. My party consisted of a rearguard of about eight or ten troops and we were travelling in a heavily laden three-tonner. In the morning the driver was down with malaria and there was no other in the party. I had no experience of driving anything of this size, but there was no option. The 260-mile route carried us to heights which, early on, were in thick mist, and it was late at night when I brought the vehicle into Lashio after driving for fourteen hours. I recorded, however, that 'between Taunggyi and Loilem we passed through the finest scenery I have ever seen in my life'. I think that distinction is still unsurpassed.

Life at Kutkai started easily. Although we had only two or three weeks in which to build a new school, it had obviously been necessary to postpone the opening course to the same extent. I spent my time well, tramping miles of countryside in quest of suitable locations for schemes and demonstrations, but finding time always to study the birds of the area. I soon had built a comfortable two-room *tawmaw*, wherein the radio, the gramophone and letter-writing filled my evenings. The Northern Shan States Battalion outpost at Kutkai was now commanded by Roddie Russell, a regular who provided amusing company. Also resident was Philip Barton of the Burma Frontier Service, a gourmet who never seemed to serve you the same self-prepared dish twice. With both of these my trail was to cross again elsewhere in days to come.

The war was now over two years old and for me, relatively, it had been mostly holiday.

The school was being erected by Kachins of the Battalion. I used sometimes to watch the sheer wizardry of their work. Major buildings, barracks or lecture rooms of bamboo and thatch went up at the rate of one a day—and never a nail used.

I went through a bad time with Paddy who became desperately ill with what I guessed was pneumonia. There was one night in particular when I thought he was going, and it was only repeated rubbing of his chest, and liberal doses of brandy that got him through.

Letters from home told me that my young sister was now wearing two more pips than I was, and that my R.I.N. brother was *en route* to England as a member of a commissioning crew for a new ship for the Royal Indian Navy. One evening I had the pleasure of playing host to Fenton Braund and about two dozen fellow-Aussies as they passed through on their clandestine way to China. Jenney finally got cleared from hospital and it was not long before we had our first course under way.

Although past and pending events reduced the school to a rather ill-starred venture, I certainly learnt as much as I taught. Jenney had first-class ideas, and soon our students were being put through the hoop with a realism that they had never remotely scented. There was never a battle but that I and my instructors were not firing live over the heads of the advance. Anti-tank raids with home-made Molotov cocktails, booby trapping and mining, surreptitious crossings of rivers, all this and more was taught with an approach to authenticity that we used to sit up late to plan. And with it all I achieved the positive identification of a species of harrier of which hitherto there had been only one officially accepted occurrence in Burma!

Then—and at last—came Pearl Harbour and, hard on its heels, the sinking of *Prince of Wales* and *Repulse*. We were in!

Soon the Japs were nibbling their way into Tenasserim and, at Kawkareik on the Siamese border, Raymond Hall of Steels ('the last of the Dandies'), with a platoon for company, fell to a much superior invading force—the first known British casualty in Burma. Rangoon was bombed on Christmas Day. At Kutkai we threw ourselves fiercely into our still sheltered task, awaiting God alone knew what summons to Heaven alone knew where.

During a long weekend break in the course I judged it opportune to reconnoitre the road to Bhamo. I motored up along a mountain road that included thirteen hundred blind bends in less than seventy miles. I stayed with Steels Forest Manager at Bhamo, Gordon Hunt, and his wife, both of whom I had known in Maymyo. Regardless—or in defiance —of events, they gave a dinner party for twelve on the night of my arrival and next day we went off on a jungle fowl shoot. That evening I dined with Chris and Nancy McDowall, old friends of Rangoon days. Chris was now in the Bhamo Battalion of the B.F.F.

On my way back to Kutkai, by prior arrangement, I crossed the border into China (with B.F.F. and Chinese Army pickets at opposite ends of the bridge marking the frontier) and spent the night at the fabulously appointed hostel serving the American-run aircraft factory at Loiwing. This was an unbelievable venture. Right in the back of beyond, and for many months now, the Americans had been assembling aircraft from components carried up the Burma Road, and delivering them to the Chinese. Of the hostel I wrote:

I'd been told roughly what to expect, but the sight of bedrooms with pile carpets, shaded lights, long baths, pull plugs, hot and cold running water and what have you was truly staggering. The place is miles out in the wilds and yet it is no exaggeration at all to say that the standard of comfort is not below that of the Grand Hotel, Eastbourne.

Later I had to express my annoyance: 'To hear them talking about the exploits of American pilots over Rangoon you'd think they'd never heard of the Battle of Britain.'

The occasion coincided with the loss of Tavoy to the North of Mergui. The same letter speculates:

I wonder if by now the ill-starred Dredge (a mere £75,000 worth) is lying at the bottom of the Yamone Chaung, a victim of the 'scorched earth' policy.

It was.

10 Scorched Earth
January 1942 to May 1942

Under my dust-laden boots the paddy stubble crunched in the darkness as I made the rounds of my platoon positions. Occasionally I was challenged, and it was by men reacting alertly to the knowledge that such things were now important. However, we were not yet being closely threatened.

Five hundred crow miles to the north, the school at Kutkai was shuttered and deserted. Hastily we had had to close down and disperse, and now, as a company commander in 'F.F.7', I found myself in the delta of the Rangoon River on operational service for the first time.

My southward journey had included a riotous farewell to Maymyo, where we had concluded our evening by emptying the club's fire-foam extinguishers over the few surviving dancers on the floor. Thence I had called in for equipping at Pyawbwe, the Headquarters of the Reserve Battalion of the B.F.F. Here I had run into George Kinnear of Steels, now in the Burma Army Service Corps, and he had taken Paddy and Tessa off me on the strict understanding that if the shape of things to come made it impossible for him to hang on to them he would shoot them. From Pyawbwe we had proceeded to the delta as one of a number of 'F.F.s', mobile two-company Frontier Force columns with the role of dealing with an expected attempt by the Japanese to capture the oil refineries intact by parachute assault. Jenney was commanding F.F.7: Christopher McDowall and I were his company commanders. We were widely deployed.

Earlier that day I had got back from a briefing session at Battalion Headquarters of the West Yorks, who were ranging in front of us in search of enemy parties expected to

153

come ashore after crossing the Gulf of Martaban, for Moulmein had fallen. I had submitted the apparently novel warning that such parties might well be dressed as Burmans, but had followed this up with a plea that Burmans were not to be shot on sight. The reception suggested that I was asking for the best of both worlds which, since the West Yorks were newly arrived, I suppose I was.

Events were moving fast, and within a day or two came the disaster at the Sittang River. After a gallant stand against heavy odds on the Bilin, the 17th Division fell back on the railway bridge across the Sittang near Mokpalin. By a tragic decision, which ended the military career of the Division's V.C. Commander, the bridge was blown when two brigades were still on the wrong side of the river. Of those who attempted to swim for it, many were drowned or shot while crossing; of those who made it, most were equipped only with underwear when they staggered ashore.

Our carefully integrated scheme with the West Yorks fell apart, for they were promptly ordered north to join the battle, which was now moving towards Rangoon along our left flank. The defence of the refineries now lay solely with the scattered 'F.F.s'.

The outcome of events was obvious, and hastily imported experts were preparing the refineries for demolition. Our time was spent in constant patrolling, but the Japs were exercising too strong a pressure in their drive on and round Rangoon to bother about pre-occupied units being left behind on their flanks. I still think it surprising, however, that an air-drop on the refineries did not form part of their strategy. They would have been a tremendous prize, and opposition would have been nominal, as can be gauged from what I wrote to my father many months later:

... it can be giving away no secrets now to say that when I was sent into the front line with my column we had a Tommy gun per section, but not a single round of ammunition for them. Likewise I and my G.C.O.s had not a single round for our revolvers. We had no compasses, and the only pair of binoculars in the column was my bird-watching pair. We had no tin hats, anti-gas equipment or medical supplies (not even First Field Dressings), and to start with I was the only man with a map. Do you wonder that the Far East was the walkover it was?

I omitted to mention, I see now, that we had no bombs for our mortars. Staff Colleges and historians of the Burma campaign please copy!

The time came when we were ordered to fall back in close defence of the refineries for the period that remained before the 'blow'. One evening, on patrol, I mapped a course that brought me back via I.B.P.'s refinery at Seikkyi. Through the tank farm I entered the residential area. The whole place was spick and span but practically deserted. I found my way to the Works Manager's bungalow and there had the shock of my life. Seated round a garden table with a newly laundered cloth on it, themselves bathed and changed into the usual evening garb of white shirt and trousers, were Charlie Haggarty and Bill Chalmers, respectively the Works Manager and Chief Chemist, and Andy Armit, who had been ordered up to join them after he had helped to scuttle the Dredge at Yamone! In attendance was a *lugalay* with a whisky decanter and cold sodas! Talk about 'the show must go on'—it was magnificent! And for me, needless to say, it was a case of 'I don't mind if I do'!

It should be explained that, though the refineries had been expertly mined, it was still required that dependable staff be on hand to press the buttons (or whatever it was they had to do) when the time came. Indeed, at the B.O.C. refinery at Syriam, the vital telephone switchboard through which the order to destroy would come from Rangoon, was manned to the last by a small team of brave Anglo-Burman girls of the B.O.C. staff.

The 'blow' was ordered for noon a day or two before Rangoon fell on 9 March. We had expected then to be ordered to make the best way we could through or round the city so as to join up with the northward retreat. This was apparently judged now to be impossible, for our final orders were that we would be evacuated by sea, along with the 'last ditchers' from Rangoon and the refineries and such military stragglers as we could round up. The means of our evacuation would be three ships which, having brought in from India a few days earlier the last troop reinforcements for Burma, had been ordered to wait down-river for this contingency.

As time for the 'blow' approached, McDowall's company was withdrawn to cover the embarkation into launches that would take the escapers down to the ships. All told there were two or three thousand people involved, though they were converging from several assembly points. My company alone was left dug in in front of Syriam. It was a gesture that did little more than provide the destroyers with a sense of company. I visited their chief and arranged with him that I would remain in position till three o'clock, as this would give him all the time he needed to get his teams away. I then returned to my weapon pit to await events.

I knew what was about to happen, of course, but I could not find it credible. Here were these monstrous, costly conglomerations of tanks and towers, pumps and power houses, with all their diversely ordered banks and swathes of pipelines, about to be blown sky high. With them would go all the 'no smoking' and 'fire danger' signs that rendered the conception unthinkable.

Promptly at noon the first of hundreds of storage tanks suddenly erupted under the compulsion of a vast ball of fire that soared and mushroomed into the sky from its bowels. Before the pursuing surge of black smoke engulfed them, I could see fragments of the tank shell that must have weighed tons, floating earthward through the heat like sycamore leaves. At some time the crescendo of that initial explosion must have reached me, but already I was stupefied by the succeeding eruptions and soon was deafened by the roar of flames and the rapid 'crump' of succeeding detonations. Down-river I could see Seikkyi and Thilawa (B.B.P.'s Refinery) leaping into self-destruction, and mentally I pictured Haggarty and Chalmers and Armit hurrying through their practised routine with the speed necessary to ensure their getaway before the holocaust scorched them.

Sickly fascinated, I watched the inverted mountains of solid black smoke writhing and billowing upward and outward from each pyre until, with an imagined gesture of familiarity, they linked arms with each other and swung and surged hither and yon to wherever unsullied, open sky still offered accommodation. Sometimes, at the base, I could still see the eruption and glow of fresh sacrifices to this awful god of total destruction, but gradually the darkness of the pit took over.

By two o'clock of this hot weather afternoon I could see the headlights of cars that were carrying the demolition squads to the jetties. Realizing the implication for myself, I sent off a section by jeep along the track of my own withdrawal, with orders that a man was to be dropped off at each fork or junction as a guide for the main body to follow. There was no guessing what conditions might be like when the time came to move.

Slowly I strolled through the area in which we were dug in, observing the men. There were about a hundred of them, equally made up of Chins and Burma Gurkhas; all of them small, tough hill men of peasant roots, none of them comprehending what their fixed, unblinking eyes were now beholding; and all oblivious of my passage.

From the slight rise that had been my observation post, I watched the all-surrounding ribbon of bright sky thinning steadily to extinction at the horizon. Still there was the roar of unseen flames and the thuds of fresh detonations. We were, as I remember it, distant from Syriam by something more than a mile, but our clothes were now wet with a perspiration that owed nothing to the heat of the day.

At three o'clock, after necessary roll calls, for it was very dark, we moved off. The lights of our jolting trucks picked out our guides who were hauled aboard as each established for us our route. Arrived at the jetties we found a jungle of motor transport, stores and nervously stamping mules; and orders to destroy the lot and be embarked by five. This was a tall order and we had to move fast. Soon blazing trucks and jeeps were providing all the light we needed to shoot the mules and to pile scattered stores and equipment onto leaping fires. It was Dante's inferno in modern dress.

We filed aboard the launch: it was a large affair that easily took the hundred or more of us. We cast off and headed down-river.

The spectacle of the blazing mess we had just created was soon forgotten in consideration of a problem ahead of us that had not bothered those who had gone before. The refineries, for obvious reasons, fronted on the river and, from fractured tanks and pipe lines, burning oil had been spewing out for some hours now. At first sight the prospect ahead of us was an unbroken sheet of dancing flames. I had visions of putting about, returning to the jetties and trying to find our way northward after all. It was only as we slowed to a cautious approach that we could see that the fire was splintered by a network of lanes of open water. Sheltering as best we all could from the searing heat, we forged a faltering course through this terrifying obstacle until finally we broke through into the open water that the oil had not yet claimed and opened the throttle.

My orders were that once my men were all transferred to shipboard I personally was to see that the cocks were removed from the bottom of the launch and then follow the crew up the ladder. As I did a round of the men to see how they had survived the frying, I found that there was a considerable collection of stores on board that had no connection with our fruitless 'campaign'. Apparently they had come from India with the division which would now be fighting for its life up the Prome road, and there had been no time or labour to unload them. Included were a number of cases of beer. Unobtrusively I slid the warm contents of a bottle down my parched throat and secreted two or three more about my person. Alas for foresight outwitted! As I climbed over the ship's rail from the foundering launch, I was frisked by a couple of ship's officers who were looking for just what I had, and I heard the over-side splashes as I moved forward to report to Jenney!

It was not long before I appreciated the wisdom of this seemingly unfriendly gesture. We, and the other two ships of our convoy, were soon headed for the open sea. At a hastily convened officers' meeting, the Master explained to us that we would be unescorted, that he had over a thousand people on board, and that among them were fifty or sixty women and the key personnel of the demolition parties: the latter were required to be flown to Yenangyaung as soon as we berthed at Calcutta to be ready to resume their destructive role there should the state of the Japanese advance make it necessary. These two categories were to have priority should we be sunk, and his total life-saving capacity, as represented by boats and rafts, was three hundred at most. In case the worse came to the worst he required that the approaches to the life boats be covered by our Bren guns trustworthily manned. So, in the darkness and as secretly as possible, McDowall and I reconnoitred our gun positions and briefed a selected group of G.C.O.s and N.C.O.s on their possible role.

That evening the Japanese radio gratuitously informed us that their support bombing from the air had been frustrated 'by more hot air over Rangoon than usual'. It had been a damned expensive smoke screen!

Our four days passage to Calcutta was uncomfortable and uneventful. As the dawn came up on our first day at sea we were out of sight of land. Not one of my Chins and Burma Gurkhas had ever set eyes on the sea before and they were completely bewildered. Unfortunately the weather roughened and soon most of them were in misery. Having had their ordeal by fire, they were now getting it by water— wherein they had my understanding sympathy.

On arrival at Calcutta we disembarked to the attempted ministrations of a crowd of well-wishers who seemed to think that they were coping with a second Dunkirk. Little did they know that none of us had seen a Jap or been under attack!

The military elements were conveyed out of town to the permanent camp at Barrackpore. After seeing my men accommodated and catered for, I had a badly needed bath and change as I had not had my clothes off for several days. Then in borrowed transport several of us officers headed for Calcutta, having agreed to meet for dinner at Firpo's that evening. Among the party, to my delight, was Derek Lewton-Brain, at last escaped into uniform, who had been a voyager in one of the other ships of the convoy from Rangoon.

I found my way to the telegraph office and sent home word of my evacuation. I learnt later that Steels in Calcutta, in their never-failing way, had beaten me to it thanks to Gordon Nicoll, who had been at the head of the 'last ditchers' from Rangoon and somehow had compiled a complete list of those of us who were in the convoy.

Then I started out hopefully in search of Maxine. The US Consulate could tell me nothing, nor could any of the banks. I visited all the likely hotels, and though there were plenty of Burma refugees milling around in the foyers in various stages of misery and filth, I could not find the one I was seeking. Presumably she was still trekking out along one of the jungle routes that spelt the end for so many. I prayed that she might be safe.

At Firpo's, utterly untouched by war, we nearly had trouble with the management on the score that we were improperly dressed. We forcibly expressed the view that the reverse was the case and trod a heavily booted way up the stairs to a well-placed table of our own commandeering. The general effect of our 'operational' appearance on the diners at large was rather pathetic. It was as though the war had come to Calcutta with our entry, and there were those who would have lionized us. We parried all questions on the extent of our martial contribution: there was little else that we could do!

Within a day or two F.F.7 was entrained for Shillong in the Khasi and Jaintia Hills of Assam. On the map it looked like a move back in the direction of the war, but there were disturbing rumours afoot to the effect that, as an unattached spawning of the Burma Army, our future role would be as garrison troops somewhere in India. Mirthlessly I recalled General McLeod's words—'In this war anybody who speaks Burmese stays on the ground'. I still had no news of Maxine and was feeling thwarted and depressed.

At Shillong we were quartered at Elephant Falls camp some miles out of the town, a heterogeneous mixture of Burma Army elements under the command of Lieut.-Colonel Bob Cook, the C.O. of the Rangoon Battalion, B.F.F., whom, fortunately, I knew.

After the usual preliminaries, I found my way into town with Chris McDowall and, inevitably, to the club, which was thronged with Gurkha and Assam Rifles officers, most of whom seemed to be in transit in the right direction.

Having carved a solitary passage to the bar and secured a drink, I looked right and left at my neighbours and found that I had been at school in England with both of them! A little later I discovered that among a number of wives and children evacuated to Shillong from Burma was Sibyl Boyt, who had been one of us at 'Ingleston' in militia and O.C.T.U. days. So, while Noel was winning himself a Military Cross in Karenni, I was squiring his wife to the twice-weekly Shillong Club dances!

Reports of casualties were coming in. Soon, of B.F.F. officers whom I knew, Roughton, Low, Wallace, Love, Edwards, Sandeman and Girling were dead. So were Bradford and Johnson, two of the Militia Company's platoon commanders. So were Morton and Chiodetti of the O.C.T.U. staff. And Braund? Where was Braund? Having spent two years railing against a fate that excluded him from the war, he had got in and out so fast that now he was drinking at the club bar of an Indian hill station!

Glass in hand one evening, before insanity or worse intervened, I was 'beefing off' to Captain Charles Davison, a casual acquaintance from the Argentine. Suddenly I detected a note of authority in his questioning of me. There were guarded references to guerrilla operations in Burma, and finally a direct question—was I interested? I replied affirmatively and was asked to be at a local hotel the following evening. I arrived punctually and, after a bit of hanging around, was collected by Davison who conducted me down a long corridor to a room into which he pushed me and then disappeared.

The room was ill-lit and the solitary occupant rose at my entry and introduced himself as Colonel Critchley. He seated me with a drink and proceeded to explain that he himself had a background of guerrilla experience in Spain and Abyssinia and had been flown out here to see what he could organize along similar lines. He understood that I had Chin troops under my command, and suggested that I might trek through to the Chin Hills with them and see to what extent I could establish and make a nuisance of myself there.

'But,' he proceeded, 'I want first your answers to four questions. What is your medical category?'

'A1, Sir.'

'Are you married?'

'No Sir.'

'Are you an only son?'

'No Sir.'

'Is anyone financially dependent on you?'

'No Sir' (and privately, 'what the hell's going on?').

'Good enough,' said Critchley, 'though I think I should add that you'll probably find yourself operating under conditions such that, if captured, you'd have no rights as a prisoner of war. Are you on?'

'Yes Sir.' And that fixed me for the next three years.

The overall plan, of which I was now to be an element, is understood by reference to a map of Burma. It will be seen that the north–south plains through which flow the Irrawaddy and Chindwin rivers are contained by a rim of hills, the Chin Hills and Naga Hills to the west and northwest, the Kachin Hills to the north, the Shan States and Karen Hills to the east. Elevations range from about three to twelve thousand feet, and while characteristics and language vary widely from tract to tract, collectively the inhabitants have far more in common each with the other than they have with the Burmese proper. It is basically the world-wide difference between the hillman and the plainsman, the one looking down on the other for his soft and easy way of life, the other scorning the first for his grime and his illiteracy.

Burma had been lost to the extent that the Japs were now in complete control of the river valleys and the plains but, at this stage, they appeared not to be prepared to face the perils of extending their domination to the hill tracts, where lived tough but naturally apprehensive peoples who yet considered themselves as free.

This state of affairs could not be expected to last indefinitely, particularly if the Japs had ideas of invading India or attacking China from the rear once they had consolidated their position in Burma. Accordingly it was resolved to feed into the hills Burmese-speaking, jungle-living

British and Anglo-Burman officers to organize, arm and train native levies for the defence of their homelands. An ancillary role was to be regular patrolling into the plains, both for the purpose of studying Jap activities and intentions and of making contact with loyal Burmese and building them up into an Intelligence network. While ambushing and harassing of Jap patrols would be fair game, this was to be confined to pinpricking rather than to aggravation such as would invite large-scale reprisals. When the time came that Allied armies re-entered Burma for the purpose of recon-quest, then of course the hills would be expected to burst into a flame of rebellion, and there would be no holds barred. Already 'Stooky' Seagrim was at large in Karenni, having lain low while the tide of Japanese invasion washed over him; though this was not yet known for certain. Others were on their way in.

The whole idea offered a wonderful escape from organized soldiering into licensed dacoity, and I knew that I had found what I wanted. Bob Cook raised no objection to Critchley's confidential request for my services: indeed he was delighted that someone was getting somewhere of his own initiative at a time of general demoralization. My F.F.7 Chins were quietly removed and segregated while they were being equipped for their role. Speed was of the essence and it did not take us long.

As a digression—but I mention it for its content of domestic morale—I would explain that some years before the war I had sent my father an excellent map of Burma, of which I was now carrying a copy. Before leaving Shillong I wrote asking him to lay his map out on a table and arm himself with a ruler and a protractor. Using as his centre 'the place where I collected malaria' (i.e. Indaw), he was to label A,B,C and so on a number of places in the Chin Hills and Upper Chindwin to which I directed him by compass bearing and distance in inches. By this device I was able later to make innocuous-seeming references in my letters to a, b and c that kept him pretty well informed as to where I was operating.

I was concerned that the route of our re-entry into Burma

should not involve us unduly in swimming against a tide of driven soldiery and civilians flowing westward. For this reason it was decided that my party would be conveyed to Imphal, whence we would travel due south along the spine of hills that leads to Tiddim, the northernmost District Headquarters in the Chin Hills, which was still under the administrative control of the Burma Frontier Service. By this route we would cross escape lines without following them. In the event, once we got well away from Imphal, our sole encounter was with a fleeing Sikh sepoy armed only with a No. 3 golf iron!

We left Shillong on 9 May 1942 by motor transport that took us to Gauhati on the Brahmaputra. Thence we en-trained for Dimapur on the single-track, one-train-a-day line that later was to be galvanized into much greater activity by American Railway battalions. At Dimapur, in the dark of a filthy wet night, we were met by Charles Davison and con-veyed to bamboo barracks in 'Penis Park'. The official name of this ghastly dump was 'No. 3 (Ruins) Rest Camp', but since, among the mouldering Hindu temples that gave the place its name, there predominated a multiplicity of massive stone linga (symbols of the god Siva), the nickname was predictable and universal.

Here, after squelching from duckboard to duckboard, I was conducted to Brigadier Felix Williams, D.S.O., M.C., who was in strategic command of Levy operations, actual and putative, in the Chin Hills/Naga Hills area. To my utter dismay, he told me that in view of the continuing Japanese advance up the Chindwin and the previous day's bombing of Imphal, it was considered that my plan to get through to Tiddim had come too late to have a fair chance of success and that, regretfully, he would have to call it off.

With how much disregard for the tenets of military discipline I know not, I disputed with this patient and kindly man the validity of what I claimed was a defeatist attitude. Recent events, surely, added up to no strong clue to Japanese intentions: they could just as easily be a smoke screen to a signing-off of continued advance. My plan had been carefully thought out, my force was supra-normally equipped, and the worst that could befall was small-scale failure. I spoke Burmese, I knew the Chindwin, my men were of the countryside, and I understood better than to court a lone, hero's death if I ran into a situation of which it was my duty to bring back first-hand information. All this and more, factual and fanciful, I argued. Finally the Brigadier instructed Davison to lay on transport to take me and my party to Imphal next day. There I was to report the present discussion to the Corps Commander, General Irwin, and request his orders.

Our mountainous trip to Imphal took us through the beautiful little township of Kohima, which later was to be demolished brick by brick in a historic battle in which the entrenched opposing forces were separated only by the width of the Deputy Commissioner's tennis court—and he did not leave his post.

Arrived at Imphal, I took prompt advantage of the Corps Commander's providential absence to organize rations and motor transport to convey me southward to Shuganu next day. I found there was knowledge of my mission but not, fortunately, of its threatened cancellation. I was even told that arrangements were in hand to replenish my ten days' rations before they were exhausted. Had I known then that I was to receive nothing more from the Army for over four months, I would still have gone forward, for the bit was between my teeth. I certainly was not going to wait for the Corps Commander's return!

Next morning, after several air raid alarms, during which Jap planes came over apparently to see what damage they had done two days earlier, we moved off. The first few miles were as I had feared. We were travelling eastward on the Imphal/Palel/Tamu road, along which was moving a human tide of evacuation. We were doubtless considered too mad or too ignorant to be cheered on our way, and passage was allowed to us only grudgingly. It was a *melee* of soldiers, British and Indian, and civilians, among whom pre-dominated petty Indian traders and the like, milling along with their women and children, and propelling wheeled impedimenta on which were piled their bundles and their pots and pans. I could not but notice the Hussars. Until their last tank had been destroyed on the east bank of the Chindwin, they had done a sterling job where much else was less than exemplary; and now, shaved and smart within the limits open to them, they were coming out disciplined and in good heart.

I had one completely unexpected encounter, in the person of a lean and hungry-looking George Kinnear marching out with a lean and hungry-looking Tessa slouching along beside him! He had had both dogs with him, George explained, as far as Kalewa; but there Paddy had disappeared, probably on the scent of a bitch. George was most apologetic over this, although he had had to share his own meagre rations with the dogs over some hundreds of miles of retreat. It was a remarkable effort, and I there and then conferred Tessa on George in perpetuity. They had established a partnership that should not be broken and, in fact, Tessa lived to a ripe old age in George's keeping.

In getting away from the human tangle we took a wrong turning, and when night fell I had to camp only three miles from Palel. After an early morning resumption we again took a wrong turning, but nevertheless reached Shuganu by mid-day. From here I sent back the motor transport and got the Chins busy on bundling our equipment into manageable loads, while I scoured around for porters and ponies. For sheer inertia I have never known such a task, and promises of assistance had to be forcibly extracted. In the evening a company of Gurkhas arrived to take up a forward position for the prospective defence of Imphal. They were commanded by Captain Villiers Dennys, a fellow Old Eastbournian, so at least I had sympathetic company for the evening.

In the morning my worst fears were realized. Nearly all the men who had promised to convey us forward were working in their fields, and no ponies had been rigged for load-carrying. Half-crazed, I routed around, forcing men and animals to the starting-post; and finally, at half-past five in the afternoon of a lost day, we straggled across the fields and into the jungle. I was obsessed with the fear that when night fell the coolies would decide that it was time to go home, and I determined to keep them going until we had passed the point of no return between villages. I allowed them a closely supervised break of two hours just before dawn, and at eleven o'clock we reached Mombi after a nightmare trek of twenty-two miles.

To pay off the Shuganu porters cost me over a fifth of the thousand rupees in silver that I was carrying. I was not going to get very far at this rate! My diary entry for the night is illuminating.

This is very expensive carrying: the reason is that at the present moment coolies are able to command what price they like for carrying refugees' kit from Burma into India. The Head-man of Mombi was anti-British in the Kuki rising of 1924(?). After an exchange of 'hooch' and a little palm oiling, however, he seems prepared to be helpful in the matter of coolies etc. The local villagers live very near the bread line indeed. The water well went dry during our stay and no food is obtainable except the odd chicken. A force of any size would be hard put to it to live on the country hereabouts.

Next day insufficient porters were available and I had to split my force and move forward in two parties, the rear one under command of my G.C.O., Jemadar Pau Chin Mang. Our needs in the way of human and equine assistance at this stage can possibly be gauged by a tabulation of our strength when we started marching.

1 King's Commissioned Officer
1 Governor's Commissioned Officer
48 Other ranks
3 Non-combatants (cooks and water carrier)
53 total force
10 days' rations
20, 000 rounds rifle and 4,500 rounds Tommy gun ammunition
3 Revolvers, 2 Bren guns, 9 Tommy guns, 44 rifles (inc. 7 surplus)
Rs.1000 in silver
Bedding
Stores and equipment, including explosives, sufficient nominally for one year's work

After only fifteen miles of marching I halted and camped beside a stream that marked the Indo-Burma border. It was a pathetic performance but I decided that I must wait for news at least of Pau Chin Mang, since he would be dependent to some extent on porters from our party making a second trip—and God knows, the physique of most of them was such as to defy belief in their ability to do it once.

I spent the afternoon hours gloomily reflecting that the facts of life as now unfolding were bidding fair to defeat my object where the Army had failed to do so. I had covered less than forty miles since leaving Shuganu; my party was dispersed; my money would be exhausted before I reached Tiddim; the assurance of further rations was obviously uttered of ignorance; villages were so small, scattered and impoverished that there was no question of feeding a force of fifty off the country even by compulsion; the track was stony, steep, sometimes near-precipitous, and ill-defined; it had rained incessantly since we left Mombi, and much of the jungle was infested with leeches that penetrated the tight folds of my ankle puttees and the lace holes of my boots until my socks squelched with blood. Worst of all, perhaps, was the growing suspicion that I might be commanding men who regarded this sodden pilgrimage as a return home by the back door rather than as a sortie against a victorious enemy. There are no fears like those that cannot be discussed with a kindred spirit.

In the morning I crawled from my roughly-fashioned *basha*, rubbed life into my chilled and cramped limbs and started the daily hunt for porters. By eight-thirty I had enough wherewith to get forward, and I also had word that Pau Chin Mang was on the move. A few minutes later I waded across the stream and was back in Burma, with an unsuspected six thousand miles and more of foot-slogging ahead of me before the Jap was routed!

11 Unto the Hills

May 1942 to July 1942

If sentiment or convention required that return to Burma called for some solemn act of oath-taking, my record is silent. I was too soon reclaiming in the three miles to Lenikot the four thousand feet that I had thrown away the previous afternoon. Arrived at the village, I arranged for porters to go down early next morning to relieve those whom Pau Chin Mang would have brought through from Mombi, toiling on myself another twelve miles to Khuangkhan where I camped.

The next march to Mualpi was a repetition—down to stream level and then a climb of nearly five thousand feet. As I plodded upward, head down under my ninety pounds of pack and equipment, my mind was at work. The Japs could have halted where I had last heard of them—on the line of the Chindwin. Even in victory they must have been strained and exhausted enough to warrant this. On the other hand no one had yet made a correct prediction where the Japs were concerned. If they still had the impetus they could be following the Allied retreat through to Imphal: after all, they had bombed the place, and Dennys's move to Shuganu was indicative of a hasty defensive plan born of somebody's appreciation of the possibilities. If, therefore, the Japs were moving on Imphal in my rear, it was prudent to suppose that they had at least occupied Tiddim, Falam and Haka to protect their flank. It was time, therefore, that I started watching my step, because I could already be the jam in a sandwich.

On arrival at Mualpi I was placed in a quandary by the presence there of two representatives of the chief of Tonzang sent north to meet me. It was evidence that my obscure passage was not proof against the jungle telegraph, but it told me nothing of whether Pum Za Mang, the chief, was a free and friendly agent or acting under enemy prompting. After feeling my way around I decided in favour of the former, but I sent two men off by a circuitous route to Tiddim, the one carrying a coded message in his underwear, the other the key in one of his puttees. Their orders were to part company before entering Tiddim but to report together to whomsoever might be in charge once they had established that the place was still held.

My next march was murderous. From Mualpi we dropped right down to the Manipur River near Kianglam and then had an unbroken climb to Tonzang at over five thousand feet. It was raining, the porters were undernourished and wilting, and it was still on the cards that we were walking into a trap. My Chins, who were of the Sokte tribe, assured me that I had nothing to fear as it was their own tribal area that we were approaching. I can smile now at my apprehension, but at that time a Chin was a Chin so far as I was concerned, and I had no appreciation of the parochial picture.

It was late when we approached Tonzang, and later still by the time I had watched the place through glasses for half an hour or so. We camped in and around the *zayat* at the entrance to the village and I planned to call on the chief first thing in the morning. However, he came to see me soon after we were settled and, since he spoke Burmese, we were able to talk without the need for an interpreter. (My troops and I had Urdu in common.)

Pum Za Mang was a large man with personality and power. Later, under enemy pressure, his loyalty was to waver, but at this stage he found it in his interest to 'string along'. He told me that Tiddim was still under Civil control, that there were troops there and that the Japs had made no move into the Hills. This was very reassuring, and after a bedtime talk with my N.C.O.s, who had been visiting in the village, I had no reason to doubt what Pum Za Mang had told me. His village, incidentally, was much bigger and wealthier than anything we had come through so far. It even boasted a well-stocked shop at which I was able to buy tea and sugar for my force.

In the morning I returned the chief's call. Pau Chin Mang had arrived with a very tired rear party, and I left for Tiddim on the basis that I would do it in two marches and he in one after resting for twenty-four hours. I camped at Twelmu on the bank of the Manipur River and, as planned, was joined by Pau Chin Mang the following day when we were only a mile or two short of Tiddim. We seemed to have been marching for an eternity, but in fact had covered little more than a hundred miles.

Our journey ended with a gentle drop down into Tiddim, and as soon as we got a clear view of the town I fell out my men and settled down to watch the place through glasses until I was satisfied that all was well. I did not have to wait long, and half an hour later—with that previously encountered mental 'click' that occurs when you drop back into speaking your own language again—I was making myself known to Norman Kelly of the Burma Frontier Service, who was still in the saddle as Assistant Superintendent, Tiddim. Norman was in telegraphic touch with Falam, the Headquarters of the Chin Hills District, so I was able to report my arrival to Lieut.-Colonel Jack Haswell, who was commanding the Chin Levies. Kelly had to pay off my porters as I no longer had the means of doing so.

My first task, after seeing my force fixed up with accommodation and a meal, was to pitch in as a male nurse. A British commando platoon, which had done sterling work during the retreat, had headed for the Chin Hills instead of going through to India, with the object of joining forces with whomsoever might be operating there, and of returning to the offensive as soon as they were rested. Unfortunately they were in appalling shape, twenty-five of them being down with Chindwin malaria at its worst. Three had already died of blackwater, including their Medical Officer, Major 'Corny' McGrath, whom I had known in Maymyo; several others were dangerously ill and there was much that had to be done for them. Some of them I knew—Colonel Dick

Musgrave (ex-*Bombine*), their commander, and Jimmie Moore, the O.C.T.U. instructor in 'Regimental Accounts' being two of them. There were no more deaths, but as soon as all were able to move they took the only reasonable course of marching out to India via Aijal, this being the easiest (*sic*) route that we could plot for them.

The greatest prize left behind by the commandos was 'Mrs Murphy', the first jeep ever to enter the Chin Hills. Complete with a good stock of petrol in drums, it had been navigated somehow from Kalemyo up to and over Kennedy Peak and through to Tiddim. Here it had been handed over to Norman Kelly by the commandos when they left. Norman was like a small boy with a new toy and I went with him on a precarious run to Fort White, which stood at the junction of the valley road from Kalemyo with the mountain road that linked Tiddim, Falam and Haka. This strategic spot had echoed to the sounds of battle on several occasions during the last half-century or more, and buried in the small military cemetery below the rest house was an early winner of the Victoria Cross.

In command of a Levy detachment at Fort White now was Peter Bankes of the *Bombine*. I had briefly met Peter in Maymyo, it being docketed in my mind that he had been the biggest monetary contributor to Kathleen Howe's concert in aid of war charities. Peter was a giant of a man, and with his curly hair he looked like a Greek god. For two years he had rowed for Oxford in the inter-Varsity boat race, and up to that time at least was the heaviest man ever to have done so. He was an ideal Levy officer and we became good friends over the months that followed.

Norman Kelly made an interesting contrast. He was a small, tough Irishman with a bubbling sense of humour and he radiated enthusiasm for the Levy cause. He had been many years in the Chin Hills, and so much of his time had been spent on inter-village touring that he knew the Tiddim area like the back of his hand. He was widely known and trusted and was fluent in several of the local dialects. Despite that he was a civilian among Army officers, the flexibility of guerrilla operations was such that his appointment as Zone Commander, Tiddim, was as unquestioned as it was right.

Norman, in fact, was magnificent. Shortly before my arrival he had been so enraged by reports of divided loyalties in Kalemyo (notwithstanding that it lay outside his jurisdiction) that, top-hatted, in morning coat and striped trousers, with Peter Bankes and two Levy Tommy gunners behind him, he had driven 'Mrs Murphy' all the way down the hill and into Kalemyo just to show who was boss!

Ultimately Norman carried a revolver or a Tommy gun according to the task in hand, but his first love was for a massive staff that had been his self-chosen badge of office for years; and when Norman raised the cry of 'bring me my brass-bound b-----ing iron' all the hills shook, and all men knew that the Assistant Superintendent, Tiddim, was on the warpath. Few men have enriched my life as much.

The establishment of a Levy organization in the Chin Hills needs to be explained in the context of a factor that was absent in the other hill tracts where irregular forces were coming into being. The Burma Frontier Force's peacetime establishment included a Chin Hills Battalion based at Falam; and whereas the other battalions were composite in structure (the Northern Shan States Battalion, for example, had had companies of Kachins, Gurkhas, Sikhs and Kumaonis), the Chin Hills Battalion, for special reasons, was comprised mainly of Chins, albeit of diverse tribes.

This Battalion now had the fortuitous distinction of being the only surviving battalion of the Burma Army—neither having seen much serious fighting nor been shattered and driven out of the country. It was virtually a 'moth ball' force.

Here obviously were the materials for effective functioning —a Levy organization backed by the 'teeth' of a fresh, regular battalion operating on its own terrain. The potential was distressingly thwarted, however, by the personality of the officer commanding the Battalion, Lieut.-Colonel Maine.

Maine was a product of the Indian Army, which is probably history's finest example of the leadership of the soldiery of a subject race by the officers of the ruling power on a basis of mutual devotion. The Army's magnificent record in war is proof enough of this. It mattered not that in peacetime that Army was a Club that protected its own. Officers lacking the personal qualities necessary to higher command nevertheless made dedicated and competent battalion commanders in a military police role in aid of the civil power in distant places; and, by and large, their men revered them. It mattered much, however, that in conditions of total war such men were not submitted promptly to the microscope of dispassionate examination and replaced where necessary.

Of such was Maine. He had been in the Chin Hills for some years and, until recently, had had his family with him. He was a disciplinarian, and his relationship to his men was that of a stern but just father to his children. If he had seen active service previously, the experience had become lost in the years of isolation from events that had shrunk his world to the compass of the Hills and their Battalion. The Battalion had acquired a mystique: it was something sacred, and his duty now was to protect it from the contamination of a world that was rending itself. The disorderly rabble that he saw in the Levies was the obvious source of the infection that he feared; and so, with a triumphant enemy in the valley below us, thirsting for more miles to add to the hundreds he had already ravaged, Maine withheld full co-operation. It was a bizarre and tragic situation that much sooner should have been recognized as intolerable.

The Battalion officers, for the most part, were Burma civilians conscripted and trained, as I had been, to fight the Jap. A minority of them caught or went along with their C.O.'s fever. The majority trod an unenviable tightrope, following the dictates of reason as and when they could or dared.

My introduction to this grotesque state of affairs came soon after my arrival in Tiddim, when Kelly showed me a two-part signal he had just received from Maine. The first part seemed to be a gratuitous personal insult to Kelly himself. The second part read:

After disposal of Soktes instruct Capt. Braund to report A.H.Q. Webula forthwith for duty.

Taking the charitable view, I would have been prepared to assume that Maine was in ignorance of my mission, but on the evidence of the first part of the signal I doubted it. Already I scented with alarm the faint suggestion of derangement.

I sent a signal to Colonel Haswell in which I quoted Maine's, recapitulated the purpose of my mission, and repeated that I was to come under himself for orders and, therefore, could not accept Maine's without his own endorsement. I then settled down to await events. The British commandos had not yet left, and as I was adding to my stock of explosives and booby traps from whatever Musgrave was leaving behind, I arranged with him that he run a brief course in their use for the benefit of my men.

Jack Haswell's initial reply to my signal alarmed me. It temporized on the note that he was unable to ration my force and would signal again later. What it did not say, of course, was that there was none to define the issue of ultimate seniority between himself and Maine.

I hastily wrote and sent through to Falam an urgent case for allowing me to remain based at Tiddim, adding that I would see to it that my force did not go hungry. I had already ascertained from Norman Kelly that the Kabaw Valley held plenty of stocks of abandoned rice, and that ownerless cattle were roaming at large. I did not add that I would be more than happy to make war with Kelly and Bankes in whatever manner opportunity offered. Haswell's response was an order to meet him at Fort White to discuss my role.

I left for Fort White a day early in order to make it in two marches. The weather was wet and miserable and, since this is not a sunshine story, I quote from my diary:

Have not referred so far to a certain degree of unrest among the troops since reaching Tiddim. The reason is not far to seek. Over the past week or two the Chins from the Burma Rifles have been returning to their villages consequent on the withdrawal of the Army from Burma. These chaps most of them have pretty grim tales to tell, but are now offered the chance of joining the Levies with the prospect of being able to get down to cultivation between spells of duty on a pay of Rs.20/- p.m. Thus my chaps find themselves the only people on full time service on no better pay. Discontent has so far shown itself in overstaying short leave, grumbling about pay advances etc.

The gathering at Fort White comprised Haswell and Mr L. B. Naylor, the Superintendent, Chin Hills, from Falam; and Norman Kelly, Peter Bankes and myself. Haswell soon made it clear that I was to come under his—not Maine's—command.

He went on to explain that the Levy organization was still only groping its way into being, and that there had been some trial and error. He stressed that the immediate problem was the rationing of any significant force. Life in the Chin Hills was a precarious struggle at the best of times and now, with trade with the Gangaw/Kabaw Valley virtually extinguished, it was going to become tougher still. It was vital that we avoid the odium that would follow any attempt to feed ourselves off the country, and essential that we make our own independent arrangements. Before they had fled from the Japs, many Indians had been settled in the Valley as small farmers: godowns in Kalemyo and elsewhere were full of rice, and cattle were freely available. As much as possible of all this must be cleared into the Hills before the Japs put a stop to it.

One windfall we had already inherited. The Burmah Oil Company, of a forethought that too many others failed to show, had established food dumps on several routes through the Hills for the benefit of such of their staff as were ear-marked to wreck the oilfields and, therefore, would be making a late getaway. One of these dumps had been sited at No. 2 Stockade and the bulk of the canned food had been used for its intended purpose. There remained, however, an inexplicably large residue of tea and sugar in sacks. This had been annexed and, at times when the source of one's next meal was uncertain, it was of great comfort to be able to down mugs of hot, strong, sickly-sweet tea more or less at will. Even so, there were to be occasions when I would call down boils and blains on the character at Imphal who had promised replenishment of my inaugural ten days' rations!

Peter Bankes was already operating a rice run from Kalemyo up through the Stockades to Fort White, whence he was dispersing supplies to Tiddim and Falam and to pre-selected dumps. Haswell now required me to do the same on the next southward route into the Hills, the road that ran from Natchaung in the Kabaw Valley to Falam. A young Anglo-Burman lieutenant named Hann was already at work in the Natchaung area, but Haswell felt that he needed a bit of armed stiffening.

Haswell I liked a lot. I discussed my morale problem with him and he predicted that I would not much longer be able to hold together, under military discipline, a force that I hoped to fit into such a loose organization as was developing.

He himself was a Regular Indian Army officer with previous service in the Chin Hills and elsewhere in Burma. Fortunately he had the flexibility of mind to see that his role was to be that of a bandit chief, and he had tempered his military dogma accordingly. Nevertheless he reduced to the ranks one of my N.C.O.s who was the senior of the malcontents previously referred to.

I had left two of my force at Tiddim with malaria, and had to drop five more at Fort White for the same reason. I marched off with Naylor, since he was returning to Falam and our route was in common for two or three stages. Naylor was a man of no outstanding talent beyond the ability to take remote frontier postings, and he was nearing retirement. However, he had reacted stoutly to the present situation and was strong in his support of the Levy movement.

After I had parted company with Naylor

. . . trouble broke out in the ranks again. The recently demoted Kam Chin was the ringleader and produced with him about 20 sympathizers. After reasoning and persuasion these were reduced to a hard core of 5. These showed no readiness to toe the line and preferred to take the consequences of desertion. The situation was clearly too delicate to risk taking them with me under arrest, so after taking from them all arms, ammo and kit I shot them out of the camp with a final warning of what they were bringing on themselves.

I wasn't doing very well!

My next hurdle was to be an encounter with Colonel Maine, whom I had never met but who, I felt sure, would be smarting from his frustrated attempt to conscript me into his Battalion! Maine had established a forward defensive position in the foothills at Webula astride the road that was to be my rice route. It was almost certain to be the line of attack the Japs would follow should they decide to go bald-headed for Falam. All day and every day Maine was grudgingly having to let pass, through his defences, convoys of Chin villagers who were humping up bags of rice from a store in Natchaung which Levy H.Q. had undertaken to buy in its entirety.

On arrival at Webula I encamped my party and reported to Maine. With him was Bobby Peebles, a fellow officer cadet of Maymyo days, but he was shaking with malaria. I was resolved against any hint of antagonism but, even so, Maine, having seated me, poured drinks for himself and Peebles and left it at that until much later, when he relented to the extent of handing me one. I could not dislike the man, but it was obvious that he was not rationally based.

I resumed my downhill march the next day, using as baggage transport thirty bulls sent down from Falam to carry back rice. On the way I met a returning platoon patrol from the Battalion under the command of Tommy West, a civilian friend of Rangoon days. I was very pleased to see him and he primed me with much that I needed to know.

On reaching Natchaung I found myself once more among Burmese and in the typical Burma that I knew. Having located Hann, I ordered the digging of a defensive position that overlooked both the village and the approaches to it, and then set in motion reconnaissance patrols by small parties so as to familiarize everyone with the terrain. Thereafter I turned my attention to the rice trade!

Hann had done a good job. Over half the stock of rice had been moved and the rest was already bagged and ready for the long haul. In the jungle away from the village Hann introduced me to some of the Burmans he had established as agents. One of them was a *Bombine singaung* who had hidden his elephants in the jungle. They appeared to be a sound lot, in present neutral conditions at least.

Coolies, bulls and now mules were arriving daily, and prospects were for an early completion of the lift. In order that the village should not be exposed to possible trouble for longer than was avoidable, I started shuttling the rice to cover in the jungle at an uninhabited locality called Pamunchaung some miles along the line of carry.

I had established a helio link with Webula, and received one day a warning from Naylor that two hundred Japs were reported to have arrived at a village called Kyigon about fifteen miles from Natchaung. The implication was obvious, so I abandoned the relatively small quantity of rice left in Natchaung and withdrew to Pamunchaung to cover the removal of the larger quantity I had lodged there. Hann I had already sent back with a report on what we had jointly learnt of conditions in the Valley.

At Pamunchaung I was camped in vile conditions, and several of my men were sick. Nearly all the rice had been moved when a Burmese agent arrived one evening to say that a Jap force had arrived in Natchaung, had learnt of the existence of the dump and had announced the intention of attacking it next night.

In the morning a scared villager delivered to my forward picket a missive addressed to 'Officer commanding the retreating forces of the British' and signed by 'The Commander of the Japanese Western Army for attacking the Chin Hills'. The letter itself was a semi-literate blend of threats, promises and cajolery, and I took it to be the homework of a Jap N.C.O. exercising himself in his enemy's language. However, the signer, Yamata, I later identified as the colonel commanding the area.

At nightfall I left the sicker half of my force—now down to about three dozen—in position near the rice dump and took the rest a mile or two up the Natchaung road to a good location for an ambush. I mined the road forward of us with a five-pound Kraft cheese tin packed with explosive and anything lethal in the way of fragments that I could muster, the mixture to be sprung by a trip wire. It was a mighty long and uneventful night, and a patrol I sent out at dawn reported no signs of life in Natchaung. I dismantled the booby trap and returned to Pamunchaung, my stomach sagging for want of hot tea and food—and there was no sign of life there either. My sick had decamped in a body! Via Colonel Maine at Webula, utterly mortified, I sent back to all concerned warning that I was no longer effective, and asking for orders. Maine lost no time: here was the 'contamination' he preached. He sent down mules and an order to 'get your unit out of the area as soon as possible'. I reached Webula after dark. I personally spent the night with Tommy West, but Maine insisted on my remnant camping a mile further up the road so that they should not infect his force. I hoped that Brigadier Williams and Colonel Critchley would ever be ignorant of my fate. My only solace was that Jack Haswell had correctly predicted the outcome of my mission.

My memories of the phase now ended are not the pleasanter for learning later that I unthinkingly caused the death of the Burmese agent who brought me word of the Japs' arrival at Natchaung. He had spotted the canvas and rubber patrol boots my men were wearing and had asked if I could obtain a pair for him as he was out of footwear. I had a surplus taken off earlier deserters and was happy to give him a pair there and then. He was later executed for his inability to explain how he came by them. My thoughtlessness is barely credible, but I did not do anything like it again. I hope that in Nirvana my friend has found it possible to forgive me.

I was soon to learn that my experience at Pamunchaung was symptomatic of something far wider. Before I left Webula with orders to proceed to Falam, Colonel Maine received copies of signals exchanged between Kelly and Haswell to the effect that the Sokte and Siyin chiefs had petitioned for the removal of Levies and the Frontier Force detachment from No. 3 Stockade and the Tiddim area generally. Their theme was that, in the event of armed resistance to the now widely expected Jap attack, they feared reprisals against the villages and were prepared to submit without a struggle. (The petition, as I later heard, included an undertaking to provide every British officer with a personal escort to see him safely out to India.)

Haswell was leaving Falam forthwith to meet Kelly at

Fort White, and Maine took off from Webula to intercept him *en route*. My orders were to continue to Falam with the rump of my force and there disband it, giving to those who had stayed with me three months advance of pay, and recording their status as men on leave. I had to drop several malaria cases at villages along the way, but ultimately saw to it that all of them got their dues.

Wondering, as I was, how Haswell and Kelly were getting on with the wavering chiefs, this was a pretty depressing march. I speculated upon possibly greater opportunities missed by my acceptance at Colonel Critchley's hands of a wild goose chase wrapped up as a mission; and I delivered myself of the following thought for the day:

> I scorned you in the day I might have had you,
> Your sleek and subtle curves just left me flat;
> But now that you so rudely are supplanted,
> Ah! that I might win you, Bowler Hat.

Falam, like so many hill tract headquarters in Burma, must have been an idyllic posting to those who had known it in peacetime. Red-roofed bungalows peered from among the pines, and flower-bedecked gardens slowed my feet at several points. I called on Naylor on arrival and had dinner with the Levy staff—such as it was. My orders, when they came through, were to proceed to Fort White to take over that Sector. The chiefs had obviously been placated.

I staged to Fort White, with none but my orderly, via Lombang, Pinetree Camp and Bamboo Camp. At this last I had a late lunch with the returning Jack Haswell, from whom I received details of how the crisis had been resolved together with a general directive on how I was to comport myself at Fort White.

On arrival at Fort White I found a full house. Norman Kelly was there with Jack Oats, the commander of the Battalion's Mounted Infantry Company. With them were three variously damaged R.A.F. sergeants who miraculously had survived the crash of their Blenheim, on a hillside newly cleared for cultivation, when they were returning from bombing Kalemyo. In misty weather they had been trying to find Fort White in order to drop a message there.

In the morning we went our various ways. Norman left for Tiddim, escorting the three airmen, two of whom were being carried in doolies; and I dropped down the hill to No. 3 Stockade where I was to relieve Peter Bankes, who was to move further north to take over a Sector based on the Suanglangsu Vum, a peak of nearly eight thousand feet.

The term 'stockade' is redolent of the glamour of receding history. Round the turn of the century, when the Chins were resisting subjugation by the Crown, the Stockades were built by the British as trenched and palisaded staging-posts along the strategic road running from Kalewa on the Chindwin to the dominant location of Fort White in the Hills. No. 1 was near Kalemyo, No. 2 at the foot of the climb and No. 3 half-way up at about four thousand feet. Little remained of them now beyond the names. No. 3, for our present purposes, was magnificently sited to command an extensive view of the Kabaw Valley, north and south. Kalemyo was central to the vista, and on clear days we used to watch it being bombed and strafed by the R.A.F.

The Sector I was taking over from Peter comprised in essence a stores base at Fort White, the forward H.Q. at No. 3 Stockade and, to north and south, two spurs running down to the Valley, on each of which was a standing picket post. These were commanded by Ted Wright and Jimmy Carpenter, two young Anglo-Burmans from Steels Forest Department. Thus, on Peter's departure, we were to be an all-Steels Levy Sector.

In the week we had together, Peter exhaustively patrolled the Valley and foothills with me, and by the time he left I was getting to know the ground pretty well. The crashed Blenheim was some hundreds of feet below our camp and, on inspecting it, we found an unexploded 500-pound bomb among the wreckage and put it up with a roar that shook the hills. The only building at No. 3 Stockade was a semi-furnished government rest house, and at this stage we had no hesitation in using it. Living under a roof made for a much easier life.

Before Peter left, Jack Oats, who had just been transferred to command of a B.F.F. company of Haka Chins, moved his own H.Q. to No. 3 Stockade. With Norman Kelly visiting us we decided on a reconnaissance in force into Kalemyo. Until the Japs showed signs of occupying it as a forward base and the R.A.F. started bombing it, the town had been something of a Tom Tiddler's ground. It had held considerable stocks of grain in Government godowns, most of which had now been removed, not only by Peter but by the Japs similarly stocking up. The Japs had taken their share eastward to Kalewa while Peter was removing his westward to the Hills, but history cannot relate an occasion when both sides did their shopping on the same day. Our mixed Levy and Battalion force (*pace* Colonel Maine, for whom Jack Oats did not have much time) entered the town at dawn after an all-night march. The place was virtually deserted and there was little worth the taking. Bomb and machine gun damage was fairly extensive.

On our return we halted at the village of Tahan, having heard from an agent that a hospital compounder had cached a quantity of medical supplies there. This proved to be the case and we annexed the lot. We then put the Levies on to rounding up about forty head of cattle and driving them up the hill. Jack's force followed while Norman and I slipped into the jungle to meet a couple of agents. Thereafter we borrowed bicycles to get us as far as No. 2 Stockade, where we caught up with Jack. We got back to No. 3 before nightfall, and Norman and Peter left for Tiddim next morning. It had been one of those uneventful sorties that nevertheless held considerable value for the future. 'Time spent in reconnaissance' as the O.C.T.U. had taught me, 'is seldom wasted'!

12 Guardian of the Stockades

July 1942 to February 1943

Jack Oats, with whom I was now to operate, I probably would not have met but for the war. After leaving Sherborne he had been turned down for the Royal Navy on the score of flat feet (of which the residual evidence was singularly to the contrary!) He had then done the rounds—felling timber for matchwood in Scandinavia, a trooper in the Palestine Police, an underground miner on the Rand, cane-cutting in Queensland and, at the outbreak of war, a teak wallah with the *Bombine*, to whose ranks he had been bidden by Billy Williams ('Elephant Bill') at the plea of Jack's parents, who were Billy's friends and neighbours at Cape Cornwall, and who had become anxious that Jack should settle down under a responsible eye.

Jack was a tough, self-reliant, slow-thinking Cornishman with a laugh that was always fun, but never more so than when it smacked of delayed action. I never saw him in a 'flap', his men trusted him completely and he had a jungle wallah's contempt for paper work. He would have been happier in the Levies than he was in the Battalion. He had won an immediate M.C. for a spirited repulse of a Jap attack at No. 2 Stockade just before the last Allied forces disappeared through the passes to India and all action had been broken off. We probably owed it to this 'bloody nose' that the Japs thereafter seemed to overrate the strength of the opposition we could offer in the Hills.

Within a day or two of his joining me, Jack was summoned up to Fort White to meet his C.O., Colonel Maine. He returned with the news that Maine, to use his own words, was 'being sacked'. I felt genuinely sorry for the man, but I knew that someone had faced an issue that none should ever have shirked.

A few days later we had quite a visitation, comprising Brigadier Felix Williams, Jack Haswell, Norman Kelly, Charles Davison and, to my surprise, Rupert Carey of the B.O.C., who was on his way to join the Levies at Haka. Rupert I knew well from oilfield days, a man to keep any dinner table in a roar of hilarity. His father had been the first Administrator of the Chin Hills after their pacification and Rupert, ever the comedian, had cast for himself the role of a one-man flag march through the ancient domains. If not being greeted precisely with 'palms and scattered garments', he was at least enjoying himself and would be an asset to the rest of us.

Felix Williams diplomatically made no reference to the force with which he had seen me off at Dimapur (nor to my avoidance of the Corps Commander at Imphal!), and he was kind enough to compliment me on my persistence in getting through to the Hills against his own judgement. He did us all a lot of good by relating our activities to what was going forward in India, and I was flattered to be told that he himself had entered the Hills along my line of march, using the route report I had sent back to Corps H.Q.

Over the weeks that followed Jack and I concerted our efforts in the matter of patrolling in the Valley. Sometimes we were out for days on end, either together or separately. There were no Japs on our immediate front, other than the occasional patrol, but we got detailed information of a concentration at Kalewa from two Indian officers who had escaped from Singapore and covered the two thousand miles to No. 2 Stockade, where they were picked up!

Occasionally the Japs moved out from Kalewa in some strength for a few days on end. On one occasion they tried to jump us into a response by opening up with a helio from Sanmyo, between Kalemyo and No. 2 Stockade. Had Jack been independently patrolling at the time, I might have fallen for this one!

Perhaps a random selection from contemporary situation

185

reports ('sitreps') will infuse some atmosphere into this period of slack water.

6–8–42   Bn patrol to Sanmyo seized five rifles and documents indicative of recent Jap contact.

7–8–42   Now that villagers are able live on own produce consider it advisable close all main roads to private traders with the plains. Believe Japs to have hazy idea our real strength and consider fog should be maintained.
(N.B. This was done.)

11–8–42   Japs reported intend returning Kalemyo near future and to have ordered fifty coolies to be ready on their arrival. Also reported to have ordered all rations in Kalemyo area to be sent to Kalewa and have threatened deal with anybody supplying Hills. Kalewa bombed Kalemyo machine gunned during afternoon. Ack ack bursts over Kalewa visible from No. Three.

19–8–42   . . . Same source reports arrival Kalewa of one hundred Jap women since transferred Mawlaik. (N.B. Falam to 4 Corps—'presumably these are *hors de combat*').

23–8–42   Unidentified single engine low wing monoplane recced this area from Eastward fifteen forty hours today.

26–8–42   Mine of 23rd pilot reported to have waved red and white flag over No. 2.

26–8–42   Two village Levies on recce Kalemyo Tuesday did not return. Reported caught by Japs Kalemyo and sent Kalewa under escort.

27–8–42   Both captured Levies escaped from Indainggyi where reported questioned by two Jap officers with ten Jap and Burman troops. Fate of one still unknown. Report of other follows.

4–9–42   Reported killed all points except Kalewa Japs 8 others 10 injured Japs 5. Three *lundwins* reported sunk including two loaded rations in mouth Ubok *chaung.* Road bridge damaged by same bomb. Damage to buildings various but no military significance.

(N.B. The above in response to a request from Corps for information on the result of recent air attacks.)

8–9–42   Repeat opinion leaflet raids giving reliable news will have good effect.

17–9–42   R.A.F. after recce planes. Urgent must speed up all reports one or more planes. Special section fighters standing by waiting your reports.

(N.B. The above from Levy H.Q. Falam.)

19–9–42   J. W. Munro reports from Yazagyo his escape from enemy territory parties sent bring him in.

21–9–42   Jap plane shot down by three British planes near Yuwa.

29–9–42   150 large dogs breed unknown brought Kalewa and 500 Thaungdut. Reported be for use in unspecified anti-guerrilla role.

3–9–42   Single engine Jap monoplane with wireless mast unretracted streamlined undercarriage and wings tapered on trailing edge over No. 3.

1–10–42   3,000 Japs and rebel Chinese Kalewa of whom 1,000 have left for Tamu via Sittaung and possible further 1,000 for Khamti N. of Tamanthe. These troops have with them fierce breed of dog in large numbers. Their role includes a bomb attached to collar . . . All boats going down Myittha being commandeered at Kalewa for transport of troops . . . Large number Japs Kalewa down with malaria.

4–10–42   Japs collecting B.B.T.C. elephants Palusawa. Villagers ordered repair Tamu road . . . Japs have ordered rations be sent Kalewa at 20 baskets per village. Approx. 22nd 70 motor boats arrived Kalewa with Japs.

7–10–42   No. 2/Fort White area recced by Jap plane for about three hours in all.

The chronicle in this staccato form could go on, but the extracts cover a period of two months and give a general picture of the varied diet of intelligence that we were sending back to India. It was during this period that the Japs passed into the Hills leaflets putting prices on the heads of British officers. In all cases names were spelt correctly. My skull was going for two thousand rupees, a pittance by civilized standards, but for none was there a higher offer!

In September Jack went sick and, after coping with him for a week, I sent him to Tiddim where he was found to be suffering from typhoid. Jimmy Carpenter at the same time was having bouts of malaria, which restricted his patrolling; so Ted Wright and I were fully extended. I had to admire Ted. In circumstances where a good pair of ears was so necessary, he was nearly stone deaf. He made no secret of this to his Levies and they knew that they had to do all his listening for him. In Jack's absence, the Frontier Force company of Hakas was placed under my command, so I was wearing two hats.

A patrol that I recall involved my searching a *phongyi chaung* in the Valley. Normally I would have removed my boots before entering the precincts, but I explained to the novice who admitted me that on this occasion I must be excused from doing so. After my search I stopped to talk to the only *phongyi* in the place. He was of middle age, he spoke remarkably good English, and one of his legs was frightfully shredded by a burst of machine gun fire from what he assured me was an Allied fighter.

I offered my distressed apologies on behalf of an unknown pilot who, I assured the *phongyi*, would be appalled did he but know the sickening consequence of the performance of his duty. I then waited for the bitterness and the invective to pour out.

Instead I was treated to a saintly discourse, quietly spoken by a man who, even though his eyes were on me, was looking through me at a Beyond that I was unqualified to discern. It was the kind of plea for holiness in man that cannot now be recaptured, though the essence of the occasion persists.

To suggest that such a response reflected pro-British or

anti-Japanese sentiment would be utterly to misunderstand the plane on which this man's mind and spirit dwelt. It should not be thought, however, that he was typical of his kind. The saffron robe all too often cloaked the evil man and the criminal.

Despite my protest, the *phongyi* insisted on hobbling alongside me to the top of the steps, where I asked for and received his blessing. It was some time before my mind was back on the job in hand.

During the four months I had been in the Hills I had been writing home weekly and dispatching by any possible means. Very little had reached me in return. Suddenly, by successive deliveries, I received two sackfuls of letters, newspapers and books, dating back in the extreme case ten months! It was a veritable banquet! Among the Indian element of the mail was a letter from John Bowerman, who had succeeded Brigadier Roughton as Inspector General of the Burma Frontier Force, the latter having died of heat exhaustion in the fighting at Yenangyaung. Bowerman wrote

I was very glad to hear that you had gone back into the Hills with a party of men to do as much as possible to harass the Jap, as it showed a spirit which I am afraid has often been lacking during the show in Burma. Most people's only desire was to get out of the country as quickly as possible and once they were headed for India few if any stopped unless they were compelled to do so.

I shall be delighted to hear of your exploits whenever you have time to put in a report.

The 'exploits' were not exactly thick on the ground, but it was a very cheering letter to receive in isolation when too often I was given to speculating whether I had been a bloody fool in ever standing up to be counted!

Periodically I wrote to Maxine care of the USA Consulate in Calcutta, but I received no replies and had no means of knowing whether my letters were reaching her.

The approach of the open season and the cold weather had brought me several visits from the Jap recce plane already referred to. I decided it was time to evacuate the rest house at No. 3 Stockade and I moved off into a jungle camp at no great distance. Naylor and Kelly visited me and the old man insisted on joining Carpenter and myself on a patrol to Tahan. I also had a visit from the Civil Surgeon at Falam, who had been looking after Jack Oats at Tiddim. David Milligan, having newly arrived from India to join the Battalion, was sent down to take over Jack's Hakas from me. David I knew from O.C.T.U. days and, until his arrival, had been mourning his reported death in action! At a time when I was making an effort to learn Siyin Chin, I was having far too much opportunity to speak English!

The reference in the quoted 'sitreps' to Japanese dogs with 'bombs' on their collars caused us some speculation until a clear picture emerged. The traditional Chin method of waging war is by ambush, and their ambush positions were always protected by a liberal plantation of *panjis* on front and flanks. The *panjis* were sharpened bamboo stakes, fire-hardened to ensure penetration, and tipped with rotting pig's liver to promote blood poisoning. They came normally in two sizes, the shorter to impale the foot (and a new army boot was not proof against it), the longer to rip the belly. By men rushing a defended position they were very difficult to see.

The Japs must have been briefed in this tactic sufficiently to be seeking counter-measures against it. The role of the dogs was to accompany patrols or attacking forces until they came under fire, whereupon the handlers would remove the pins from the grenades fixed to the dogs' collars and tell them to go to it. Detonation, supposedly, would occur while the dogs were struggling among the *panjis* and a passage would thus be breached. The technique may have been tested in training but I never heard of it being adopted in action. I should imagine that damage done to the *panjis* would fall short of what was required.

One of our number came up with the novel piece of information that dogs could be totally distracted by the smell of aniseed, and we asked that two pounds of the stuff be dropped to us. The reply we got from some promotion hound at Corps (lacking, alas, a grenade round his neck) made little more sense than if he had told us outright that 'aniseed, dogs, for the distraction of' was not an Army issue.

We let it go at that. The lesson that, whatever your forward units ask for, you give them, was being learnt but slowly.

The pace now started to quicken. To the south, in the Haka Zone, 'Jamie' James of the *Bombine* came under fire some fifty miles from Haka from a Jap force advancing into the Hills from Kan in the Gangaw Valley behind a screen of press-ganged villagers. He returned their fire but withdrew to forward of Shimpi, the village immediately in his rear, when the Japs opened up with mortars. Here he was attacked again, but he inflicted casualties before withdrawing further to a strong defensive position forty miles from Haka. Once more the Japs attacked, but this time they were routed after sustaining something like fifty casualties.

Simultaneously with this action, Joshua Poo Nyo, a Karen who was Kelly's opposite number at Haka, was attacked by a small enemy party further north and withdrew behind the Dawngva River after blowing the suspension foot bridge on his route. A third enemy party was reported to be moving towards Haka from the south, and Tommy West, with a Battalion force, was on his way to intercept it.

There seemed to be no corresponding activity on my front, but I had numerous patrols working the Valley, manned all ambush positions and laid a network of pre-planned booby traps on the tracks entering my Sector. At the same time I asked that the R.A.F. bomb a specific building in Kalemyo which the Japs were using as a forward Intelligence H.Q.

In the Haka Zone the Japs withdrew as suddenly as they had arrived. Probably they had never intended more than a probe in force to test defences but, from the point of view of the Chin villagers in the southern areas, the Japs had attacked and been routed. The effect on morale was electric.

The matter of feeding the Levies was an ever-present problem. I was still getting supplies in from the Valley but the activity at Haka warned me that my staging dump at No. 2 Stockade was too large and too vulnerable. My diary records:

Pretty good progress made today with the clearance of rice from No. 2, but there is still a lot to move. In view of Jap tactics S. of Haka of advancing behind a screen of coolies, this traffic on the road is a nightmare; and if it were not in so essential a cause, would stop it immediately.

I was dispersing this rice in jungle dumps throughout the Sector, because if the Japs did decide on a cold weather push through the Hills it would be the Levy role to lie doggo until the tide had passed and then start operating against lines of communication.

News from Falam told us of the Anglo-American landings in North Africa.

I used to speculate sometimes on the fact that my No. 3 Stockade camp was only some sixty miles as the crow flies from the Indaw Oilfield, and I had recently enrolled as a Levy the Chin who had been night watchman on the Agent's bungalow during my time there. One day I composed a message to the Indaw Burmans over my signature as Agent of the Indaw Oilfield, not as an Army officer. The message conveyed personal greetings and instructed the recipients to produce it to liberating forces as a token of their readiness to co-operate. I sent the message back to Corps and they dropped ten thousand copies of it at Indaw, Lawtha and Pantha.

Travelling home by sea on leave after the war, I narrated this episode at the breakfast table and found that sitting opposite to me was the Lysander pilot who did the job! I, in my turn, was securing copies of various Jap leaflets being dropped in the Kabaw Valley.

Of one of my Levies caught while on patrol, I received word that he had been 'stripped, cut about with dah, bayonetted and disembowelled before others'. We captured three of a party of *thakins* (Burmans recruited as levies by the Japs), and questioning of them yielded a picture of generally increasing Jap activity. From Falam I learnt that

As direct result our ARP system Jap plane that passed Fort White area about six weeks ago was located and shot down.

I think this was probably the character who used to wave a Jap flag from his aircraft when on low-level reconnaissance of my Sector. We were becoming puzzled by increasing evidence of signalling from the Valley towards the Hills, and I proposed

If night flying planes not ours suggest patrolling of all telegraph lines for possible tapping by isolated parachutists whose presence might explain helio reported from Myohla.

I was learning fast that the booby trap is a two-edged weapon. With the advent of fine weather and an unclouded moon, detonations by night became a frequent occurrence, requiring a stand-to and the dispatch of investigating patrols. In one case we killed a Chin soldier who had escaped from a prison camp in Rangoon and who died thus tragically on the front doorstep of his homeland. We also killed a tiger and other animals.

On the left flank of my camp was what we knew as Telegraph Spur, because it carried the poles and the cleared alignment of the telegraph line that used to link Kalemyo with Fort White. Hard on the heels of reported Jap patrolling in the vicinity of No. 2 Stockade, and in the early morning of a waning moon, the booby trap near the foot of the spur went up with a roar to shatter all silence.

On this occasion I took out the patrol that was to make the frontal investigation. I had four thoroughly drilled men with me and, after a silent approach to within fifty yards of where the trip wire had been, I could see from a prone position that there was a body lying just beyond. If it was a Jap, then it meant that he had been left there deliberately as bait to an ambush. Covered by the rifles of my party, I inched the most paralyzing fifty yards of my life, snaking the last few until I could reach out and touch the still warm flesh. A few minutes later, with the deer slung on a pole, we were humping our next day's meal up the spur! This sort of thing, under multiplication, was hard on the nerves, and in a mood of self-pity I wrote:

> Lord, stifle the moon. This is playing their game.
>   If only they'd sleep and let me do the same.
> The track, wanly gleaming, is peopled I swear,
>   By Japs? Or my scouts? Or with ghosts of the air?
> The radio's hidden: the codes are with me:
>   The—Christ! Something's shaking a branch on that tree!
> (For God's sake shut up! If you're running this show
>   And start at each whisper, the whole crowd will know).
> There's half an hour gone since the booby trap sprung.
>   It's cold, but I'm sweating and scared and unstrung.

> Tomorrow I'll laugh as at all false alarms?
>> Tonight—not for nothing the gun in my arms!
> My arms! What a vision to trouble me now!
>> Cascade of her hair from that sensuous brow.
> Is it she who is come? Her voice that I hear?
>> Across the wide world has she caught at my fear?
> No! That way lies madness. Far better the rum.
>> And swift comes the answer. Stand to! Here they come!

By contrast, nothing inflamed my resolve more than a letter I received from Donald Moxon, a priest on the staff of Rangoon Cathedral. He was writing in reference to an orphanage with which I had had some association:

We have just had news of *Bishops Home* who were most unfortunately left behind, largely through the Army collaring their transport. The head-mistress and her 2 sisters and John Derry [a priest] have all died. Of the party of senior girls who tried walking through the Hukawng Valley about 35 strong, all have died except 5. 'Higgi' [Higginbotham, another priest who studied Burmese with me in London] died as the result of wounds inflicted by a Jap Officer to whom he protested because the Japs were looting his kit which had in it a large sum of Diocesan money.

Jack Oats returned from sick leave in India early in December, and I had a visit from the Chin Hills Battalion's new C.O., Roddie Russell who, since I had last seen him at Kutkai, had won a Military Cross at Yenangyaung. Roddie was in his thirties, and was an excellent choice to succeed Maine. At the same time Jack Haswell was elevated, with the rank of Brigadier, to the overall command of the Chin Hills Area, still with his H.Q. at Falam. His successor in command of the Levies was Lieut.-Colonel Frank Ford of the Burma Rifles. This also was a first-class choice because 'the Assassin', as Frank was known, had all the qualities for the role. I had known him briefly in Maymyo.

From mid-December onwards Jap activity increased, and on the twenty-third a force reported to be a company strong moved into Tahan and showed signs of staying there. This was too near for comfort, and the conjunction of Christmas and a waning moon was suggestive of something more than passive intent. We decided, therefore, that we would have the first say and that we would make it a combined operation.

We bivouacked that night in the jungle near No. 2 Stockade and moved forward at dawn, Jack on a southward and I on a northward arc. We were to attack simultaneously at noon and, if results favoured it, Jack would go in with the bayonet under my covering fire. (Be it noted that the Levies were not equipped with bayonets: their role, not always ingloriously, was hit and run.)

Despite our knowledge of the terrain, we underrated our ability to make the approach in secrecy within the allotted time. Five minutes before zero I got my platoon-strength force into a perfect position, with twenty or thirty Japs in full view in the main street of the village, which we commanded from an angle of enfilade. A tree-top sentry was the worst factor in our final approach. Jack, unfortunately, faced not only this same obstacle, but a broad stretch of open paddy land complicated his final run-in. When I opened up at zero hour I was not to know that Jack was still distant by a mile or more.

Our opening shot toppled the sentry from his tree like a sack of potatoes. None of the others in view was carrying a weapon that I could see, and they sustained casualties while running for cover. Thereafter we ourselves came under fire from the balconies and upper storey windows of the street-side shops, though I'm sure that the Japs never got a sight of a man of us. We mixed it until we appeared to be on equal terms, whereupon I pulled out northwards leaving the Japs to continue firing for quite a time after we were gone.

Jack made a rapid bee-line for the road midway between Tahan and No. 2 Stockade in order to cover my withdrawal should the Japs follow up. They did not do so, and my only interruption was provided by a R.A.F. Lysander which made an abortive attempt to machine-gun us as we made for the Hills.

The action described, microscopic though it was on the tapestry of current battles, rated a mention on the B.B.C. News bulletins of 26 December, and I received a personal complimentary message from the Army Commander. Apparently it was claimed for the affray, with what truth I have no idea, that it was the first time since the retreat from

Burma that the Japs had been attacked—as distinct from resisted—at ground level. It was of more consequence to me that after nearly forty months of war I had at last had my baptism of fire!

On our patrols back to Tahan during the following few days, I had meetings with broadly smiling agents whose tails were well up in consequence of the action. They reported that the Jap casualties had included twelve dead transported by bullock cart to Kalemyo for cremation, and that the rest of the force had withdrawn before nightfall of the same day.

A few days later, Peter Bankes did even better. From his eyrie on the Suanglangsu Vum he was patrolling in the Kabaw Valley when he learnt that the small Burmese village of Nansaungpu, north of Kalemyo, had been occupied by sixty Japs and that the villagers had fled. Peter positioned his Levies so as to provide a cross pattern of covering fire. Then by night, with never a sentry in view, he raced an armed party down the track separating the two rows of houses, firing the roofs with bamboo torches as he went. The Japs were shot up as they fled, and Peter returned to the Hills with our first Jap prisoner. Unfortunately the man broke and ran for it on the way up and was brought down by a shot that killed him.

From Frank Ford one day I received a heavily sealed envelope, the contents of which were a missive addressed to himself by Corps H.Q. Attached to it was an intercepted letter of mine in which I had made strictures against 'column dodgers' in New Delhi, whose qualifications for levy work were at least as good as mine. The burden of Corps' theme, as I remember it, was that 'this officer has been guilty of uttering remarks calculated to throw into disrepute an honourable branch of His Majesty's Armed Forces and, pending a decision on disciplinary action to be taken against him, he is to be reprimanded'. Frank's covering reprimand, written in pencil on Army-issue toilet paper, read: 'Dear Harold, I agree with every word you said, but don't be such a bloody fool in future.'

Beyond this, I remain unpunished!

Japanese activity throughout Burma was now pointing the way to a renewal of their offensive on a large scale, and a few days after the action at Tahan I was joined at No. 3 Stockade by a company of the 2/5th Gurkhas under Captain James Crombie. At the same time British battalions were being transferred from the Western Desert to the Burma Front. As a first step towards getting these new arrivals trained for the very different kind of warfare they would now have to wage, small parties, each comprising an officer and twelve other ranks from two separate battalions, i.e. twenty-six men in all, were sent through for attachment to me at No. 3 Stockade for a period of four weeks per party, after which they would be returned to their battalions to impart what they had learnt. They were to be referred to as commandos while they were with us, and my orders were:

Braund will instruct commandos in general tactical dispositions and methods as employed in Chin Hills in guerrilla role.

Over the next three months I received three such parties, drawn from the Beds & Herts and the Yorks & Lancs (first party), the Essex Regt. and the South Staffs (second party) and the Black Watch and the Border Regt. (third party). No. 3 Stockade, thinly spread of course, was becoming quite a base, and, to an extent that I could not welcome, I was having to assume responsibility for administrative procedures that had not been of my world hitherto. Years ago, on my first arrival on the oilfields, I had heard Rupert Carey define his current portfolio as that of 'Dan, Dan, the Lavatory Man'. It was a cap that seemed to fit me pretty well now!

The British troops, my countrymen, confounded me. They had most of them seen violent action in Crete, Greece, North Africa and elsewhere. They were tough, but when it came to feeding them they were collectively a complex of pre-conceived and prejudiced ideas. For eight months now I, in general terms, had been eating whatever was in the camp pot. There was always a base of rice: what went in with it you did not have to question, though I admit that my first confrontation with curried monkey, when there was nothing else, had a cannibalistic connotation that turned my guts over and I never came back for more. Ignoring this extreme departure, however, there was always a damned good feed.

The B.O.R.s, with a few intelligent exceptions, would not look at the stuff. It was 'native food', and they moaned like hell if they could not have a twice-daily meal of bully beef and potatoes, served up as a mush that I never envied them. Nevertheless their presence made a change from isolation that in many ways was not unwelcome and we had some pretty good fun together.

The officers made it their business to learn their new trade with less compunction, and they normally messed with me. Lieutenant Johnson of the Yorks & Lancs, a peacetime school master, had seen action against the Germans, the Italians and the Vichy French. He was desperate for an encounter with the Japs so that he could lay claim to be the first British officer to have done battle with the Axis in all its elements. He had his wish fulfilled in a small-scale night skirmish with a Jap patrol east of Tahan just before his party was withdrawn from the Hills. There was a bonus thrown in. A pair of tiger, maintaining a steady marching interval in his rear of about a hundred feet, followed him and his men for some miles along the track they took back to No. 2 Stockade!

A week or so later, the Japs reoccupied Tahan as a cover to whatever was going on in the Kalemyo area. This unfortunately came at a time when Corps had placed a veto on any large-scale aggravation of the Japs. Nevertheless, with commandos, Gurkhas, Frontier Force and Levies to draw on, we were getting through a tremendous amount of patrolling which led to a number of minor encounters and skirmishes. I never ceased to be astonished at the casualness of the Japs in forward positions. They must have known that there were now British and Gurkha troops in the Fort White area, yet the following are 'potted' extracts from observational patrol reports:

Crombie with four secs Gurkhas recced Tahan close range. Sentry seen tree top outside Yakub Ali's shop left without being relieved. Troops in streets in partial undress, slovenly and without arms . . . Saw presumed runner on bicycle leave in direction Kalemyo waving and shouting . . . At long range twenty men seen apparently doing PT . . . Jap seated typing outside Yakub Ali's house. Runners reported to him with salutes . . . Sentries on ground and in tree top outside Yakub Ali's house. Former smoked and occasionally threw stones at passers by.

Among recent additions to the Levies was Charles Davison, who had wearied of being Critchley's aide in India. While spending a day or two with me, he took a small patrol down to the Valley and cut the telegraph line running north from Kalemyo. He chose a spot in the middle of an open paddy field to avoid suggesting an ambush, but he did replace the pins of two grenades with the severed ends of the wire. From a distance he watched two Japs, hung around with repair equipment in addition to their rifles, approach the break and start pulling in the trailing wire. One of the grenades exploded within feet of the two men and Charles set off in quest of identifications. As he approached the prostrate Japs one of them fired a round in his direction. Charles rushed him and finished him off with his Tommy gun. He found that the man had already had his right arm blown off, since when he had fired one round and had been trying single-handed to reload when he died. The other man was already dead.

Now, with little enthusiasm on my part for such promotion, Haswell phoned me to say that the increasing 'militarization' of the Hills rendered it impracticable that Poo Nyo and Kelly should retain command of their Zonal Levies, and that Rupert Carey and I respectively were to take over from them. I was to hand back the Fort White Sector to Peter Bankes as soon as he could get across from the Suanglangsu Vum. I left No. 3 Stockade on 5 February, thus ending a seven months tenure of the Sector. From Fort White onwards I marched on frost-bound roads. They matched my mood.

13 The Storm Breaks

February 1943 to August 1943

A day or two after I left No. 3 Stockade, the Japs attacked
Jimmy Carpenter's Levy picket on the Ngalzang Ridge to
the south. They came up the hill shouting in Urdu that they
were friends and that the Levies should not shoot. On
hearing the firing Jack Oats quickly deployed his company,
one platoon into an ambush position on the road below the
Stockade, another to work round to the rear of the attackers
and a third, under his leadership, straight up the ridge in
support of Carpenter.

Both parties put up a spirited defence in the face of
enemy rushes which appeared to cost them a number of
casualties, but the defenders withdrew when they came
under accurate mortar and, for the first time, artillery fire—
the Levies virtually fighting their way out of encirclement.
Jack was slightly wounded and had one rifleman wounded
and another missing from his platoon. The Levies had three
wounded and three missing believed captured. The attack
had come late in the evening and at dawn all elements
available scoured the ridge, but the Japs had gone, leaving
behind in a deep *chaung* a mule loaded with 70 mm. shells.
The affair seemed, once again, to be nothing more than a
testing of defences or a foray in quest of prisoners.

Life in Tiddim promised to be pretty prosaic. On the
Civil side Norman Kelly had been reinforced with an
assistant in the person of Philip Barton, with whom I had
last consorted at Kutkai. Philip still seemed to be able to
conjure glamorous meals out of an ill-served pot, and I
found the quality of my messing rising by leaps and bounds.
He and I boarded with Norman in the Assistant Super-

THE NEW LIGHT OF BURMA

PUBLISHED EVERY MONDAY, WEDNESDAY & FRIDAY

Chin Hills—Allied propaganda leaflet

Chin Hills—Japanese propaganda leaflet

Chin Hills—Captain Braund and 'B' Levies o:

the Kamhau tribe by Captain Anthony Gross

Chin Hills—A Haka Chin Levy by Major Fry

Chin Hills—The Author with Mr P. T. Barton, M.B.E.,
Burma Frontier Service

intendent's bungalow. There were in addition a Public Works Department bungalow for the peacetime use of touring officials, and a now abandoned Mission bungalow. In the quickened pace at which life was now moving, neither of them was ever unoccupied for long.

As a prelude to the Japanese offensive which was surely coming, I thought it highly likely that Tiddim, among other places, would be bombed; so I made it my business, while settling into my new role, to improve the passive defences of the place. I built in the jungle a camp for the main force to follow James Crombie's advance company of the 2/5th Gurkhas, who were expected at some unspecified date. I even organized a soccer match between the Levies and one of the outgoing commando units.

R.A.F. Dakotas had been dropping supplies at Tiddim since September. The inaugural, experimental drops had been made by faster-flying Hudsons, sometimes with dramatic results. At that time I had been on a brief visit to Tiddim when we got delivery, *inter alia*, of fifty thousand rupees in coin (it being a fact of life that paper money was totally discredited and unacceptable). The coin was bagged in six thicknesses of gunny in units of about two thousand rupees per bag. The bags were dropped on the football field at high speed, and they exploded like anti-personnel bombs, scattering a cloud of coin in all directions. The graded field had a steep slope alongside one touch-line that led down into thick jungle. Protection that was adequate to stop a football was certainly not up to barring the progress of rolling coins, and this accounted for the tally being about three thousand rupees short. Something approaching thirteen thousand rupees, however, was unusable because the coins were distorted beyond acceptability as legal tender.

On 17 February I received from my parents a Christmas greetings telegram that had been despatched seventy-two days previously. India was getting to grips with the problems of war! A few days later I had my first bottle of beer for seven months, but the occasion was qualified by the distressing comment—'Unfortunately there's no more where that came from!'

It was a matter of pride to the Civil authorities that, with Burma officially enemy-occupied, the post offices at Falam, Tiddim and Haka were still functioning on a nearly 'business as usual' basis. One day, however, there came an edict that they were to be absorbed into the Indian Postal Service for the duration. With effect from a notified date, Burma stamps would cease to be legal tender.

When the day came, I went into the post office at Tiddim and variously stamped several envelopes, some of which I postmarked with the date immediately following invalidation. I packed and sent them off to my father. He never received them.

As soon as I could get away, I took off from Tiddim to visit the northern Sectors of the Zone. It involved a round trip of a hundred and fifty miles through country that I had not previously travelled, and two of the three Sector Commanders I should be visiting I had never met. It galled me tacitly to be welcomed by each as a 'base wallah' and I made a point of taking patrols down into the Valley in the hopes of an encounter that would show me up in better light; but all was quiet on their fronts.

During my absence from Tiddim I had had myself built a stilted hut under a clump of pines at the extremity of Norman's extensive garden. Though I continued to mess with Norman and Philip, I had grown wary of living in recognizable targets, and in any case wanted the peace and quiet necessary to the enjoyment of a portable gramophone and records I had just had sent through to me from India. Perhaps instinct played a part also, because I woke one night to the roar of flames and, running down my steps, saw Norman's bungalow ablaze and Philip, as he leapt from his bedroom window at that precise moment, demonstrating convincingly that it was his habit to sleep in the nude! In very truth he got away with nothing! Norman had got clear on the other side of the house, and within minutes the fire had got such a hold that there was nothing we could do but watch the blaze against a background of detonations from the arsenal of ammunition and explosives that Norman harboured in his bedroom.

The Levies were now to suffer a distressing blow. 'The Assassin' was regarded as a Kachin rather than a Chin expert, though, Lord knows, the touring around that he did during his tenure in the Chin Hills must have come near to qualifying him as the latter also. He was transferred at short notice to the newly vacant command of the Kachin Levies, who were operating in the Fort Hertz/Sumprabum area.

A jeep road, which had been pushing forward from Shuganu along my original line of march into the Hills, had reached Tiddim. One morning, bearded and stripped to the waist, I was actively helping with the unloading of Levy supplies for which dispersal transport in the shape of porters and ponies was standing by. Another jeep arrived and discharged a Lieutenant-Colonel who introduced himself as Hayes, the new commander of the Levies. I greeted him warmly, introduced myself and escorted him up to my *basha*, where I added a shirt to my person and ordered tea.

After an agreeable briefing session, Hayes said that he would like to visit Fort White next day to meet the officer commanding that Sector. I signalled Peter and made the necessary arrangements. I watched Hayes go with a nameless apprehension that was fulfilled on his return. During a carefully modulated summary of his impressions thus far, Hayes reproved me, having officer status, for manhandling stores with my Levies, and then said that he was not at all impressed with Bankes as a Levy officer!

We had been sent the wrong man!

In time of war there is no excuse for this sort of thing. Granted that Hayes had had some limited previous Burma experience, he had made no mark and carried away no nostalgic memories. There was plainly that in the air which suggested that a reject for battalion command had been shunted off to a remote posting where he would be out of the way. Obviously our affairs were no longer in the hands of such men as Felix Williams and Critchley.

In my tentative notes for a manual on levy warfare, with which I never proceeded, there was something to the effect that the choice of the commander should be a matter for consultation with the senior officers of the force. The suggestion is no more irregular than the role. If the rules of 'the Club' require that command postings must go to regular soldiers, it is a fact that the Burma Army had by no means been milked dry of talent. If, on the other hand, no strings need be attached to imaginative selection, it is equally the case that there were available at the time at least three jungle wallahs who had reached command rank, any one of whom would have brought to the job an expertise that Hayes could not approach.

Instead 'the Club' continued to look after its own, even with the enemy at the gates. With one or two exceptions, Hayes never lacked the loyalty of his officers in the months that followed, nor was he aware of the protection accorded to him against the ridicule of others. Personally I got on with him well—indeed I was the only one of his officers whom he habitually addressed by his Christian name. He had the deplorable habit of referring to the Anglo-Burmans amongst us as half-castes. He never remotely understood the Chins, nor they him.

In fairness I should add that Hayes was awarded a D.S.O. at the conclusion of the Chin Hills campaign, so there is that much at least to support a contrary assessment.

During April Jap activity in front of the Fort White Sector assumed the proportions of a gathering storm. The full battalion of the 2/5 Gurkhas (the best fighting force I ever knew) was now based on Fort White. The rest of 48 Brigade was moving into the Hills and going the same way.

Early in May the Japs assaulted in battalion strength with artillery support. They came up two-pronged via the Stockades and Telegraph Spur and occupied No. 3 Stockade after a fierce battle with the defenders comprising two companies of the 2/5th, still with three platoons of Levies under Peter Bankes in support—though badly out of role.

I had taken off for Fort White with a platoon of ex-Burma Rifle Levies and reported to the Brigade Commander, a man with a personal reputation for near-suicidal courage. When he learnt that I knew the ground behind the battle, he told me that he was preparing a counter-attack on a scale that would drive the Japs down the hill and that, from a position at the foot of the Pimpi Ridge near No. 2 Stockade, I was to do what I could to harry them as they withdrew.

It took me some hours to get down by a necessarily circuitous route, and as I travelled I could hear the intense fire that marked the counter-attack. One of the assaulting Gurkha companies was commanded by Captain Villiers Dennys, with whom I had bivouacked at Shuganu on my way into the Chin Hills. In this action he won a Military Cross and suffered a leg wound that ended his military career, while one of his platoon havildars, Ghaje Gale, was awarded the Victoria Cross.

By the time I got down the Pimpi Ridge it was evident that the counter-attack had failed, but I waited for a resumption. The Japs had placed strong flank protection on the road through No. 2 Stockade and it was not easy to get a sight of what was moving. Such as we did glimpse was all one way—upward. The Japs were plainly reinforcing. Occasional outbreaks of sporadic firing encouraged me to think that a renewed attack was coming in from Fort White, but by nightfall all was quiet.

Without food or blankets we stayed in position until dawn when I sent two scouts up to Dimlo, between Fort White and Tiddim, to reconnoitre southwards along the road in search of the Brigade. They returned with the news that the Gurkhas were digging in on the slopes of Kennedy Peak astride the Dimlo/Fort White road. This confirmed my suspicion. The Japs were in possession of the field. I took my party back to Tiddim and reported to the Brigadier. He was not only in a mood of angry mortification but appeared to have forgotten my existence.

In an otherwise excellent book, which includes a description of the battle of the Stockades by two co-authors who could not have been present, there occurs a travesty to be corrected. The passage runs:

The Chin Levy contingent, sent to reinforce the Gurkhas, broke, leaving only their commander and a few men. As a result the Japs were able to establish a strong footing within the position.

The question of who reinforced whom, of course, is a

matter of fact, and to this extent the passage requires reversal. Peter's Levies at No. 3 Stockade had come under the orders of the Brigade Commander who, one must assume, knew them to be without bayonets in a situation where the *kukri* and the bayonet were the weapons of the day. Some of them lacked the status and the training of soldiers and a minority, I would expect, would still be armed with flintlocks. The ungenerous stricture, fortunately, carries its own repudiation.

I had returned from the Pimpi Ridge with what might have been taken for mumps. In fact an abscessed tooth that had been bothering me for weeks had flared to the point where I was maddened with pain, and I sought and was granted permission to jump a jeep returning to Imphal. There I had the offender extracted by the dentist at the base hospital.

Before returning to Tiddim I decided that I should find out whether anyone was interested in anything I might have to say about conditions in the Hills. I regretted this at my first interview, which was with a supercilious Intelligence Colonel who told me that it was his practice to delete the last nought from Levy reports of enemy strengths. I flared at this and suggested that perhaps we had a clue here to the loss of No. 3 Stockade. We parted less than friends! Later, at a brief discussion with the Corps Commander, I thought it my duty to retail this statement of policy, though this time I employed more tact. The G.O.C. dismissed the matter lightly, and a month or two later I saw the Colonel gazetted for an O.B.E. Presumably his methods had official approval, but my 'sitreps' continued to be factual.

I only laughed once while in Imphal. I had ascertained from the dentist that 'Poona' was the password I required to get me into Corps H.Q. As I threaded my way through the grove of trees that harboured the H.Q. *bashas*, a Gurkha sentry, with fixed bayonet at the ready, jumped out and demanded the password.

'Poona,' said I.

The sentry, correctly gauging my standard of Urdu, replied

'Poona *mat bolo* Patna *bolo* pass friend'.

The dentist had been twenty-four hours out of date!

I returned to Tiddim as I had come, save that a Major's crown had displaced my Captain's pips. Steels were no longer having to make up my pay! Military conditions at Tiddim were such that I found myself alternating between a desk and liaison duties. Practically the whole of 17 Div. was now concentrated in the area. I had some personal contact with the Divisional Commander, Major-General 'Punch' Cowan. My memories are of a first-class soldier and a fantastic memory for names. Attached to the Division as an interpreter was an American Japanese who enjoyed the privacy of a goldfish. His most innocuous sorties—visits to the latrine not excluded—required that he be escorted by a section of troops to ensure that he was not picked off by some trigger-happy warrior!

Coincidental with an unexplained lacuna in my diary, made good only in part by my letters, the Japs, who had consolidated at No. 3 Stockade, resumed their offensive, occupied Fort White and dug themselves in on Kennedy Peak. In some venture, of which memory recalls nothing, I slept wet for several nights and lost all the equipment I was carrying.

I was rotten with scabies, infested with round worm, having periodic bouts of malaria and bacillary dysentery and subject to occasional 'black-outs'. So, when ordered out on six weeks leave exclusive of travelling time, I shaved off my beard, reached for my hat and went. I had had fourteen unbroken months of it, and now that the Tiddim area had become militarily operational I resolved to apply for a transfer to the Kachin Levies, who were still waging war in the manner to which I had become accustomed. Later, after my sense of proportion had returned, I changed my mind in favour of seeing through to finality a show of which I had been a founder member.

Since I propose to substitute for an account of how I spent my leave a chapter on the Chins and their way of life, I will confine myself to saying that my time was divided between staying with my brother in Bombay and Madras (he was transferred from one to the other while I was with him) and with Ben Braund and his family in Calcutta; and in dodging in and out of doctors' consulting rooms and hospitals. I was cleared of the scabies, the worms and the bacillary. The 'black-outs' were correctly diagnosed (in view of my subsequent freedom from them) to my being allergic to the anti-malarial Mepacrin, which was the current prophylactic. The malaria I had already learnt to live with.

I made no little effort, via the USA Consulate and otherwise, to find out what had happened to Maxine Strong: but she had disappeared without trace.

14 Interlude

The Naga, the Chin and the Lushai Hills—and below them the Arakan Yomas—are a submontane confusion of hills hanging like a bunch of grapes on a vine from the eastern extremity of the Himalayas. Within their ample bosom they nurse the Indo-Burma border. Viewed on a map, or even from an aircraft, the run of the ranges is generally north/south; but at ground level this distinction is too frequently illusory: the pursuit of a nominally ridge-top route can involve, with sickening frequency, a plunge down to and a haul up from an intersecting stream bed.

The Chin Hills attain their highest peak at Mount Victoria, which tops ten thousand feet; but this lies to the south, outside the limits of Levy operations. Kennedy Peak, at just under nine thousand feet, is the highest feature of the area the Levies sought to dominate.

Civil control of this same area radiated from Falam as the Divisional Headquarters via sub-Divisional outposts at Tiddim and Haka, to the north and south respectively. These three places are linked by a ridge-top mule track and are at an average elevation of about five thousand feet. Parallel to the track to the east, and occasionally visible from it, is the Kabaw/Kale/Gangaw Valley succession. The dominant feature of the Valley is the Myittha River flowing tortuously from the south to join near Kalemyo the smaller Neyinzaya coming down from the north. The two in combination plunge through a gorge in the lower range of hills that separates the Valley from the Chindwin. Into this major waterway they spill at Kalewa.

In peacetime the Chins, an impoverished people by

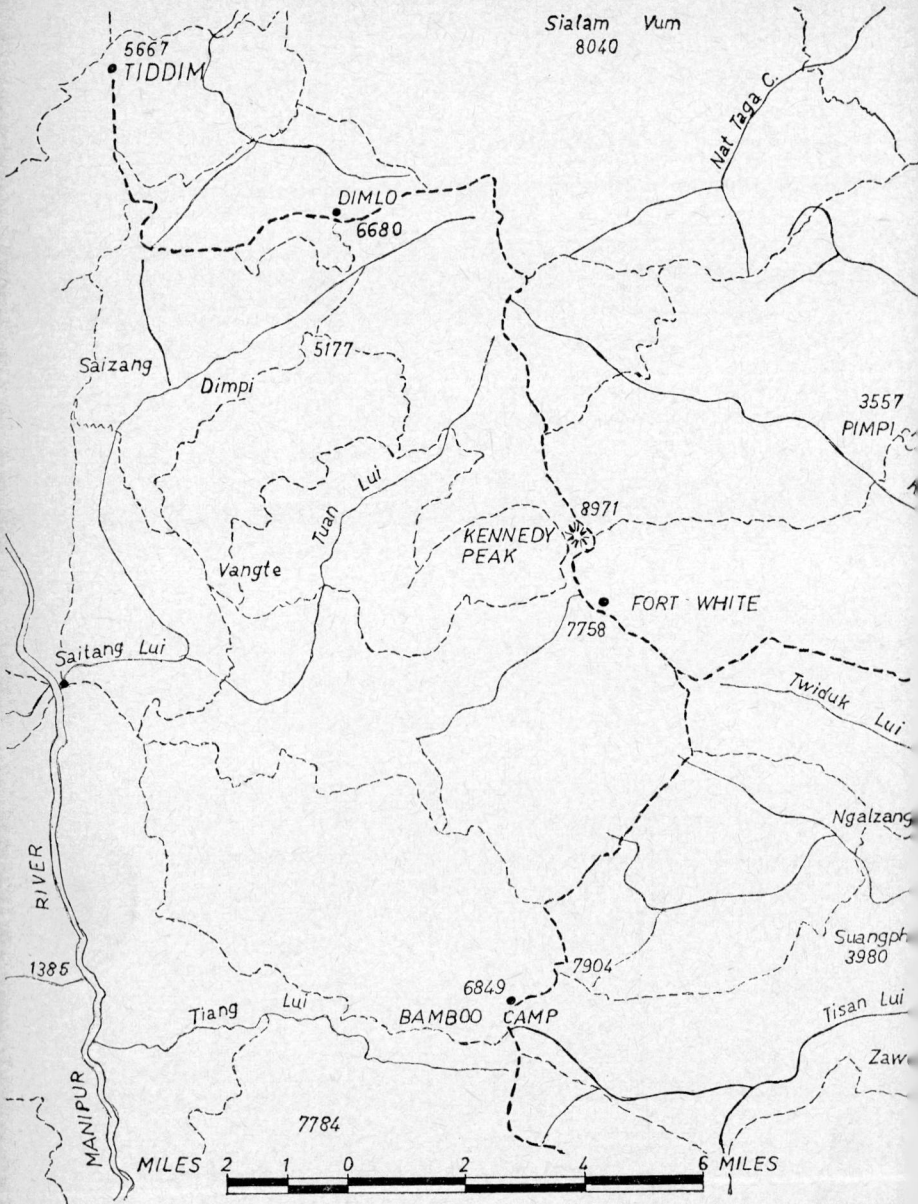

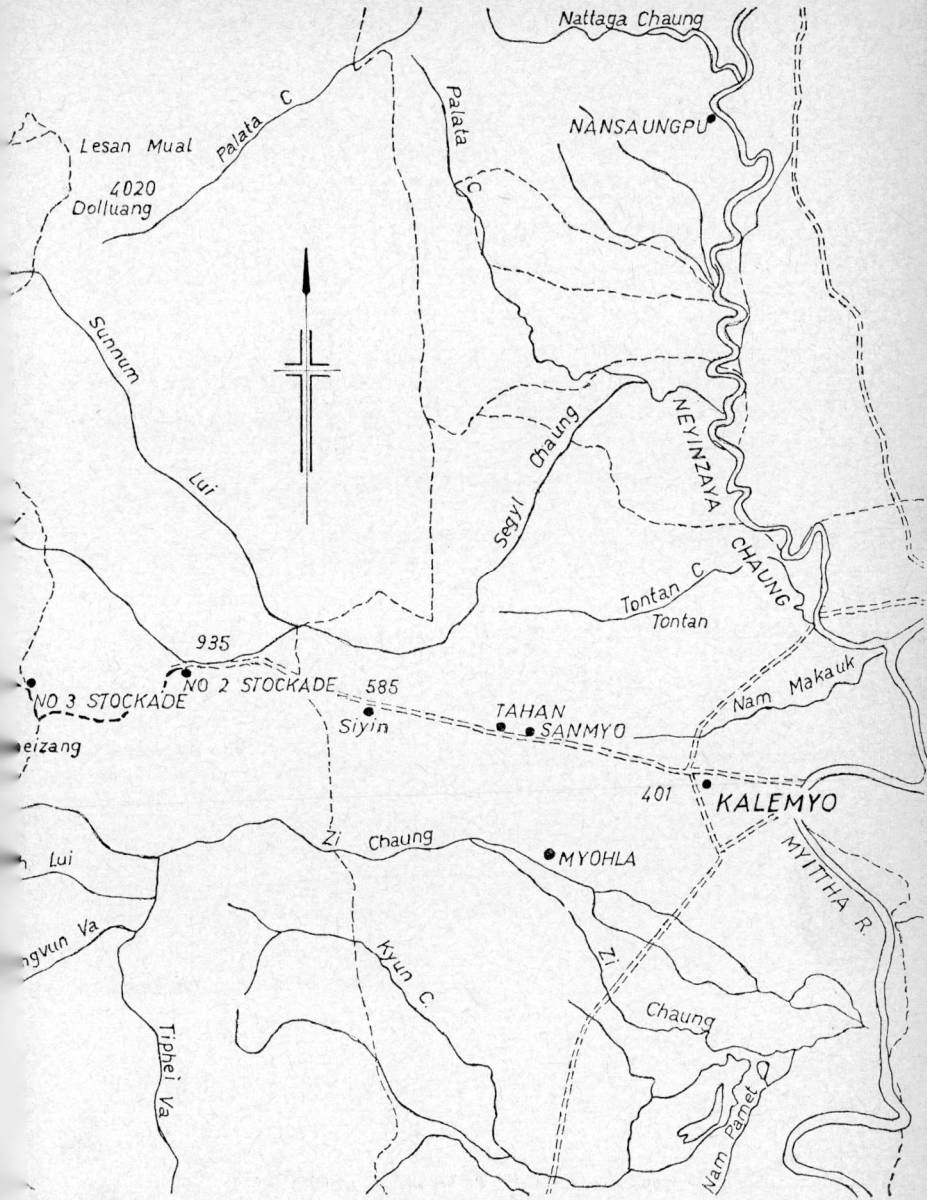

CHIN LEVIES - TIDDIM ZONE - FORT WHITE SECTOR

comparison with the plainsmen, used to visit the Valley to buy food to supplement their own meagre produce, together with such minor comforts of life as they could afford. From the Tiddim area they would go via Fort White and the Stockades, from Falam via Webula to Natchaung and beyond, and from Haka by less strategic tracks to Myintha and Kan. There was virtually no reverse traffic. The Hills had nothing to offer the Valley dweller; and the Chins, but newly weaned from head hunting, were distrusted on their own ground. Occasionally, elsewhere in Burma, one met a Chin who had been lured away perhaps as a personal servant or for some other special reason; but by and large they stayed in their Hills.

The Hills were sparsely populated because a hard way of life kept them so. The unit of living was the village, owing obedience perhaps to a tribal chief, and the general pattern was that villages were distant from each other by a day's march, which would be represented by an average of about twelve miles according to terrain. In such conditions neighbouring villages would have established as their territory a rough circle of six miles radius with the village as the centre. From this territory would come their crops and their livelihood. It would also provide grazing for the village's herd of mithun, a domesticated bison of sometimes enormous size and always fearsome mien. These animals were kept mainly for sacrificial purposes. Despite their bulk and aspect, I never knew them other than as the most mild-mannered of creatures.

In the longer administered, less sparsely populated and more enlightened Lushai Hills, cultivation of village terri-tory would often be carried on by the method of terracing, with its concomitant of timber conservation. In the more backward Chin Hills there was profligate waste of natural resources, with which the Civil authorities were constantly wrestling. A *taung-ya* (a patch cleared for cultivation) would be opened up by felling and burning off, the soil initially being rich in wood ash. Crops would be grown for a few years until the soil soured, whereupon another *taung-ya* would be cleared. Some villages were surrounded by almost complete denudation and, if the worse came to the worst, the entire village would emigrate, literally in search of pastures new. That way lies ultimate soil erosion, the protection against which is education; and education is a ladder for the lowest rung of which the Chin foot was but groping at the time of the Japanese invasion of Burma.

Outside of Falam, Tiddim and Haka, village populations that could be numbered in four figures were but a handful. The typical was from fifty to five hundred. The houses were shambling, smoke-blackened, stilted affairs of hewn timber with grass or bamboo leaf roofing. Christianity—and Burmese Buddhism for that matter—had made very little impact on the animistic superstitions of the villagers. The verandahs of the houses would be hung with the skulls of animals, either mithun or the spoils of the chase. Those of human enemies were not so obtrusively displayed, because British rule had outlawed the practice. This does not mean that in wartime, after a convivial round of *zu*, they were not available for private inspection, particularly since we had found it politic not to discourage a revival of head hunting— provided they were Japanese heads. After all, Colonel Yamata had placed a price of two thousand rupees on mine!

Passing across the verandah, one entered a large council chamber or family room according to the occasion. Further within was the communal sleeping chamber, having at its extremity the 'convenience' via which the pigs corralled below the house were fattened for consumption on human excreta.

The village was governed by a headman, sometimes having the status of a chief, and a council of elders. To a very large extent the British Civil authorities left in council hands the administration of law and order according to tribal custom. Only in matters of life and death and other major crimes was jurisdiction transferred to the Civil courts at Falam, Tiddim and Haka. Even in these spheres, trial and punishment reverted naturally to the councils of elders at the height of our pre-occupation with the Japanese; and I have personal knowledge of one case of a jealous lover condemned to death for a murder that involved two neighbouring villages. In the presence of the elders of both, his throat was ceremoniously cut on the rock platform that marked the divide between the two village tracts. This did not imply necessarily that the two villages were on friendly terms. Tribal law was being implemented.

When the tide of Japanese invasion lapped against the fringes of the Hills, the Levy organization was brought into being with an eye to tribal custom. Resistance must have an underlay of village protection if anything more communal was to succeed. Accordingly two cadres of Levies were established, the 'A' and the 'B'. Taking the latter first, the 'B' Levy was not normally a professional soldier, though military pensioners were frequently to be found in his ranks. His role was to defend his village and to provide such personal service to the wider cause as made it possible to include his village effectively within a further flung defensive net. This required, firstly, that he be armed and, secondly, that he be reliably on call at rotational intervals to ensure that each village possessed a pool of runners from which inter-village messengers or porters could immediately be demanded at any hour of day or night. It followed from the implied divorcement from regular agricultural pursuit that the 'B' Levy, while on duty, had to be rationed and paid. The 'B' Levies were numbered in many hundreds and, in most areas, could be counted on for as much as or more than they were paid for.

The question of arms was partly answered by history. During the years when the European Powers were vying with each other for the mastery of the Indian subcontinent, the Chin Hills, among other areas, were a vacuum into which one Power would feed arms to the embarrassment of another. These arms, for the most part, were flintlock rifles, and to the Chins they were the most priceless of all possible gifts. Passed down from father to son, and preserved in immaculate condition by both, they now aggregated a powerful arsenal in the hands of men skilled in their use. Gunpowder they had learnt to make for themselves, and a couple of hundred yards of telegraph wire pillaged from the Valley could be cut and fashioned into a more than sufficient supply of ammunition. The British redcoat, perfected in the use of the flintlock, was said to be able to get away three rounds per minute. Peter Bankes and I, after a morning of hard practice, never bettered one round.

This, however, was not the point. In the Chin Hills, a fusillade from behind a protective screen of *panjis* was followed by a fade-away to the next ambush position, where reloading could be done at leisure. In the forties of the twentieth century Japs died in the Chin Hills of wounds inflicted by weapons made before the battle of Waterloo! Rifles we provided as and when we could to those trained in their use; we even distributed shotguns sent through to us from India.

The 'A' Levies were a full-time force, and to a large extent they were still embodied soldiers officially. Many of them were survivors of actions in Burma that had ended in the extinction of their units. Weaponless, and with their equipment lost or jettisoned, they had found their way back to the Hills, with or without detention in enemy hands *en route*. Silently, and frequently shamefacedly before their pensioner elders, they had returned to their villages and reverted to the agricultural pursuits from which they had been weaned by the recruiting officer years previously. Thus they had remained, in many cases until a Burma Army pay party visited the Hills and, with no questions asked, called them to various points along the route and paid them their arrears in full.

Now, deserter, looter and he who had kept his nose clean, they were serving in the ranks of the Levies in the defence of their own Hills. None of us had any illusions as to how the bulk of them would react if the Japs invaded the Hills and overran their village tracts, but, for the most part, we were not encumbered by considerations of regimental tradition. If today's fighter is to be tomorrow's deserter, then get full value from him today. Guerrilla warfare is not soldiering, and guerrilla officers need have no inhibitions beyond due observance of their oath of allegiance.

In appearance the Chin is typically Mongoloid, his way of life giving him far more in common with such as the

Gurkha than with the less rigorously nurtured Malaysian. The men wear their hair long and gathered into a bun, with a variety of style that is generally indicative of tribal area. Thus, a bun worn at the back of the head would normally denote a Siyin, a Sokte, a Kamhau or a man from one of the other Tiddim area tribes. The Falams wore their buns on the top of the head, and the Hakas in front so that it overhung the forehead. In each case the head would be wound round with a cloth puggree designed to keep the bun in place and, by way of anchorage, a large hair pin would transfix the bun, from which it would protrude on either side. These hair pins were wrought from crude silver and frequently would be a more-or-less scale model of a flintlock rifle, or a double-barrelled shotgun, or the animistic totem pole that guarded the entry to the wearer's village.

The women likewise wore their hair long, either hanging or loosely done up at the neck. Their dress was a plain or embroidered black skirt, of knee to ankle length, worn with a black or dingy white bodice. An indication of her husband's status or wealth was the amount of crude silver belting that a Chin woman wore. This belting was usually fashioned from melted down rupees, and could sometimes extend from the waist to well down on the hips, in which case she would be carrying quite a weight of metal around with her.

The women had few inhibitions. They did a share of work in the *taung-yas* as well as their own housekeeping, and they mixed freely with the menfolk even when a visiting Civil or Levy officer was present. They were as tough as the men, and I once knew a woman to be working in her *taung-ya* in the afternoon having given birth to a baby that morning. I have no notes on infant mortality, but it must have been very high.

The Chin characteristic that must have been the bane of the missionary was his prowess as a drinker. Heaven alone knows how large a proportion of his hard-won *taung-ya* produce went into the distilling or fermenting of his alcoholic beverages; but the social implications of his drinking were considerable. The drink came in two forms, a distilled spirit of somewhat gin-like clarity known as *zu-riel*, and a rice beer resembling in appearance a thin and pallid pea soup. This was known as *zu*. For me the drinking of *zu-riel* had always the quality of a self-inflicted wound. *Zu*, on the other hand, at its best (and it could be extremely variable) was a nectar which I came to relish. During periods when we were hard put to it to feed ourselves, I am convinced in all honesty that, from the point of view of vitamin or other nutritional content, it was the most valuable constituent of our diet.

The other chapters of the Chin Hills part of my tale are concerned primarily with the anti-Japanese facet of our role. It needs to be understood, as a background to this, that keeping up the morale of the Hills as a whole made demands on us that were less spectacular but certainly no less vital. In quieter periods we all of us were committed to wide-ranging 'flag marches' that took us, an officer and no more than a section of 'A' Levies, from village to village over hundreds of exhausting miles of climb and descent.

Imagine me, if you will, humping my ninety pounds in the late afternoon of a day burdened with rain and leeches towards a crest that twice or thrice would turn out to be false. Ahead of me the mule track traverses in hair pins, in advance of each bend of which my mind has to make a decision. Am I to play the mule or the man? For, twenty yards short of the bend will probably be an up-hill scramble dclineated by the feet of porters who, perhaps for generations, have considered that particular corner to be worth the cutting. Am I to gain by this precipitous, rhythm-breaking diversion? Or will the steady, head-down plod that I have established leave me better able, despite the extra forty yards, to make a right decision with regard to the same problem that will face me at the next bend?

In driving rain, or clinging mist, or biting cold, or blinding sweat—according to season—I reach the top and lurch round a corner that gives me a mile-distant view of my objective for the night, one of the hundred and thirty-six villages that I personally visited at least once. Immediately in front of me are the stone platform, the poles and the skulls that mark the village boundary; and there, nursing a bottle of *zu-riel* for my consumption, is the village headman with some of his elders. I have long since learnt that to protest that I can't stand *zu-riel* and would prefer to wait for the *zu* is going to damn my visit before it starts; so somehow I get a slug of the stuff down.

Head up and shoulders back, though it kills me, I enter the village to the stares and the giggles of an ill-nourished crowd. Maybe on this occasion one of my escort is a native of the place, in which case they all are swept away to hospitality before I even have time to observe the etiquette of seeing to their accommodation.

I am led up the steps of the headman's house. My orderly's and other helping hands strip the equipment off me and remove my boots and socks—the eleventh, shall we say, of the fifteen pairs of boots I wore to destruction in this fashion. I burn off the leaches and retire to nourish the sub-structural swine. I linger in retirement long enough to plug the more stubborn of the leech bleeders with strips of paper torn off *The Times* crossword puzzle, of which I have a number about me in various stages of completion. Then I proceed to remove the more accessible of the ticks, to lather my scabies-infested groin with sulphur ointment, and to lubricate my bleeding piles with vaseline. Trousered again, I pause, perhaps, before a mentally mirrored reflection of a young officer-cadet in white tie and tails tap dancing on the floor of the Maymyo Club. Then I enter the council chamber to discharge my duty at the *zu* pot, which I find already positioned centrally with the assembled company, seated decorously in order of precedence, awaiting my pleasure and my lead.

With a '*nang-ma na dam maw bawi-nu?*' to my hostess, the headman's wife (or the equivalent phrase according to tribal area, this example being 'how are you, madam?' in Haka Chin), I lower myself onto the wooden stool beside the *zu* pot and then, head down, am drinking. Later I shall be served food from the family pot. If they have done me the honour of killing a pig—well, what is one more worm among so many!

For a fuller picture of the *zu* drinking ritual I cannot do better than borrow from an account of my stewardship, which the Directorate of Public Relations, G.H.Q., India, published at the end of the war in the Journal of the United Service Institution of India:

Zu has already been mentioned. The part it plays in the life of the Chin is really astonishing. No wedding or funeral would be complete without it. No business can be transacted or dispute settled except around a pot of the stuff; while the shooting of a bear by a member of your household is the immediate signal for two or three pots to be broached. In fact any excuse for a party, and as the arrival of an officer in the village for the night was invariably such an excuse, one had to get used to marching in the morning with a hangover!

The *zu* is served in large earthenware jars resembling in shape those in which the forty thieves are pictorially depicted as meeting their end, and averaging about three feet in depth. The already fermented rice or millet is held down by a platform of banana leaves, so that when the water is added the grain does not float. A hollow bamboo 'straw', through which everybody present has to suck in turn, is pushed down through the leaves and the grain to the bottom of the pot, and beside it a sliver of cane, the top of which is two or three inches below the water level. All is now set for you to be led to the pot to drink your way down until the cane breaks surface; and then, because as an officer you must show your calibre, to have the pot refilled and repeat the performance.

The setting for this bibulous scene is a low-beamed, smoke-filled Chin house lit only by the flare of burning pine chips. Round the drinker a circle of as many men and women as the place will hold, all talking hard and expectorating through holes in the floor: an outer circle of children, dogs and chickens all giving tongue in their fashion, and paddling around under the house two or three grunting pigs to provide the bass note. If the occasion is a 'proper do' dancing will be a feature of the evening—as big a circle as possible of alternate lads and lasses, holding hands and shuffling their way round to the beat of a drum and the strains of a monotonous chant. Rate of progress I found to be just slow enough that by the time I had worked my way round as far as the main beam supporting the roof, I had forgotten the crack on the head it gave me on the previous circuit and so got another one.

The routine of *zu* drinking becomes endowed with a refreshing variant when the 'belles' are present, as you are then led to the pot with one of them as a partner and, with your arm around her, suck your way down to the cane alternately before leading her back into the dancing circle. Should the officer pass out during the course of the evening the success of the party is thereby assured, and he is made as comfortable as possible for the night on a bearskin and under a Chin blanket.

I would now add to this account that, if the visiting officer

219

was new to the game, the Chins knew how to exploit the occasion. Instead of preparing the *zu* pot for drinking some hours in advance of the guest's arrival, the water would be added just before he was led thereto to drink. This resulted in an expansion of the contents of the pot that operated in direct opposition to the drinker's attempt to consume his prescribed ration. I was caught only once. On that occasion, when I was just about 'half seas under', I found that the pot was overflowing!

In this manner, with these people, lacking the opportunity for weeks on end of speaking my own language, I spent three years of my life that in peacetime would have been devoted to raising a family, perfecting myself in my profession, and generally in 'keeping up with the Joneses'. I have no sense of loss; I would ask for nothing back; and I have not known more stimulating company.

Belonging to this wayward chapter are one or two other aspects of life that cannot specifically be docketed elsewhere.

The financing of our multifarious activities was done entirely in coin. Paper money simply was not acceptable when military reverse could render it valueless. The fact was a curse that lengthened the transport train, be the occasion active or passive. We were required to keep accounts, but on the basis that they must not be revealing of anything significant. If in the gloom of an *indaing* jungle in the Valley you handed over fifty rupees to a Burmese agent, the cash sheet merely indicated 'Intelligence'. If, in the cause of morale, it was necessary to summon headmen to a meeting that called, as they all did, for the broaching of pots of *zu*, the cash entry suitably concealed the fact. It goes without saying that such licence proved highly offensive to the gentlemen of the Department of the Controller of Military Accounts in India, at whose querulous expense we had considerable fun.

As instruments of barter or personal reward, I should mention two other media that had the power of currency. My copies of *The Times* and *The Statesman* were held in the highest esteem as cigarette paper. A double sheet of either would buy a chicken or a dozen eggs anywhere. Then there was parachute cloth. We were ordered, quite impossibly, to return all parachutes to the supply dropping centre at Agartala in India. Instead we used to confer them on village headmen in return for hospitality, or to others for miscellaneous services rendered. Gradually one became accustomed to seeing women and children wearing new blouses or shirts, betrayed for what they were by the seams, irrelevant to the garment, of the parachute panels. Though the Chin women wove coarse cloth for skirts and blankets, cotton yardage was obtained in peacetime from the shops in the Valley villages now barred to them; so a parachute was a tremendous prize.

Finally, because in this I detect a thread of near-consistency, I would make a comment relative to the choice of suitable Levy officers that by some nevertheless will be disputed. To start off with we were all of us pre-war Burma jungle wallahs of one sort or another. As time went on it became necessary to supplement our numbers, frequently with newly commissioned youngsters from home for whom the Chin Hills was a fortuitous posting. This involved a few outright failures and, above them, a mixed bag whence potential emerged quickly or slowly, I aver, according to background. In general I found that the better the education, and specifically if it included boarding school, the quicker did the man become a dependable and self-reliant Levy officer. He it was whom you could risk sending out to relieve as a Sector commander after no more than a few days under your wing. The other tended to be the man you had to entrust to someone's care for some weeks while he absorbed, shock by shock, the depths of what was required of him and of what he had to put up with. Officering of a guerrilla force, after the original source of supply is exhausted, should be by fully-primed volunteers only.

15 The Battle for Haka

September 1943 to January 1944

After my leave in India, I returned to Tiddim via the route along which I had struggled when I first entered the Hills. I marvelled, in a sense sorrowed, at the transformation. No longer was it a leech-ridden, rocky hill track. Here now was a strategic road, strung with supply dumps and transit camps and culminating, for the final climb to the Tiddim ridge, in the historic 'Chocolate Staircase', the brown, loamy, hairpin approach up which even armour was eventually to find its way.

On reaching Tiddim I was astonished to find Rupert Carey installed as Zone Commander, and orders waiting for me to proceed to his old 'stamping ground' at Haka and to take over that Zone. Later, in Falam, I was to be told by one of his staff that Hayes had determined on this exchange in order to separate Peter Bankes and myself. In combination, apparently, he distrusted our influence! With Rupert at Tiddim were Philip Barton and Peter, and, since rum was a ration issue by this time, we had a pretty good party before I began my southward march.

I reported at Levy H.Q. in Falam for only the second time since I had entered the Hills. I had had to travel from Tiddim by a circuitous westward track because the Japs were heavily dug in astride the main road in the Kennedy Peak/Fort White area. Onwards from Falam to Haka I journeyed by the normal peacetime route through magnificent country.

I arrived at my new Headquarters in time to put down a rum ration that had arrived simultaneously with Italy's surrender. Among those present was Jack Oats, whom I was delighted to see; but when I saw him off a day or two later it was to be my last view of him as an able-bodied man. In a tragic jeep accident in Shillong while he was on leave, his back was broken and he was crippled for life. Jack of all people.

I took up residence in the sweeper's quarter of the Public Works Department rest house. The bungalow itself was unoccupied, but I decided that a single-roomed hovel would more easily be kept warm, and the cold weather was not far away. As an office Rupert Carey had taken over the Haka school building, which was closed for lack of staff in present conditions. Administratively he had done himself proud, and I quailed at the long-forgotten sight of files and a typewriter! However, I was not to be burdened with such things for long.

Measured on a map, the Haka Zone commanded a north–south front of little more than seventy miles, but in such a wild tumble of hills this becomes an index of little meaning. The inter-Zonal boundary with Falam started at Sihaung Myauk in the Kale Valley, whence it followed the Manipur River westward to its junction with the Pao Va: from that point it marched, still westward, with the latter.

The Northern Sector was based at Hata, to the east of Haka and near the riverine Zonal boundary. It was commanded by Dick Rees, recently joined and straight out from home. He was very unmistakably a Welshman and had been an instructor in physical training before the war. Bodily he was a man of tremendous strength, and as a Levy officer he proved to be one of the best we ever had.

The Centre Sector, with its base at Zokhua, was—and had been since the inception of the Levies—under the command of 'Jamie' James of the *Bombine*. He it was who had given the Japs their first drubbing in the Hills a year previously, and he was a very seasoned campaigner. He had taken a poor view of Colonel Hayes before he had even met him. Under the old dispensation, Zonal orders to Sector commanders had tended to be of the 'you might get off your backside' variety. Innocent of its changed origin, Jamie had received an order prefaced by the words 'you will'. He marched off in execution thereof, but only after dispatching an ack-

223

nowledgment which read 'please say please'. Whether Hayes was still around to see the reply I know not.

Far to the south at Lungngo, in a total isolation that he maintained for over a year, was David Cozens, an erstwhile accountant in the B.O.C.'s Rangoon office. Translated from the city lights to a remoteness that represented the maximum possible contrast, he took to the change with a missionary zeal that was quite astonishing, and he did a tremendous job as a listening post where all otherwise would have been silence. With me in Haka was Ian Hillis, a young Scot from a Glasgow shipping office, whose resolution in all that he did rounded off a first-class team of officers.

By the end of September it was evident that the Japanese were poised for a renewed advance through the Hills into North Eastern India at least; and, in accordance with the appreciation I had made on my first entry into the Hills, signs were not wanting that they intended to occupy Tiddim, Falam and Haka to protect the flank of their main attack. In Haka the Levies had the backing of a Gurkha company from the Chin Hills Battalion, Burma Frontier Force, under the command of Frank O'Donel, an Anglo-Burman of great dependability.

So far as the Levies are concerned, any account of the events that follow must necessarily be prefaced by an explanation of the overriding qualification that governed our operations. We, the officers, were playing a microcosmic role on a world-wide stage of march and counter-march in foreign lands. The Chins, on the other hand—and any one of them could have enriched himself by the betrayal of any one of us—each had a vested interest in any local withdrawal that exposed his own village, and, therefore, his wife and family, to occupation by the advancing Japanese.

Consequently, in a way that no regular campaigner can be expected to understand, we had to plan for piecemeal defection as an accompaniment to each mile of ground yielded. Not desertion in the sense of disillusioned men throwing away their arms and submitting to the enemy, but a quiet fading away by trusted men who, having collected their families, food and blankets, would slip away into jungle hiding and there await events. It was not a thing that was discussed: we knew it: they knew that we knew it; and until their individual moments of decision came, they and we would continue as comrades in arms.

The Japs moved against Falam and Haka simultaneously; and, in their extraordinary way, they advanced noisily, without precautions, like a crowd on the way to a football match. With twenty-four hours notice of the departure from Tintha of an enemy force comprising about three hundred Japs and a hundred Burmese levies, Dick Rees from Hata crossed the Netpian Va to meet them with a hand-picked force of fifteen men, most of whom were armed with automatic weapons. Meanwhile I sent Hillis forward to Sihai with a platoon of Levies, and myself moved to Dauchim with my reserves.

Dick found the enemy force, unprotected, heavily laden and flat out on the ground after a stiff climb. From easy hand grenade range he tore into them with all that he had until it was time to go. For long after he had pulled out, the chaos was clearly audible, and the Japs were watched as they spent the next five hours cremating their dead at the foot of the descent west of the ambush.

Lest distance be suspected of lending enchantment, let me borrow, for Dick's next contribution, from my more than twenty-five-year-old account published by the Directorate of Public Relations, G.H.Q., India.

The following day the Jap force reached the village of Hata (not to be confused with Haka itself), and there, thanks to thick jungle extending almost up to the walls of the houses, another ambush party was lying up in a position to cover the compound of the headman's house in the hopes that at least a patrol would visit it for information if nothing else. The gamble succeeded beyond expectations. The entire enemy force entered this very small village, and into a fenced-in compound packed with Japs, the ambush party threw every grenade and fired every round of Tommy gun ammunition it was carrying before pulling out.

These two actions were later reported by the Japs themselves as having cost them 132 killed and wounded. Dick's only casualty was a wounded Levy. This man must but recently have graduated from a flintlock to a rifle. He shot one of a patrol of three Japs he met on a jungle track, but was himself then shot through the shoulder while trying to discover how to get another round up the spout! His disgust at being thus let down was all he could talk about when he was carried through my H.Q. *en route* to hospital in Haka! For a very great performance Dick Rees was awarded an immediate M.C.

Meanwhile Colonel Hayes, who had made his H.Q. just west of Haka, sent forward Frank O'Donel's Gurkha company, two platoons of which I moved forward to Sihai to support Rees who had had to fall back there in the face of enemy reinforcement of the Hata ridge. Hillis I moved from Sihai to Rinpi as soon as it became apparent that the Jap advance on Falam was being covered by enemy patrolling on our side of the Pao Va. I joined him a day or two later, leaving Rees and O'Donel to harry the Japs on the Hata/Haka road.

From Rinpi our patrols across the Dawng Va made several contacts with the enemy in the Haiphai area but, of intent, we left unanswered their attempts from the east bank to draw the fire of our picket on the west bank at the Haiphai/Rinpi ford. We were very well placed to ambush them if they crossed. To the north of our Rinpi base we tried to disrupt the Jap Line of Communication to Falam but, though we inflicted some casualties, the supply columns were too strongly escorted for us to make an effective impression.

One night we did goad the Japs into sending a fighting patrol across the Pao Va and it attacked us at Rinpi. It was the briefest of actions, for Ian and I, with only two hundred yards to run to the picket that had been bumped, arrived after the Japs had precipitately withdrawn. The picket commander, astonished at so facile a rout, made no claim to have inflicted casualties; but the Japs left such a welter of potential identifications as to suggest complete panic. It comprised a steel helmet, a Japanese flag, a soldier's identity disc, a hand grenade, fifteen rounds of ammunition, a Japanese manual on the Indian National Army, a guide book on Indaw (Katha District, not the oilfield), five occupation currency notes and two field message forms.

Rees and O'Donel were being no less active to our

immediate south, and for four weeks we lost no more ground, though continuously in contact. Unfortunately the Falam Levies, operating in concert with the main body of the Chin Hills Battalion under Roddie Russell, were having a rougher time on the Jap Line of Communication; and Pat Rathbone, with the elements of three Levy platoons, was ordered by Jack Haswell to cross the Pao Va and join his force to ours after being harried by artillery fire as cover to a determined Jap advance. This left virtually a straight fight for Falam between the Japs and the Chin Hills Battalion.

Falam was lost on 7 November, leaving the main road from Falam to Haka wide open in our rear. Hayes accordingly ordered the withdrawal of my Rinpi force to Hranhring and of O'Donel's Gurkhas to the proximity of Haka. Rees, still with the benefit of flank protection from these moves, fell back westward from Sihai as and when enemy pressure forced him to do so. From Hranhring Hayes ordered me to send Rathbone to Pioneer Camp on the Falam/Haka road to reinforce a newly arrived young officer whom Hayes had sent there before it became threatened by the fall of Falam.

Hillis with his Levies I sent to the high ground between Hranhring and Hniarlawn as a potential cover for both Rees and Rathbone. Hayes had moved his H.Q. westward from Haka along the Klangklang road and now called me back there for a discussion on policy arising from the fall of Falam. While I was talking with him, the youngster from Pioneer Camp arrived in alarm to say that the Japs had attacked him there and that his Levies were dispersed and no longer under command. He had seen nothing of Pat Rathbone and his force.

Hayes promptly sent me off up the Pioneer Camp road to locate Rathbone and, if possible, to organize resistance. (Be it remembered that Pat's Levies were Falams and that Falam was now in enemy hands.) I found Pat about four miles short of Pioneer Camp with a few Levies and a platoon of Frank O'Donel's Gurkhas under his command, the fruit of prompt unguided liaison between the two of them. I sent messages of recall to Hillis and Rees, and to Frank an order

227

to find a defensive position on the main road two miles to the rear of Rathbone, whence he was to take over the duties of rearguard if and when Pat was forced to withdraw through his position. I joined Frank and soon had the good news that Hillis was through and, with very few men, was in a defensive position in my rear.

Pat was attacked at dawn next day, 11 November, with machine guns and mortars, to which he was able to reply in kind; but he withdrew under the threat of encirclement and, after another attempt to stand and fight, passed through our position. I stayed with Frank, hoping for word from Rees, but had had none up to the time when I received orders from Hayes to withdraw Frank's force to the site of what had been Hayes's H.Q. just west of Haka.

The Japs attacked Haka with mortars in the small hours of 12 November, and before dawn they also attacked an earlier base camp of Frank O'Donel's at the point where the Klangklang road left the Falam/Haka road. At dawn a section patrol of Gurkhas, which I sent out to investigate this latter bombardment, surprised the enemy rummaging about among abandoned stores. The Gurkhas attacked with rifle and machine gun fire, and then went in with their *kukris*. Their shouts were audible from my position, and also —a strange background—was the celebratory clamour from the Japs as they overran Haka.

Quickly my mind ranged over what I had left in the sweeper's quarter: there were, of course, my gramophone and records and a few volumes of carefully chosen reading; but there were no diaries or documents that could have got anybody into trouble. A grievous loss was a still more than half-full demijohn of gin that I had brought back from leave with me!

Hayes had withdrawn Pat Rathbone and his remnant before this latest fracas, and I was now left with O'Donel and Hillis and a depleted company of Gurkhas. My own force of Levies had been men from Haka itself or from villages to the east of it, and predictably most of them had faded away to find and secrete their own families. I was very worried at having had no word from Dick Rees.

I split the Gurkhas into two platoons under the two officers. Ian Hillis and his platoon I took back to the next north–south valley behind us. Along it meandered the Timit Va, and if the Japs were to try to get in behind us, a quick detour into the valley from the south was the way to do it. I left Ian digging in and went forward again to rejoin Frank O'Donel. I quickly decided that his position was fast becoming dangerous and that no purpose was to be served by attempting to hold it. Accordingly I faded him away, ordering him to prepare a night laager for both platoons a mile or two south of Ian down the Timit valley at a point where the Klangklang track, having followed the river thus far, suddenly climbed upwards into the jungle that clothed the slope of the next ridge. It was clearly a defensible position and my orders still were that I was to maintain contact with the Japs. Two hours after Frank vacated his position, the Japs attacked it with mortars.

With Frank digging in for both platoons at the chosen site, I left Ian in position southward along the Timit until after dark, when I pulled him out silently and brought him back to the laager. I reckoned that the Japs would probably attack his abandoned position when the moon rose and that, finding him gone, they would wait for daybreak before reconnoitring further. To prove me wrong, they could of course have conscripted Haka villagers as guides, but later information pointed to their use of dogs.

By midnight there was no indication that the Japs had made any move since their abortive attempt to attack Frank O'Donel. However, as I bedded down with Ian Hillis, I should have known better than to risk qualifying as an involuntary contributor to the Anthology of Famous Last Words.

'Ian,' I said, 'I've heard a hell of a lot of mortar bombs go bang in the last twenty-four hours, but not one of them has been aimed at me.'

At two o'clock, under a nearly full moon, the Japs attacked us with two and three inch mortars, L.M.G.s firing green, red and yellow tracer, Tommy guns and rifles. The Gurkhas were first-class, and we were soon responding with all we had—and we were at no disadvantage so far as fire power was concerned. The Japs made several attempts to rush our forward pickets but were driven back on each occasion.

As soon as I found myself pushing wounded back along the road, I decided to break off. There was no knowing for how many more miles my pitifully small force would be required to repeat this sort of thing, and there was none to relieve or reinforce us. I withdrew O'Donel's platoon under a heavy cover of fire, and as soon as he was in position on the track within the jungle to our rear, the rest of us, still exchanging heavy fire, followed and went through him. The Japs continued firing for some time after we were leap-frogging our way towards the summit of the ridge. As soon as I could manage a roll call I found that we were four Gurkhas short and had six wounded, most of them able to walk. I later learned that the Japs had suffered no less, but they were better able to afford it.

By dawn we had reached the top of the ridge at nearly seven thousand feet, and it was fiendishly cold. We found ourselves looking down on Klangklang, comparably situated atop the next westward, but lower, ridge. It was from there that I had had my last word from Hayes, and I now sent him a report to the effect that we still had a small reserve of ammunition and were in fair shape except for lack of food and a desperate all-round need for sleep. I myself had scarcely been off my feet for seventy-two hours.

I reconnoitred an excellent position commanding the debouchment, into a ridge-top *taung-ya*, of the track up which we had climbed after breaking off the action; and once more we turned to digging in. From a forward position, as daylight came, I was perplexed to hear bugle calls and two bursts of L.M.G. fire from the direction of the scene of the night's action. It sounded ominously like prisoners or wounded being ceremonially executed.

During the morning Pat Rathbone, looking extremely ill, arrived from Klangklang to say that Hayes had moved further west to Thlualam and that I was to withdraw my force thither without further attempt to maintain contact with the enemy. This order came as a great relief, though I was surprised then to learn that we were no longer to try to keep a finger on the pulse. In the light of after-thought, however, I realized that this could not be done indefinitely by a small, diminishing, weary force for which there was no relief available. In the event, as it turned out, the Japs made no further westward move after the action at the Timit Va. Probably they considered the Timit an adequate limit as a cover to their occupation of Haka. It was at Imphal to the north that the high stakes were to be played for: and it was there that Japan was to suffer the greatest defeat on land in her military history. We were very small beer!

Pat also brought me the more than welcome news that Dick Rees was with Hayes. Through the failure of my runners to reach him, Dick, with an ever-dwindling force, had fallen back on Haka in complete ignorance that it was Jap-occupied. He was actually dropping down the face of the ridge that overhangs the town when he saw Jap soldiers strolling across the parade-ground. In full view he belted for the jungle and, after a wide detour with no news of what was happening, he arrived in my rear and found Hayes.

We double-staged to Thlualam, for there were no stores or rations left in Klangklang. With the pressure off, we were most of us stumbling along in semi-sleep. I was marching with Ian Hillis on a track that had a ten-foot drop alongside it. As I rounded a bend I saw him, from the corner of my eye, go straight on and over. By the time I got down to him he was fast asleep and I had the devil of a job waking him. He was quite unhurt.

On arrival at Thlualam, I reported to Hayes who seemed, I thought, excessively pleased to see me until he explained that, from a medical orderly who had left the 'party' at the Timit Va somewhat precipitately, he had had an eye-witness account of my death! However, I did sustain one personal loss at the Timit. The blast from a mortar bomb, apparently, removed the camouflage netting from my hat. There were no tears wasted there, but, tucked into the netting, had been my last surviving pipe. I made such an issue of this before Hayes that, in order to shut me up, he gave me one from his own private reserve. It was a good one and I still have it. Before typing this paragraph I stuffed its eroded bowl with tobacco and lit up.

From the timeless sleep that followed, I awoke and took stock of our position. Apart from Frank O'Donel and his depleted force of Gurkhas, there was a handful of Levies who apparently had ignored or were lacking the call of family. There were Levy officers on the scale of about one per Levy— Hayes plus Rees, Hillis and myself from the Haka Zone; and Rathbone, Bryan Smythe and Joe Byrne who variously had come south to join us after the loss of Falam. Within a day or two we were joined by Jamie, who had been harried out of his Sector but had heard on the jungle telegraph of our whereabouts. Of David Cozens there was no news, which was not surprising as his Sector was a long way to the south.

We had little ammunition, no rations and no blankets or spare clothing: the night temperatures were near to freezing. Bryan Smythe, with phlebitis, and Pat Rathbone, with pneumonia, were both stretcher cases from here on. Hayes still had his radio, and by that means we were ordered to march south-west to Tuipang in the Lushai Hills across the Indian border. We were promised a ration drop at Salen two marches distant, though out of desperation we had to tackle it in one. It was the usual murderous up and down hill going and we were weak and exhausted by the time we got there.

Mercifully we received our drop, and made it the occasion for a day's 'breather', for we still had six marches to go and would have to add sufficient rations to our weary backs to cover that distance; and we now had a lot of sick in addition to the stretcher cases. Painfully and slowly, up and over those unending ranges, we slogged—a journey of which I carry not a single pleasant memory. Tempers were frayed, the C.O. was petulant and the Gurkhas were downhearted. At least we were not under pursuit!

My mind ranged uneasily over the question of whether Hayes had done the right thing in pulling us Levy officers out at all. The original concept had provided for our going to ground when the Japs invaded, and the Levies themselves, whom I think Hayes regarded as having deserted, had done precisely that.

In the after-light of the useful revivalist role that yet lay ahead of us, I believe that our withdrawal served the better purpose, because I don't think many of us would have survived had we stayed. If we had not been given away by the small minority of disgruntled informers that there was bound to be, the Japs might have forced our surrender, as they did in the case of Seagrim in Karenni, by atrocious reprisals against the village communities suspected of harbouring us.

However, I don't give Hayes credit for seeing things that way. He regarded the Levies only as troops, and since his arrival in the Hills had even started issuing Part I and Part II Orders in the accredited regimental fashion!

It was indeed a blessing that the dispersal of our campaigning was such as left Hayes with little more than nominal control at times when things were popping. I don't think any of us ever disobeyed an order, but there were established means of evading receipt if the right thing to do was obvious to the man on the spot. Undoubtedly it adds up to the same thing, but we, with lives to live in Burma, owed more to the Chins than we did to the fostering of a basically unsympathetic stranger's military reputation.

After an eternity we reached Tuipang where, with medical aid, dry accommodation, food, blankets and a few creature comforts, we found ourselves adequately ministered to. Hyde, the Assistant Superintendent at Lungleh, whither we were next due to proceed, had sent news out to us of how our and other campaigns were progressing. For me the most shocking item was that Peter Bankes had been killed on the forward slopes of the Suanglangsu Vum which he had policed so effectively and for so long. Peter, since last I saw him at Tiddim on my return from leave in India, had himself had a spell out. Pru, his wife, bore his son months later. Nor did Peter live to know that his brilliant raid on Nansaungpu had won him the Military Cross. David Milligan too was gone. He had died gallantly during the withdrawal from Falam, and this time there was to be no 'resurrection'.

From David Cozens, in his southern solitude, came two runners to say that the Japs had not come so far and that his Levies were holding together. He added that he was out of rations, but that for so long as he could feed his force of a hundred men off the villages, he proposed to continue operating. In the event, he did so for over two months; and he was the only Levy officer not to leave the Hills at this time.

For our tedious but unthreatened trek from Tuipang to Lungleh (the equivalent in the Lushai Hills to Tiddim or Haka in the Chin Hills), we split into small parties so as not to overstrain the accommodation facilities in the intermediate villages. During my leisurely, bird-watching progress I studied with fascination the visitors' books in the village rest houses, most of which exuded history going back as far as the last century. The more of them one leafed through, the more the story of personalities emerged. Thus, during the First World War, the Resident of the Lushai Hills was revealed as a Colonel Shakespeare, who seldom seemed to tour without his wife. Of Mrs Shakespeare one derived a mental picture of an indomitable and exacting woman. A no less regular traveller was the Superintendent of Police, an officer named Macdonald.

Three things were clear. Firstly that Colonel Shakespeare was an ardent fisherman and his wife a domestic perfectionist. Secondly that Macdonald and Mrs Shakespeare shared a mutual antipathy for each other. Thirdly that Macdonald made a point of never occupying village accommodation with the Shakespeares: he was usually two or three days march behind them.

Typically, the rest house book would contain a catalogue of the Colonel's catch from the stream preceding the final climb to his night's lodging (thus—one Mahseer 60 lbs, one Mahseer 48 lbs, and so on). His lady's entry would be a criticism of some shortcoming in the domestic arrangements. Macdonald's subsequent contribution would be a counter-criticism of whatever Mrs Shakespeare had written. In one case Mrs Shakespeare had complained that the seat in the outside privy was too far off the floor and that the aperture was too small. Macdonald's immortal gift to poesy was:

> This must invite the obvious retort
> That your face is too large
> And your legs are too short.

What fun formal dinner parties in Headquarters must have been when both factions were present!

16 Jockeying for Position
January 1944 to August 1944

I had spent my thirtieth birthday exhausted and flat on my back at Tuipang. For Christmas we were at Lungleh, basking in the kindness we received from Hyde. In his company I felt, as I had done with Norman Kelly at Tiddim, that here was a man with a near-perfect peacetime job, though now, of course, things were different.

The qualifications for Hyde's service I assessed, in an hour of leisure, as, firstly, a wife who could adapt herself to the civilization of isolation without pining for the rat race of Civilization; secondly, a love of reading and music; thirdly, richness in hobbies—the scope for a painter or an ornithologist, for example, was limitless; fourthly, some talent for languages; fifthly, a pride in the people under your care; and finally (I suppose it should come higher) good health. In the main the Indian Civil Service chose its men extremely well; and, through such people, the record of Britain's one hundred and fifty years of administration of multitudinous Asians is one of which informed men cannot be other than proud. I would like to have been of their number.

We idled away our time in Lungleh while Corps laboriously assembled a conglomeration to be known as 'Barforce', having as its task a re-entry into the southern Chin Hills and the conduct of active operations in the Haka area. The composition of the force was the 1st Battalion of the Bihar Regiment, Frank O'Donel's Gurkha company of the Chin Hills Battalion, B.F.F. (now made up to full strength), various support units, and Levies 'up to limit air supply'.

The commander of the Bihars was a Devon man, Lieut.-Colonel J. R. S. Tweed, D.S.O., M.B.E., M.C. His second-in-command was a giant Pathan, Major Habibullah Khan. In a distant future my trail was to recross Habibullah's in his capacity of Chief of Staff to the Pakistan Army. The other officers were British and Indian wartime soldiers.

The Bihar Regiment had been formed, for political reasons, from one of the less martial races of India, for which cause there was some excess of prejudice against it. This was not alleviated later when troops of the renegade Subhas Chandra Bhose's 'Indian National Army' replaced the Japs in Haka, and incurred the hatred of the Chins by setting a standard of behaviour worse than that of the men they had relieved. Lest this itself should smack of prejudice, let me say of the hundreds of thousands of Indian *jawans* who remained true to their salt that, in my view, there never was a finer army.

John Tweed was a delightful character and an apt leader of a mixed force. He was also the most gifted water diviner I have ever known. He had been disturbed by the accidental discovery of his talent, for he had previously regarded such a thing as belonging to the realm of Mumbo Jumbo. He had therefore sought and studied the scientific explanation of the water diviner's metabolism and, having satisfied himself that there was nothing abnormal about it, had proceeded to the enjoyment of his fortuitous ability. Some years previously, as an officer of the Burma Rifles, he had been invited to Yenangyaung where, with some success, he had differentiated between oil and water bearing strata at shallow levels. That, in fact, is how I had first heard of him.

Hyde's bungalow boasted an immense lawn, beneath which ran a pipeline carrying water to Lungleh town. Hyde himself, alone of those present, knew its precise alignment. Jamie, Hayes, I myself and others fruitlessly tried our hands with the customary forked stick. Tweed, with an accuracy that Hyde could only describe as 'bang on', tracked the water flow without difficulty.

At last we got moving with my modest dispatch to Bungklang near the Chin Hills border. Hayes had already taken off to find what he could of the Falam and Tiddim elements of his command. Bungklang stood at the junction

237

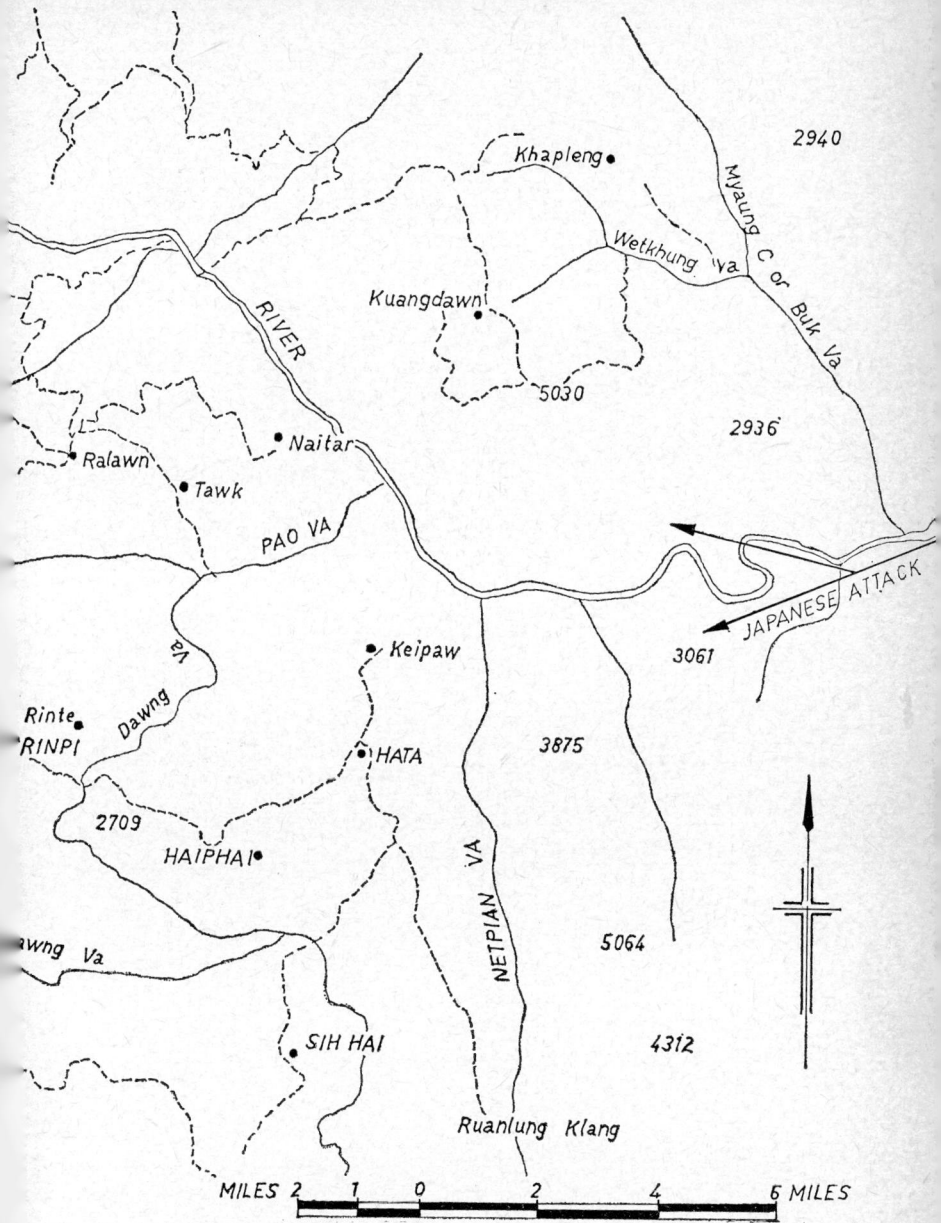

2940

Khapleng

Wetkhung Va

Myaung C or Buk Va

RIVER

Kuangdawn

5030

2936

Naitar

Ralawn

Tawk

PAO VA

JAPANESE ATTACK

3061

Va

Dawng

Keipaw

Rinte

RINPI

HATA

3875

2709

HAIPHAI

NETPIAN VA

5064

awng Va

SIH HAI

4312

Ruanlung Klang

MILES 2   1   0   2   4   6 MILES

CHIN LEVIES – HAKA ZONE – HATA SECTOR

239

of four tracks, two of which meandered in, northerly and southerly, from the Chin Hills. My task was to call in to me what I could of a nucleus of our Levies, and also to organize sufficient porterage to move Barforce forward.

While at Lungleh we had already established communication with the Levies lying low round Haka, and I started off at Bungklang with a small force which had trusted sufficiently in our intentions to make the westward trek to join us. Soon I was asking that Jamie, Dick Rees and Joe Byrne be sent out to join me, as a prelude to moving them forward with small parties that I felt sure would snowball into larger forces with each day's march. Ian Hillis, unfortunately, had gone out sick. Rationing was going to be our main problem, but we preferred to take the risk of having to signal back that we were resorting to partial disbandment for lack of rations rather than start off with an authorized strength that we might well find inadequate for our purpose.

At the beginning of January Dick Rees crossed back into the Chin Hills with about thirty Levies. His orders were to set up a base at Hriangkhan, midway between Klangklang and the Indian border; and then to establish a strong, mobile picket in the neighbourhood of Thlualam whence small reconnaissance patrols would investigate the state of the game in Haka. A few days later Jamie left to feel his way back into his old 'lease' in the Zokhua area, and Joe Byrne I sent off to operate towards Haka from Rees's north.

Joe has barely been introduced. He was a Shan who, having been orphaned as an infant, had been adopted and educated by an Irish Civil Servant and his wife, whose name he had taken. Joe was a tough little warrior and an excellent companion who, after a session of *zu*, could always be counted on to sing with fervour the song about the little fishes who 'swam and they swam all over the dam'. There's a man I'd like to meet again.

Both Joe and Dick Rees had been briefed in regard to persistent reports we were receiving that the Japs were holding a British prisoner in Haka. If he existed, it was no one that we could account for, and none was ever found.

The Bihars arrived at Bungklang a day or two after I had

completed my thinning-out there. I waited long enough to get Tweed's views on future operations and then took off for Thlualam to base myself with Rees. Travelling with me was Gilbert Turnbull who was relieving Joshua Poo Nyo as Assistant Superintendent of the Haka sub-Division. I saw a lot of Gilbert in the weeks that followed. He was a man full of energy and dedication to his task. His experience of hill tribes elsewhere soon put him *en rapport* with the Chins, and he made a welcome marching companion.

At this same time, the elderly Naylor had been relieved as Superintendent, Falam, by Noel Stevenson, whom I had previously known. Stevenson, from very early on, had been one of the most forceful champions of the raising and training of Levies in the Burma hill tracts. He was a man of considerable personal courage, and in his ideas was radical, unorthodox and spectacular. His theories had great potential and, in the right 'climate', would have been successful in practice. Unfortunately, Stevenson himself was possessed of a volatility of self-expression that rang up 'no sale' when it came to preaching to the unconverted in high places. Accordingly he went his way frustrated and a nuisance to others.

By the time we reached Thlualam there was that in the wind to show that the Chin Hills had been moved up the priority list by quite a few notches. We were able to call on the air dropping service to an extent that we had never yet approached: in fact we were almost totally rationed by this means from now on.

Typically what was required of us, once a drop had been arranged for a given date and location, was to clear a ridge top for about a hundred yards or so, or make use of an existing *taung-ya* if one were suitably located; and then to display prominently a white X at the approach end and a T at the departure end of the strip, using parachute cloth for the purpose. An hour or two before the arrival of the dropping Dakota, we would be instructed to place two identifying letters near the centre of the strip.

The aircraft would arrive, circle the dropping zone once or twice in order to establish any possible navigational hazards, and to verify our bona fides, and then proceed to drop. Down first would come the 'free' drop, bags of rice and *atta*; then would follow the parachute loads—perishable edibles, ammunition and equipment and, by all that's merciful, rum. A wave from the crew through the dropping doors, and the aircraft would head westward with our blessings. We knew these boys as 'Manna'.

Needless to say, top priority in this welcome treatment had to be given to David Cozens, who was still holding his Levies together down at Lungngo. He got his first drop early in January.

Gilbert Turnbull was soon faced with a rationing problem of another order. Levies from the Haka area were rejoining us in considerable numbers, but many of them were bringing their families with them. This created a situation beyond our scope, and ultimately we moved Corps to enlist the help of the Lushai Hills authorities by establishing a refugee camp across the Indian border whither we sent our horde of non-combatants. The effect on the morale of the Levies was wonderful, and we soon had something like three hundred and fifty men in the Sectors that semi-circled Haka.

Militarily our orders were:

Barforce general plan as follows. Jap defensive positions will not be attacked. Ops will be conducted against L of C with object forcing Japs come out to attack us and ambushing them when they do so.

In mid-January I received a somewhat delayed report to the effect that a Jap force had left Haka southward in search of Cozens. With little hope of reaching him in time, I nevertheless sent runners off to warn him. Fortunately David independently had received timely news of the same move and, after a two and a half days chase, he caught and ambushed a Jap patrol as they were wading across the Boinu River. His signal reads:

. . . ambushed patrol of ten Japs and one Chin interpreter near Phaipha Khuathar PC 7917. Jap casualties one officer eight OR's killed one escaped. Chin interpreter wounded. Own casualties nil. All Jap bodies and full identifications recovered. Booty includes one MG one mortar with bombs one revolver seven rifles plus grenades ammo papers . . .

This was levy warfare as it should be, and the news acted like a tonic on the rest of us.

I was ordered to send the arms and identifications to Divisional H.Q. at Tiddim, where their delivery coincided with the arrival of Lord Louis Mountbatten, the Allied Supreme Commander, South East Asia. Lord Louis witnessed a demonstration under firing conditions of the machine gun and the mortar included in the haul, but I was told later that no credit was given to the Levies for their capture. Here was a minor example of the professional self-seeking that seemed so often to scar the business of winning the war.

Hayes himself, unfortunately, was not helping matters. He had taken off, first to Tiddim, and then to Corps H.Q. at Imphal where, apparently, he had infuriated everyone by arguing a role for the Levies in the Tiddim Zone that took no account of the fact that a division of regular troops was now in the field. I think he was haunted by fear of the possible dissolution of his fortuitously acquired command.

My attempts to keep in touch with Hayes, by addressing coded sitreps to him via Stevenson's Civil radio, were squelched by a strongly-worded request from the latter to pipe down, followed by a sarcastic comment on Hayes's prolonged absence. So, in liaison with Tweed, I was left to get on with it. This suited me admirably, for Tweed was a man without preconceived ideas and easy to work with.

In addition to Ian Hillis, who had been a non-starter in our return, both Rathbone and Smythe had been evacuated sick, leaving us very thin on the ground for all that was required of us. One of my signals read:

... If any truth rumour officers for Levies now learning Burmese Imphal can you get this formality waived and officers sent through without delay.

Remembering the many months of slogging that had led me to a minimum competence in the speaking and understanding of Burmese, it seemed a curious prelude to a posting to a Chin-speaking area, but I was no longer easily surprised.

One event occurred that cheered me no end. We had frequent patrols keeping Haka under observation, but one I sent out with strict instructions to get into the town by night and find out everything they could about the strength of the enemy and where they were sleeping. The patrol leader carried out his mission to the letter but must have had doubts about my believing his subsequent report. Imagine my delight, therefore, when he and his men returned to my camp bearing as evidence of a mission accomplished my gramophone and six unbroken records and the ruins of my leather writing case!

The case, a present from a family friend when I first sailed for Burma, had been with me throughout until I was forced to abandon it in Haka. Finding it locked, the Japs had slashed off the corners sufficiently to make it possible to extract the contents. The ultimate bill for repairing it, as I was forewarned in the shop in Calcutta where I got the job done, was about three times the cost of a new case. That, I explained, did not affect the issue, and I have it in use today.

The wintry conditions in which we were operating now were a terrible strain. I wrote home:

The last day of January provided an experience I shan't forget—an eighteen mile march along ridge tops in intense cold made really hellish by driving wind and icy rain. Never in my life have I known what cold is until now. Though we kept moving the whole time, one of my party died, another nearly went the same way and I should say I was about third! I had to have my clothes peeled off me.

Not surprisingly I was getting recurrent bouts of my old Indaw malaria, and again I was shot through with worms. In February I was writing:

I've had a miserable week, my cold having turned into a sort of 'flu which I haven't yet been able to shake off. I'm now admitting myself beaten and am lying up in the jungle for a few days to give myself a chance. I'm also getting toothache again. Luckily I've got a good medical outfit, so it's just a matter of combining the duties of doctor and patient for a few days and I shall be all right.

I was still receiving in very irregular batches *The Times* from London and *The Statesman* from Calcutta. They were invaluable for more than the reading they provided. I always had a reserve of crossword puzzles for periods of sickness, while the exchange value of the sheets as cigarette paper I have already described.

One day I received a letter from Billy Rivers. Many years previously he had been a recruiting officer in the Chin Hills, and some of the older men who remembered him knew me by this time as his kinsman. That same evening one of his old friends, now a 'B' Levy, wandered into my camp. I showed him the letter, told him whence it came, and invited him to write something to Rivers *bawi-pa* for enclosure with my reply. The old boy was tickled at the idea and laboriously scratched out a message of greeting, which Billy would have had no trouble in reading, for he was fluent in Haka Chin. Perhaps the censor was not!

In March, during what looked like a settled lull, I made the long southward trek to visit David Cozens. I had to plan mostly for double marches, and even so would have time to spend only two days with David in a round trip of twelve days. I took with me what had now become my permanent, personal section of twelve men. We travelled as nearly transport-free as we could. It was a rewarding pilgrimage from the propaganda point of view if nothing else. Each night's stop was at a village *en fete* in our honour. We drank *zu* until the small hours, a behavioural pattern that added mightily to the burden of each day's march—particularly when beset already with occasional bouts of fever.

At last we reached the Sector H.Q. near Lungngo, and a gaunt, unsmiling character came out to meet me and introduced himself as Cozens. There must surely have been some echo of Stanley's meeting with Livingston about the encounter. I don't know how long it had been since David had spoken English. Jamie had been his last visitor months ago. David's attitude during our first few minutes together was something between suspicion and embarrassment. His Levies, of course, revered him as the only *bawi-pa* who had stayed with his men during our recent reverses, though, apart from his spectacular killing on the Boinu, he had been able to contribute little beyond invaluable intelligence.

David was a man of tremendous self-containment. It was this alone that explained his ability to exchange the city lights for the stark loneliness of a remote jungle in the way he did. He loved what he was doing and was resolved, when the war ended, to resign from the B.O.C. and qualify for the Burma Frontier Service. In the event, post-war Burma elected to go her own way and David never got his chance. He did make, however, a sentimental peacetime journey to revisit his old friends among the Lungngo Levies before the mists of Burmese Nationalism came down and laid their dankness on the Hills.

We had much to talk about. The Levies and the local headmen threw the inevitable celebration, and the atmosphere boded ill for any further Jap patrols that might venture their way. It was one of those occasions when I too rejoiced in the job I was doing.

I left David with a selection of reading matter and some minor amenities and set off northward again. I was feeling far from fit, and the daily alternations of climb and descent—frequently twice over—were becoming harder and harder to take. For the first time, I think, I was having to lighten my load by distribution among the others, willing helpers though they were. At least when I got back to my H.Q. camp it was to find that the Levies had been at work improving my lot, and I now had a comfortable couch to sleep on.

The news was very bad. The Japanese offensive against Imphal, which had seemed stalled at the time of my departure, was now in full swing. They had driven 17 Div. out of the Hills and were in occupation of Tiddim. Most unfortunately, a group of Haka chiefs, who had been invited to Tiddim for a propaganda view of Allied armed might, arrived back in their own area just in time to hear that the town had been lost. Morale dropped badly, and many of the Levies were asking us if we thought we should have to leave them again. Stoutly we denied any such intention, and some of us at least meant what we said.

I was doing worse and worse, and soon found myself incapacitated by illness that roused me vomiting in the morning and had me paralyzed from the hips down by mid-day. These symptoms worked themselves out after about two weeks, but I was left feeling desperately weak and depressed. It was mighty hard to act the part of a leader poised for retribution! Apparently I had been suffering from a form of typhus, and a week or two later I was writing home:

I've just had a visit from a Doctor of well above the average standard of M.O.s in these parts and he has left me some Santonin which, apparently, is the dope for worms: so if there are any left they'd better make the best of the time left to them. Incidentally he was intensely interested in the symptoms of paralysis of the legs combined with sickness, fever and giddiness which I was having a month ago. He says that, despite the fact that it has not been recorded since the last War, he is convinced that it was 'trench fever' and he is writing me up as a freak case to the Army medical authorities! I suggested that my leave be doubled so that I could go on a lecture tour of hospitals, but he didn't hold out much hope of that!

It was not long before the Japs in and around Haka started to thin out. They were meeting their Waterloo at Imphal and Kohima and were having to throw in there every man they could round up. To a very large extent they were being replaced in the Chin Hills by Indians of Subhas Chandra Bhose's 'Indian National Army' (the I.N.A.).

Bhose at that time, of course, was universally scorned as a traitor to the Allied cause. He inevitably became that by the path he followed, but many Asian and some American historians see him now only as a selfless patriot dedicated to the cause of '*Jai Hind*'—Free India. His final place in posterity's annals, in fact, is not yet discernible. He himself died in an air crash before the war ended, but even after India attained Independence his fellow-countrymen were still arraigning at minor Nuremburgs the military officers who had followed him. The mantle of patriotic martyrdom is still withheld by many of his people. Had Japan won the war, of course, it would probably have been a case of

> Treason doth never prosper, what's the reason?
> If it doth prosper, none dare call it treason.

Whatever the truth about Bhose, there is little to be said of dedication or selflessness about the bulk of the Indians he led. The greater part of them comprised a minority of those who had been captured in Malaya or in Singapore: they had accepted service in the I.N.A. as an alternative to the rigours of continuing captivity. Among their ranks were three elements of, I would judge, roughly equal representation. Firstly, there were those who shared Bhose's belief in the rightness of what they were doing. Secondly, there was the badmash element—freebooters attracted by the open door to loot and rape. Thirdly, there were those who saw in feigned enlistment a golden opportunity to escape and get back to their regiments.

The situation had an extraordinary implication. Since becoming enemy-occupied, Burma had declared herself belligerent on the side of the Japanese. So here were the likes of myself, leading forces of a country (Burma) that was at war with Britain against the soldiers of another (India) that was allied with her!

The badmash element of the I.N.A. incurred for all their fellows the bitter hatred of the Chins. The Japs, for all their unpleasant ways, pursued at least a nominal policy of representing themselves as liberators. The I.N.A. displayed no such inhibitions: they were high-handed, brutal and lascivious—a fact which involved us in much preaching of restraint in all cases where Indians were encountered singly or in small parties under circumstances possibly indicative of loyal men seeking escape.

The lesson generally was well taken, and we had some amusing incidents. On one occasion a Dogra section found themselves detailed for night duty at a machine gun post the I.N.A. were maintaining on the ridge that overlooked Haka. It was the chance they had been waiting for. After dismantling the machine gun and scattering the parts, they skirted Haka and set off westwards, still with their rifles.

Soon after daybreak they were spotted by one of my patrols commanded by an Urdu-speaking Burma Rifles havildar. The Dogras laid down their arms immediately they were challenged. Their N.C.O. explained to mine that they had been imprisoned at Singapore, and during captivity had attended lectures by Indian officers who sought to persuade them to join the I.N.A. They had not been convinced but, after a common oath sworn in secrecy, had decided to join and escape when they could. Now here they were.

Under escort on the way to my camp, the Dogra naik asked the havildar if he would halt the march to permit of his making a request. Guardedly the Levy acceded. The Dogra then pointed to the rifles that had been taken off his men and asked if the bolts might be removed and the rifles returned to them. He and his men were soon to be paraded before the havildar's officer, and they wished him to see that their discipline was not broken. I have always been glad that my N.C.O. gave credit for a soldierly request and complied.

He had his prisoners well but not too blatantly covered as they marched up to where I was standing. They were dirty and tattered but advanced smartly to their N.C.O.s shouted step. They halted, formed up and ordered arms. The Naik stepped smartly up to me, slapped his rifle butt in salute and reported his section's return to duty.

I knew enough to believe that a lean time lay ahead for these men. I certainly had gone through the motions of taking them at their face value. For all I could tell they might have been despising me for being taken for a chump so readily! The wheat took a lot of separating from the chaff in cases of this sort, and it could take weeks or months of questioning in detention before such men were cleared as loyal or trapped into giving themselves away. That, however, was someone else's task. Nevertheless, as they were escorted rearward next morning, I watched the Dogras go with a feeling of sympathy. Peasants turned soldier they may have been, but I was pretty sure that they were gentlemen of their word.

The Bihars by now were operating in close support of the Levies in the Haka area. I met some pretty good N.C.O.s amongst them—men keen to start establishing something in the way of the regimental tradition they yet were lacking. I think the Levies might have taken to them more kindly had the Jap alone been the common enemy, but in the circumstances there was disdain and occasional friction.

I now started to receive some replacement officers. They

were mostly youngsters out from home, but there was a nugget amongst them in the person of George Wilson!

There was nothing accidental here. After I had seen George off at Mergui, he had been sent to England. As soon as he was commissioned (or rather, recommissioned) he applied for the Indian Army and came out as a Gurkha. I had met him in Calcutta when I went out on leave from Tiddim, and it was then that we had set in train the various applications that at last had borne fruit.

While in Calcutta I had introduced George to my kinsfolk, the Mitchells, who had been doing much for me since I entered the Hills by sending through small parcels of tobacco, toothpaste and other comforts. On his way to join me now, George had called on the Mitchells, and Thomas had unloaded onto him four bottles of gin for delivery to me. Manfully George had accepted the additional burden and, on handing the bottles over, he only claimed one as his commission!

Nowhere could I have found a more appreciative listener to the tale of my recovered gramophone; and soon, with gin gently swilling in our mugs and Ludwig van Beethoven casting his spell upon the mountain air, we were back where we came in.

George left next day, ultimately to take over Jamie's Sector, as the latter was due to stand in for me while I went out on leave. As I watched George swing off on his way, I saw in him that indefinable something that stamps the man who is no stranger to jungle living. My pre-war memories of his military perspicacity had been freshened by the overall appreciation of the war situation to which I had been treated after Beethoven had bowed out the previous night. How fitting it would have been had George arrived to relieve Hayes instead of, incongruously, to take station under me!

Continuing sickness was impairing my judgement, and each new threat to my getting away on leave used to plunge me into the depths of depression. When one of my newly arrived officers accidentally shot himself through the shoulder (I was beside him at the time), I was sorely tempted to kick his backside before dealing with him medically. I wrote home that night.

I'm waiting to hear now whether I am to get away or not. It's the very devil. Among the thousands of 'chairborne troops' in India there are hundreds who *could* relieve chaps out here, but, of course, it would mean no punkahs and no cold drinks—and that's a hell of a price to pay.

Next week it was:

This week I celebrated the 10th anniversary of my arrival in Burma, and it's over 5 years since my one and only leave. I wish Grigg would stop mouthing in Parliament about all men with over five years service being on the way Home. It makes me rather mad. But I get madder still at some of the correspondence in the 14th Army newspaper. The number of men who seem to think they have the right to be repatriated before the Jap has been beaten is truly astonishing.

Another thing. Some of the 'hardships' that receive the eulogy of the Press really don't compare with some of the difficulties that people here have learnt to take in their stride. If all this self-pity could be turned into Jap-hatred we'd start getting somewhere.

Noting now, as I must, that I was not exactly short of self-pity myself, and regretful of the ill-humour that the extract throws up, I think it serves, nevertheless, to show the moods that assailed me when there was no one to whom I could let off steam.

Personal hygiene posed interesting problems.

No more malaria. I've kept fit all the week. My worst problem these days is personal hygiene, and I shall have to get myself thoroughly deloused before I enter any private houses in India. I've just had a blitz against my clothing and bedding by boiling everything that could be crammed into a 4-gallon petrol drum. Unfortunately I no longer have soap to spare for washing clothes, so my underwear remains a uniform shade of battleship grey no matter whether it has just had a wash or is in need of one. What a life! What a hell of a life!!

And again:

I'm having another go of scabies. I'm glad to see that Medical science no longer attributes this to failure to wash, but puts it down to a bug. Nevertheless, it's an unpleasant thing to go on leave with, and I'm lathering myself with sulphur ointment for all its worth—to the detriment, needless to say, of what's left of my clothes.

Came the day, and I handed over Haka Zone command to Jamie, who himself would be coming out on leave on my return. Jamie had had his fill of Hayes, even under conditions of remote control, and I think he had already decided to put in for another posting, which he in fact secured.

I started on my twelve marches to Demagiri on the Karnaphuli River, which would take me into India via Chittagong. For some days I had for company an Indian Flying Officer, whose Hurricane had packed up on him while he was escorting a ration drop. His baling out had been observed, and he was located and brought in by Levies with little delay.

He was luckier than others, particularly those who baled out or crashlanded in the Kabaw/Kale/Gangaw Valley or beyond, of whom we rescued about six. The R.A.F. itself was at fault here through erroneous briefing of pilots who might have to make their way out on foot.

In the Chin—and other—hill tracts life moves along the ridge tops, few of which can be crossed without cutting an inter-village track. Yet the briefing stressed only the frequency with which streams entered the Myittha from the Chin Hills. Follow any one of these and return to India must surely be the end result.

I remember the case of a chap called McGregor, when I was operating in the Tiddim Zone. He crashlanded his damaged fighter in the Kale Valley under observation by a brother pilot who saw him leave the wreckage, wave his thanks and head for the Hills. I got the news and moved off with three or four patrols to search for him, added to which all village headmen in the area were instructed to send out parties of 'B' Levies to look for a British officer.

It took us six days to find McGregor, and then only because, exhausted and bleeding, he had climbed to a ridge top to get away from the leeches which were bidding fair to kill him at *chaung* level. His feet were like raw steaks because he had taken off in a 'scramble' in soft shoes instead of flying boots and they had by now been ripped to ribbons. He was hauling himself along on a stick, a picture of agony. When I produced a tin of bully beef from my pack, his reaction was such that I thought he was going to dispense with the preliminary of removing the container.

McGregor's ordeal had been needless, but I received no response to a recommendation I made that the next Levy officer out on leave should visit the relevant R.A.F. stations for the purpose of disseminating a few home truths.

The Americans' problem was different but equally of their own making. A Super Fortress had received extensive damage while bombing Rangoon. As it limped homeward, losing height, the crew jettisoned everything they could in an effort to lighten the aircraft and, by the time it crash-landed in the Gangaw Valley, six of the crew of eight had themselves baled out in pairs. The survivors, the pilot and another, were likewise reported as having left the aircraft and headed for the Hills in the area of Jamie's Zokhua Sector.

Jamie got his rescue drill moving, and within a day or two received word that the two men had been found and were being escorted to his Sector H.Q. Like the rest of us, Jamie had got used to two square meals a day—curry and rice at noon, and curry and rice at sundown. On this occasion, with two hungry Allied guests in prospect, he threw into the pot every embellishment that he could dream up.

On the arrival of the Americans, Jamie dispensed rum and other necessary medicaments and then ordered the Levies to serve up his *magnum opus*. To his disbelief, his guests apologetically excused themselves from participation on the grounds that their orders in regard to the consumption of 'native' food were of the strictest. Before Jamie's incredulous gaze, the Americans then opened two little boxes and dined on pills! At least they had the delicacy not to invite the shocked Jamie to join them!

On arrival at Demagiri, I found the place militarily in the charge of Ian Scott, late of Steels, as transit officer. Ian and I had been fellow-inmates of 'Merry Helenside' on my first arrival in Rangoon ten years earlier. I hadn't seen him for a long time as he had left Steels before the war and disappeared from my ken. We had a convivial evening together, and in the morning I boarded a launch that would take me to Chittagong *en route* to Calcutta. It was the last week of August 1944.

17 Counter-Offensive
August 1944 to February 1945

As on the previous occasion, leave in India had as its base a procession that led in and out of dentists' chairs, doctors' examination theatres and private bathrooms, where one subjected oneself to nauseatingly intimate procedures in the cause of dispelling bacillary dysentery, scabies and worms within the allotted span of four weeks. For good measure, Steels showed sufficient interest in the prospective post-war return of my body as to submit me to a top-to-toe 'medical' on their own account!

Steels, in exile from Burma, had established their Eastern Head Office in Calcutta. Sir John Tait had but recently retired as General Manager, and I enjoyed on more than one occasion the hospitality of his successor, Percy Salkeld. Both men earned the gratitude of us all for the painstaking manner in which they passed on to the London Office any news of staff on service that came their way. On two or three occasions my own people answered the phone to a reassuring passage of information that otherwise they might not have received for weeks.

While in Calcutta I stayed variously with Ben Braund, desperately overworked as Chairman of the Royal Commission inquiring into the Bengal famine of the year before, and with Kathleen and Thomas Mitchell, my benefactors aforesaid. My brother Jim was still in Madras and, when I joined him there, I was most kindly accommodated by the Berringtons, whose son-in-law, Glen Gaudie (of Steels), was then serving with the Chin Hills Battalion, Burma Frontier Force, somewhere west of Falam. My only regret was that I brought no recent news of him.

I found, as I had done a year previously, that there was a keen 'market' for my Burmese-speaking services, and that a transfer from the Chin Levies presented no problem. Indeed, I was medically advised against returning to the Hills. So why should I? Though, unaccountably perhaps, I liked Hayes personally and got on with him well, I still deplored his lack of talent for this particular task; and if I joined others who already were seeking means of avoiding further service under him, perhaps good would result.

I couldn't do it. I recalled a discussion I had had with my own Levies after the fall of Tiddim. More in sorrow than in anger they had suggested that I would soon find it politic to duck out from under again. I had sworn that I would go to ground with them, even if in defiance of orders. Without intended blasphemy, it would seem too much like a case of 'before the cock crow twice' were I not to go back.

I returned to the Hills, in reverse, by the same route as I had followed to get myself out. At Chittagong, Steels Manager was Bill Morrison, to whose serious illness in 1937 I had owed my colourful interlude at Thayetmyo as Acting Manager of the Burma Cement Company. Bill was one of those who was older than myself by the narrow margin that dictated whether you were put into uniform or toiled the war through doing the civilian work of three. In Bill's case this was a regrettable dividing line, as he was a tough and redoubtable character. After a shared bottle of whisky he was about ready to purloin a uniform and join me on the trek that lay ahead.

Next morning I 'launched' my way up to Demagiri and took once more to my feet. With two or three marches behind me, I had cast myself down for a rest after a climb of nearly six thousand feet. Within minutes an equally exhausted Lushai mail runner joined me and, with that lack of embarrassment that had come to mean so much, he dumped his bundle and sat down beside me. I assumed that his mails were destined for Lungleh, but when he said that his bag was to go through to Haka I sat up and got to work.

The first letter that I found addressed to myself was from Maxine Strong! While on leave I had renewed my efforts to find out what had happened to her. I had darkened the doors of American Consulates and banks, but there must have been that in my personal appearance that suggested irrelevance to the American way of life. I had certainly drawn blank all along the line.

Now, here was her handwriting! Furthermore, she was writing from England whither, as a member of the American Red Cross, she had been posted in a recreational capacity, her task being to organize concerts, clubs and so forth for large bodies of bored G.I.s awaiting the launching of the Second Front. After her walkout from Burma she had returned to the States as a refugee, and had then worked for a year in a factory making bomb sights near New York. She had become disgusted with the complacency that surrounded her and had applied for and been accepted by the A.R.C. for overseas service. Now she was in England! I hoped that she might still be there if ever I got the chance of home leave.

Militarily, October of 1944 brought not merely the end of one more rainy season, but the Fourteenth Army's counter-offensive as an established fact. At Imphal/Kohima —*pacé* American opinion—the Japanese sword had been broken in the biggest and most crucial land battle of the Far Eastern war, and the Japs were now in retreat all along their Indian front.

The Levies I found to be moving eastward at a speed that made of my return from leave a pursuit! By the time I caught up, they were already in reoccupation of Falam and Haka. Both places had been evacuated virtually without a fight, but the I.N.A. suffered many casualties by ambush and in small-scale battles before they extricated themselves from the Hills. No prisoners were taken. The Falam Levies lost one British officer killed. I had not known him.

To set the seal on the eviction of the enemy from the Chin Hills, the Haka Levies were now given the promising task of harrying them in the southern end of the Gangaw Valley which, via Tilin and thence Pakokku on the Irrawaddy, was one of their certain escape routes.

We were formed into three columns of about two hundred

men each, commanded, north to south, by Wilson, Rees and Cozens, each of whom by this time had the help of recently arrived junior officers. I was to be independent with my section of twelve on a roving commission that I hoped would enable me to see something of everyone.

My immediate problem was transport. Villagers who two years ago had willingly humped bags of rice into the Hills could not so readily be counted on to return to the Valley as porters to a para-military adventure. I had about seventy pack ponies which I distributed among the columns as best I could. I then set off in search of elephants.

Our Intelligence consistently had included reports of the Japs making use of *Bombine* elephants along the whole line of the Valley. If they could do it we could, though I feared that most of the beasts would be in poor shape by now. With Jamie's departure, my brother-officers no longer included a teak wallah and there was little enthusiasm among them for a proposition that they regarded as unrealistic. However, my earlier experience of elephants persuaded me that the thing was worth a try.

I marched with George Wilson's column, which was headed for the area of Gangaw. Within no time at all of our arrival in the margin of the Valley, his patrols reported a small Jap supply column moving north with elephant transport. The escorting troops were effectively ambushed, and we left-wheeled the three elephants up the jungle track by which we had come down. The *singaung*, the *oozies* and the *peijeiks* all came with their beasts and, after a brief period of apprehensive panic, there was no concealing their delight at their 'capture'—in fact the *singaung*, with a small Levy escort, slipped away into the jungle and returned within an hour or two with three more elephants, the remainder of his charge, and their followers. Thus far I had proved my point pretty dramatically!

There were obvious risks inherent in the absorption of Burmans into our force, and I think that some of the Chins at least were doubtful of my good sense. However, after a long talk with the *singaung*, who was obviously a man of the old school, I was convinced not only of his own integrity but that he spoke for all of his men, who were in fact a team of some years standing. The *singaung* expressed shame at having been caught carrying for the Japs, but perked up when I told him that his first responsibility had been to his elephants, and that if service to the Japs had been necessary in the cause of keeping them fit and fat, he had done the right thing.

I did not immediately realize it, but my automatic use of the words *ma de wa de* (fit and fat) had told the old *singaung* that I was no stranger to the working elephant. Next day, in the upstream clearing that I had allotted to the elephants, there was much scrubbing and sluicing of hides and cleaning of chains and harness. I was asked to inspect and, having done so, was offered the individual log books for entry.

To the *singaung* I said:

'*Singaung gyi*, why do you ask me to do this? If the Japs return and drive me away, there will be much trouble for you all when they find that I have signed these books.'

The old man replied:

'*Thakin*, we have had much trouble already: but we have heard that in India the *Asoya* have defeated the Japanese in a big battle and that now the Japanese are running away. We know now that they are finished.'

'*Singaung gyi*,' I pursued, 'I am not of the *Bombine*, nor am I a *Thit Bo-gyi*. Is it right that I should sign?'

'*Thakin*, you speak Burmese: you understand about elephants. It is enough.'

'*Singaung gyi*, if I sign there is one thing that you all must understand. It will be a contract between us that you serve me and that I look after you. You will become not-fighting Levies. I will pay and feed you for your service, but you all must accept my orders as soldiers do. Go now, and when you are ready to tell me what your men have to say, come back to me here.'

After a huddled *pyaw zaya* under the trees, the *singaung* returned.

'*Thakin*, we are all of one mind. Please sign the books.'

I had anticipated the outcome, and during the period of waiting had mentally composed an entry, which I now wrote into each of the six books. It read

> That you are back, my Bombay-Burmah master,
> Is not the reason for the pride I feel;
> For though I bear your brand upon my backside,
> I'm *ma de wa de* by the grace of Steel.

The *singaung* was somewhat puzzled by this lengthy entry, though the *ma de wa de* was in Burmese characters. I explained that I knew a lot of *Bombine Thakins,* and that my entry was no more than a fraternal greeting in conditions where letter writing was not practicable!

The jungle telegraph did the rest. Within a week or two, somewhat to my embarrassment, I had forty elephants, all fit and equipped for work. In some cases *oozies* had been carrying for the Japs when the word reached them. They gave them the slip by night and joined us deviously. There were, I knew, those who thought me a fool for inviting betrayal. I rested my case on the human quality of the *singaungs*; old and trusted *Bombine* servants, known to each other for years, they were in fact a guild and would not have brooked the presence of a Judas.

The bond between man and beast can be a wonderful thing. Here were these professional elephant men, dependent for years on an organization—in this case the *Bombine*—for the provision of gear, medicaments, rations and a programme of work for their charges. Came a day when everything crumbled and disappeared. Since then life had become a day-to-day problem of increasing complexity. The Japs had grossly over-worked elephants, and blamed their resultant exhaustion or death on *singaungs* accused of working for the British. The *singaungs* themselves had had to bear the problems of fodder and physic. The implications are endless. Yet two years later, here they were, the Burmese cheerfulness seemingly unimpaired, and the elephants fit and fat or reasonably near it.

I left George Wilson with a suitable reserve of elephants for his base transport requirements and for the clearing of air drops, and moved off south with the rest to find Dick Rees. Lest it be thought that the succour of elephants had now become our main concern, I had best draw again on my contemporary report to G.H.Q. for the broader perspective.

The nature of the country and the general conditions under which we now had to operate were very different from those of the Hills. In the flat *indaing* jungle of the valley I soon found to my surprise that the Chin's sense of direction which had guided us in the Hills was not an instinctive bump of locality, but merely a matter of visual recognition of familiar land-marks viewed from high ground. In the valley where, except in the immediate neighbourhood of the villages, there was little such visibility, Levy patrols began losing themselves in a most disconcerting manner and to a great extent we were forced to abandon our policy of small and numerous patrols in favour of patrols in strength under an Officer with a compass.

Nevertheless, some of these were conspicuously successful, notably a raid by George Wilson with a force of a hundred men on a Japanese supply dump some twelve miles in rear of their positions at Gangaw, which at this time they were strenuously defending. Wilson got his large force across the Myittha River and through the jungle to the dump, which was a large one comprising bags of rice, crates of biscuits and tinned fish, ordnance stores of all kinds and a godown full of nothing but ammunition of every calibre the Japs were using on this front. A platoon of Japs guarding the dump was driven off with the loss of four killed and at least two wounded, and by the time they ineffectually counter-attacked every building was blazing. Wilson got his force back intact, he himself resembling a Christmas tree, with samples of just about everything the dump had contained slung about his person, in addition to the identifications from the dead Japs.

Over fifty miles further south Cozens was also achieving results. The small town of Tilin was evacuated by a garrison of about five hundred Japs on Christmas Eve after they had burnt large dumps of their stores. Cozens got into the place before dawn on Christmas morning in time to catch a small rear party in the Post and Telegraph Office. He surprised and drove them out, and the identifications he recovered from two dead were, we learnt later, of the greatest value. Cozens withdrew his force from Tilin after the action, and the town was then reoccupied by a company of about two hundred Japs until it was captured by Fourteenth Army at the end of January.

At about the same time, Rees in the Minywa area midway between Cozens and Wilson, had the unpleasant experience of being attacked while a plane was actually dropping supplies to him. The crew apparently did not see the bursts of the mortar bombs, so that until the sortie was complete and the rations dragged away to safety Rees had to continue the action in conditions unfavourable to himself. Fortunately the attacking force was not a large one, and Rees got away with it for the loss of only one Levy killed.

Having spent Christmas with George Wilson, my south-ward trek continued to Dick Rees's camp in thick jungle within six miles of the main Valley road near Minywa. Here we were joined by Colonel Hayes for a couple of days, our first sight of him for many moons! He was in time to participate in a New Year supply drop that included whisky, sherry, beer and live poultry. Changed times indeed!

Dick was anxious to get his force moved further south in order to be able to operate in conjunction with David Cozens against the Tilin area, as it was hereabouts that the Japs could be expected to make a stand if they still had the means and the will to do so. Transport had been Dick's problem but, with the arrival of elephants, a move became possible. I decided to tack myself on to Dick's column, as my next move was to see David Cozens anyway to deliver his share of the elephants.

Our first march involved a tricky crossing of the Myittha River near the point where its eastward tumble from the Chin Hills becomes a northward meander down the Gangaw Valley. The ford was about eighty feet wide, the water fast-flowing and armpit deep to a Chin. The elephants we sent across loaded and strongly escorted to wait for us in the jungle. The ponies had to be unloaded before they could be driven to make the crossing. A rope tautly stretched across the river provided purchase for fifty or sixty braced backs, while the broken-down loads were laboriously passed from hand to hand—with here and there a mishap as a foot slipped and man and load went down and had to be rescued.

During this conspicuous passage of the crossing, a pair of Hurricanes flew over us, their subsequent manoeuvre showing that the pilots had seen us. My mind, leaping to an attempted reading of theirs, identified my force as Japanese retreating southward clear of the perils of the Valley road six miles to my east.

The Hurricanes were now some miles away, coming down one behind the other with the valley of the river as the axis of their approach. Their intention was obvious.

Downstream, twenty yards from the rope, a large boulder reared out of the river, creamily cleaving the race of the waters. I ducked under the rope and flung myself towards the rock. I clashed violently and painfully with it but, as one with the encounter, dragged myself asprawl over its summit. I heaved myself to my feet, with the fighters now within a mile or so and at little above tree-top level. I dragged myself out of my sodden, clinging shirt, raised my arms above my head in a wide 'V' and prayed that my torso might be larger and whiter than life.

The Hurricanes went over with a roar that shook the valley, and the human chain of Chins, just now waking to the implication, started to break for the banks. I shouted them back to their positions if they valued their lives, being certain that the pilots, startled into staying their hands on the first run, would come back for a second look. This they surely did, but my renewed waving reflected, I believe, something more confidently casual than the panic of my original antics. Anyway, the visitors sheered off.

The laborious and interrupted crossing of the Myittha had considerably shortened our day, and I camped the whole force for the night at the top of the climb that followed the crossing.

During the day's march my mind had been busy establishing a 'drill' governing the use of elephant transport in enemy-dominated territory. Beyond his magnificent contribution to the load-carrying problem, the elephant was clearly a liability all along the line.

Firstly, the elephant has completed an honest day's work before any other element of the column. Therefore he is a brake on mobility.

Secondly, the elephant is crewed by Burmans (i.e. not by Chins) as fortuitously recruited as the elephants themselves. Therefore there is a security risk.

Thirdly, the elephant's nocturnal habits are the ultimate negation of secrecy of location. On a still night, the snapping of bamboos by a foraging elephant can be heard for miles. Therefore the elephants must be laagered at night some miles from the armed camp; the location of the armed camp must be unknown to the elephant men; the loads allocated to the elephants must be those that most readily can be sacrificed, or at least done without for days if necessary.

Finally, a minimum knowledge of the working elephant is necessary even to reason thus far; and I alone of the present

Zonal officers could lay claim to that minimum knowledge. I was not a teak wallah, and what I knew about elephants had been incidentally learnt at Indaw. Mercifully it met the needs of the two nights that followed.

On arrival at our camp site, Dick Rees took care of the military side of our dispositions, while I briefed one of his young British officers in the matter of where the elephants were to be accommodated, using, incidentally, the weather-beaten map that is beside me as I write. We had twelve of the beasts with us and I had left them all under guard at the bottom of the hill. The officer's job was to conduct them upstream to a bend in the river that suggested suitable foraging. He took with him an interpreter who was to tell the *singaungs* that in the event of trouble they were to stay put until they heard from me.

I then proceeded to the one and only experience that inclines me to belief in telepathy.

For the first time in my Haka Zone service, four British officers were camped together under the same canopy of stars. Someone had produced a pack of cards and, in a *basha* that betrayed no chink of light, Dick Rees had set the stage for a game of bridge. We had dined and moderately wined, our New Year drop not yet being exhausted, when something clearly—very clearly—went 'click' inside my head. It was quite indisputable and, to the disgust of the others, I pleaded weariness and left them to a threesome.

I wandered off into the darkness, frightened by something that wasn't fear. I made a complete round of pickets, warning each N.C.O. commander that this was a night of a waning, or Japanese, moon. I returned to my own *basha* convinced that I had done everything but that I had missed something. I invoked the medicine man in myself: I decided that my nerves were shot and, having been in my clothes for many days, that I should strip right down and get a good night's sleep. I set out to do just that.

Soon after two o'clock I was abruptly awakened by grenade explosions and by the spectacle of tracer flowing through the camp. (Tracer does seem, somehow, to travel slowly.) I hauled on a pair of trousers and my jacket, grabbed my Tommy gun with one hand and the balance of my whisky ration with the other, and set off to do battle—my mind curiously vindicated in respect of its bedtime fears.

For a description of the action, I rely on my verbatim report to Colonel Hayes (written three days after the event) because it differs so materially from an account of the same action published some years later by a non-participant.

The action opened at 0210 hours when the Japs fired on a Levy picket East of the camp on the road Thanbaya/Sinbon (PJ2968), slightly wounding one of the picket. The picket fell back to its position on the edge of the perimeter. The Japs then deployed very swiftly, sending up red Verey lights as they worked their way round the perimeter, and firing into the perimeter with, as far as could be judged, one discharger cup, one (possibly more) LMG, hand grenades and rifles. The distribution of Verey pistols must have been on a handsome scale as they were being fired in profusion from all round the perimeter. The object of this tactic was not apparent, but it is opined that it was intended either to impress the Levies with the fact of being encircled or to inform the commander of the attacking force where attempts made to pierce the perimeter met with opposition.

Within half an hour of the start of the action all five defending platoons were being engaged from close range (in some cases only 30 to 40 yards). At this stage fire from both sides was very heavy indeed, and the presence of much natural cover in the form of small nullahs, rock outcrops and tree trunks was undoubtedly the reason for the lightness of casualties. The Levies 3″ and 2″ mortars were both in action, firing at short range towards the rear of Jap positions as indicated by their Verey lights.

Except for an all-round failing to blaze off needlessly after Jap probings had been repulsed, and, in some cases, as a matter of routine whether enemy were in sight or not, the Levies behaved on the whole with commendable steadiness. At no point was the perimeter pierced or withdrawn, and at one stage, when the two forward platoons were being closely engaged (with—to them—unexplained firing 100 to 200 yards in their rear, and Jap discharger grenades falling behind them) the Levies were answering the jabberings of the Japs with shouts of '*kukri nikalo*', '*dushman maro*' etc.

At 0400 hours (after the last round of reserve .303 ammo had been issued!) the enemy withdrew. The camp stood to until first light when four B.O. patrols went out and cleared the village and tracks leading away from the camp area. No enemy was encountered, but there were Jap footprints going away from the camp along nearly all these paths, and it is evident that they dispersed in small parties, probably to a pre-arranged R.V. There was no apparent signal of withdrawal at 0400 hours, and it is conjectured that that hour was pre-determined as the time for withdrawal in the event of the attack not being successful.

My casualties were very light—one dead (Levy Chia Hnin, of my own section) and four wounded, mostly by grenade fragments. The Japs left one dead and a badly wounded lieutenant, who coughed his life away soon after we found him. This abandonment was not typical of the Japs, and I surmised that the two could not be found or had not been missed at the time of the withdrawal. A welter of blood and bandages, documents, identity discs, water bottles, bayonets, a helmet, a cap, belts and a pack were testimony to a larger number of casualties dragged away, the scored and blood-stained dust of the tracks providing corroboration of this. I later learnt on good authority that the wounded had included the commander of the Tilin garrison, a major, and that he had died.

The occasion illustrates, as so often before, the sheer profligacy of encounter by moonlight in thick jungle. For a total of perhaps twenty to thirty casualties, I would estimate expenditure of ammunition of all arms and from both sides at thirty to forty thousand rounds. The Japs in particular, and as they always did, were firing absurdly high. I found a nick out of the brim of my hat that presumably had been caused by a bullet or a grenade fragment. My half-bottle of whisky I had totally consumed during the two hours of the battle!

The attacking force, I later learnt, had come from Kinban on the main Valley road four miles distant. I imagine that they had been witnesses of the Hurricanes' performance and had drawn an accurate inference there-from. They must then have come up to Thanbaya and forced villagers in the *taung-yas* to pinpoint our camp for them. We had of course hoped that our presence in their vicinity was unknown to the Thanbaya villagers, but this is too often a doctrine of perfection. There is always a village idiot or a pair of lovers on the wander, and once the news is out it spreads like wildfire.

I was now almost completely out of ammunition, and it was vital that I hurry into hiding until I could secure an air drop to restore the position. I sent a party off to clear a dropping zone on a ridge in the jungle six miles to my south, and signalled for an emergency drop at that point. The elephants, I was delighted to find, had been marshalled and harnessed for departure. Under cover of patrols, we loaded and sent them off on their escorted way. Finally I withdrew the rearguard and led them off in the same direction.

On making camp in the late afternoon, I disposed of the elephants on a *chaung* in a valley bottom two miles in my rear, received instructions to expect two Dakotas at nine next morning, issued all ammunition on a scale that amounted to less than ten rounds per man, checked our defences and turned in.

In the small hours of the morning my picket on the Thanbaya track exchanged fire with a Jap patrol which instantly withdrew. Soon afterwards a friendly Thanbaya villager arrived to say that a Jap force was in his village preparing to attack us before we received more ammunition. This was right on the bone, and there was nothing wrong with the Jap reasoning!

I stood the force to, vainly tried to cancel the morning's double drop, and sent word to the *singaungs* to the effect that we were moving off without the elephants, which they were to keep closed up and silent until they heard from me again. Most of the elephant loads were at the elephant camp, but such items as bags of rupees and spare arms and equipment were with me, and hastily I had to hide them in the jungle. Then quietly we moved off southward again. As we passed the dropping zone I put out the letters 'NO' instead of the 'AH' which was required of me.

By nine o'clock I was eight miles distant from and two thousand feet above my hastily abandoned camp, feverishly but unsuccessfully trying to establish the radio contact necessary to divert the Dakotas. Right on time they arrived over the dropping zone and, like spectators at a football match, we watched them circling.

'NO' in place of 'AH' could surely mean only one thing to the dimmest wit; but the Dakotas continued and repeated their leisurely round. After ten minutes or so I realized that the 'NO' had been removed, and that the pilots would be cursing the lazy bastards who were oversleeping on their sylvan couches instead of giving them the all clear. There had been earlier occasions of identifying letters not being received in time for display to dropping aircraft, when welcoming waves from the ground had satisfied the pilots that all was well and the drop had been made. Latterly, however, the R.A.F. had been getting tough on the point, and we had been warned that drops would not, 'repeat not', be made in the absence of identification. The question now was—were these chaps going to stand by their own rules, or were they going to present the Japs with two plane loads of booty?

Half an hour had gone and still the Dakotas were circling. At each approach to a dropping run I found myself closing my eyes and praying: and each time I opened them it was in the faithless conviction that I would see the parachutes floating down. After the longest forty minutes of my life— and to the enormous relief of us all, a silent throng of crouching, gazing Levies, the Dakotas broke their circling and headed westward.

After ordering the clearing of a new dropping zone at our present location, and having received word that the Dakotas were being sent back to drop to 'AQ', I redistributed our slender supply of ammunition in order disproportionately to equip a strong fighting patrol, which I then took back to the scene of the night's alarm.

The situation at the dropping zone, which we approached through the jungle, was as I expected to find it: the 'T' and the 'X' were still out, but the 'NO' was gone. The loads we had secreted in the jungle, at no great distance, were still there. We stalked on, past our abandoned camp, until two Burmans emerged from behind trees in our path.

They told us that they had been conscripted as guides to a force of Japs that had searched our camp and then moved on to the dropping zone. Here the officer in command had ordered the removal of the 'NO'. He had then scattered his men round the zone and all had hidden among the trees, where they had remained until the aircraft flew away. The officer had then ordered his men out again, fallen them in and marched them back to Thanbaya, whence they had carried on eastward along the Kinban track.

This sounded plausible; it could also be the setting for a trap. Accordingly I detained the Burmans and put the bulk of my force into a position covering the track to Thanbaya. Under this cover I sent a small party to summon the *singaungs* and their elephants. Once again there appeared to have been no panic in a situation that had lain outside my briefing and, after everything had been loaded, we marched off back to camp 'AQ', where the Dakotas had delivered by the time we arrived.

I have tried to put my feet into Japanese shoes over this cat and mouse occasion. As I see it, a junior officer would have taken over at short notice from the force commander mortally wounded in the affray at Thanbaya. Instead of calling it a day after receiving a bloody nose, he had probably surmised correctly that a jungle-routed force could not be left with much ammunition after such a heated exchange, and had followed us up while our pants were down. Our hurried evacuation after completing preparations for an air drop would have strengthened his belief. Having some knowledge of English—perhaps just that bit too much—he had faced a difficult decision on the dropping zone. Was 'NO' valid or a warning? Weighing up my problem of trying to cancel a drop but lately laid on, he decided on the latter and removed the 'NO'. When the Dakotas came over, my forty minutes of sweated apprehension were shared by himself, until my prayer was answered at the expense of his. He then decided that to continue the chase deeper into the Hills would be to stick his neck out too far, and accordingly called it off.

Nor should I withhold praise from the elephant men. Having been, on successive nights, the listeners to a pitched battle and the victims of an abandonment, no matter the assurance that it was temporary, they were still intact and marching with us.

My reference to an experience of telepathy I attach to my inexplicable sense of unease before the Thanbaya engagement, and the personal behaviour that it prompted. Nothing manifest had occurred to promote so acute a sense of foreboding.

At the time when my mind went 'click', I think now that the attacking force was sneaking its way round our perimeter, their orders being to observe strict silence until the commander's Verey pistol heralded the attack.

Thus, the collective thoughts of a hundred or more men, all radiating evil intent towards me, tangled as one with the atrophied stump of my antenna of instinct sufficiently to jar it into a pale performance of its primordial role.

There are doubtless more down-to-earth theories!

18 Farewell to Arms

February 1945 to May 1945

Within a few days of our replenishment on hill 'AQ', we were filtering into the Valley in small parties bound variously for Tilin; but now there was nothing but anti-climax in front of us as the Fourteenth Army drove southwards.

Soon, and with no little pride in the venture into faith that had made such a thing possible, I was handing over my 'fleet' of elephants to a senior Royal Engineers officer for use in the vital task of restoring blown bridges. He listened, with what I know was silent admiration, to the words of thanks and congratulation with which I took my leave of the *singaungs*.

With the alteration of one word and the insertion of another, I find that the closing paragraphs of my 1946 account to the Directorate of Public Relations conclude my story of the Chin Levies in terms that seem to me to be as valid now as they were then.
Accordingly I fall back on them—

Now, since foot-slogging Levies cannot for long keep ahead of an Army Corps moving in motor transport, we near the end of the tale. The leading Brigade of East Africans caught us up near Tilin towards the end of January. It was an entertaining meeting, since very few of the Levies had ever seen as much as a bicycle. They were now treated to the spectacle of lorries, carriers, artillery etc. rolling southwards down the same road that three years previously had witnessed the tragic scene with which this story opened.

Till mid-February we continued to patrol a large area of country south of Tilin so that 4th Corps could go through and eastwards to Pakokku without themselves having to detach a force for this purpose. When the dust behind their last vehicle had settled our job was done, and the enthusiasm with which the Levies, after almost three years of continuous service in the field, set out on the long march back to Haka needs no description.

Before leaving the valley, however, there is one subject that, in justice, calls for comment. To what I have always considered a most discreditable extent, our historians of the Burma campaign of 1942 placed a major share of our failure on the shoulders of the 'traitorous' Burmese. That there were such traitors no one who knows Burma will attempt to deny: but then the 'fifth column' was not coined in Burma; it has been an universal phenomenon wherever the scourge of the late war was laid. In Burma, as elsewhere, it was an unfortunate fact that the traitor's power for evil was out of all proportion to his numbers, but that the incidence of traitors in Burma proportionately was greater than, say, in Holland or Norway, to name two Allies who have earned our respect, is, I consider, a ridiculous assertion, particularly since it comes so often from those who do not know the country nor had any part in the campaign.

Even though the Gangaw Valley is traditionally one of the most peaceful areas of Burma, the fact that, with the exception of one established and one possible instance of treachery, I met with nothing but friendliness and co-operation (despite that in many cases, notably those of the elephant men, guides and agents, such co-operation was attended by no little personal danger) goes far to prove the argument.

A further point to be stressed if this account is to be appreciated in its true perspective is that the humdrum in everyday life gains nothing in interest by being translated onto paper. If these pages read like a racy account of life at high pressure, it is because the long periods of inactivity, the innumerable negative patrols and ambushes and the tedium of administration are there, but with so little story value as necessarily to be assumed by the reader to lie between the lines.

It has been, furthermore, a strictly personal account, and in no sense a complete history. Levy Officers, whose trails never crossed with mine, could doubtless write just as interesting an account without featuring any of the incidents that I have related. The frequent charge of exaggeration or 'line shooting' is best countered by the record of honours won by the Levies to date. They include 1 D.S.O., 1 O.B.E., 2 M.B.Es, 8 M.Cs, 5 B.G.Ms (that I can recall) and a number of 'mentions'.

As to what was achieved in concrete results, I have had too incomplete a contact with the Tiddim and Falam Zones to give more than the figures for Haka, which are that for a total of probably more than 400 casualties inflicted on the enemy we lost 8 killed in action or died of wounds, 8 more by drowning, accident or illness, while of 7 wounded in action only 2 are incapacitated for further service. These scarcely credible figures speak volumes for the policy of fighting always, as far as possible, in conditions of our own choosing, and even then by the inglorious tactics of hit and run. That these are the right tactics for Levy warfare is indisputable when, with every member of your force a local, the effect on morale of heavy casualties would be disastrous.

What we achieved as a screen of intelligence covering for nearly three years a large extent of the land frontier between India and enemy-occupied Burma only G.H.Q. are in a position fairly to assess. The respect in which we were held by the enemy came most interestingly to light in an Intelligence file found in the Japanese civil office in Tilin after our occupation of the town. The reports from enemy agents which it contained gave us credit for performances and force of numbers that would have cheered us up no end had we known of them twelve months earlier, and they well illustrated the value of mentally putting yourself in your enemy's shoes and trying to sense his difficulties instead of too readily assuming that the only difficulties are your own.

At a time when the Press is busy extolling the partisan movements coming to light in countries attaining liberation from their oppressors, there seems to be a tendency to exclude such classic examples as lie within the borders of our own Commonwealth. Among these the record of the Chin Levies may well provide as fine a story as any. Through the greater part of their campaign they (speaking particularly of the Hakas and Falams) had no regular backing other than their own Chin Hills Battalion. Despite the accent on 'we' which underlies this account, the fact remains that Levy officers were so few in number as utterly to have been unable to counter a general throwing-in of hands at any of the two or three periods of crisis when this was possible. To a great extent we were present as advisers and co-ordinators of effort, and as liaison and administrative agents (or, as one officer put it, to see that when a week's rations were dropped to the Levies they did not eat everything on the first day!).

Many ventures led by officers had actually been proposed and planned by the Levy leaders themselves and, while privately reserving the right to veto any scheme that appeared to be too wild and woolly, we pushed for all it was worth the atmosphere of War for the Chins by the Chins themselves. It was not an easy role to learn and we had our share of failures; but that the end justified the means is a claim that none of us feels need come from himself.

(N.B. The B.G.M. is the Burma Gallantry Medal, for which all indigenous ranks of the Burma Army were eligible.)

The march back to Haka took us twelve days, with one day's break for a rest half-way through. It was a triumphal procession; with much *zu* drinking at the village halts and loosing off of occasional *feux de joie*. Here and there, illicitly secreted in pack or bedding roll, reposed a Jap head.

At a general assembly soon after we reached Haka, Colonel Hayes announced that he had been ordered to raise two battalions from the Levies as a contribution to the new

Burma Army, one of them to be comprised entirely of Hakas; and that this move was to be regarded wholly as a measure of reward to the people of the Chin Hills for the loyalty, steadfastness and courage they had displayed during the three years of threat to their homeland.

This news was received with the greatest acclamation, sweetened for me by Hayes's subsequent word to myself that in the matter of selecting officers for the new battalions he had been told to count me out as my services would be required elsewhere. In my own eyes my debt to the Chins was now fully discharged and, despite frustrations, I felt that I had adhered pretty closely to Colonel Critchley's mandate as he had defined it in Shillong nearly three years ago. More important, I had gone stale. Any change now would be welcome even if, as seemed likely, it was a posting to the newly-formed Civil Affairs Service (Burma) which, during the inevitable period of pacification that lay ahead, was to function under Army control.

Gradually we all accustomed ourselves to a life without pickets or sentries, alarums or excursions. I wrote home:

I am sitting on my bottom all day paying out money, settling claims and complaints, and drying the tears of widows who come to see what they can expect from their husbands' deaths in the way of hard cash. Not a dynamic form of existence. I further have an unending road of Courts of Inquiry, Courts Martial etc. stretching out ahead of me, and they look like keeping me busy for months. The joys of three years in an irregular unit are quickly dispelled when it comes to winding up in a regular manner, and I'm heartily sick of it already.

But there was another side to the penny.

Meanwhile the weather is grand, I have no worries and plenty to read, so compared with the poor devils fighting in the heat of Mandalay I suppose I'm well off.

As a variant from my chair-borne role, I organized and played a lot of football and, as might be expected of so bibulous a people, *zu* parties were frequent and uninhibited.

I'm expecting another heavy party this week. The *piece de resistance* will take the form of a frenzied dance round the clothing and equipment of some Japs killed some while back. Sounds unpleasant, but I shall be just as barbaric as everybody else I have no doubt!

After several weeks thus spent in compiling records, writing recommendations and reports (including the one for G.H.Q. from which I have occasionally quoted) and squaring up the Hakas generally, I was ordered to Falam to preside over further Courts of Inquiry there.

I had a final party before leaving Haka. I sat in the throne of honour immediately underneath a Jap head! I was more than a little sorry to leave the place, but it is just as well, as if (as I begin to suspect) there is no such thing as Home leave, then a change of atmosphere will be the next best thing . . . The atmosphere of the last three years will, after tomorrow I fear have gone entirely. In fact I expect to sink to the ultimate horror of an Officers' Mess.

I left Haka early in the morning to a noisy farewell, which included much 'discharge of ordnance'. At the point on the road where begins the gentle drop to Pioneer Camp, I sat for a few minutes alone with my thoughts, memorizing a last view of Haka. I thought both of achievement and of failure, to stand to my credit or to be laid at my door. I wondered what the future might hold for these tough, untutored people, whose destiny thus far had been a harshness of living unknown to the majority of the human race. Would they be better off under the debilitating shield of civilization or by returning to the demanding life that had bred them? The choice, I supposed, would not be theirs. On which reflection I waved my farewell and left them.

Pioneer Camp and its rest house were a shambles, and this was to be a sadly repeated experience during the hundred-odd miles of marching in the Chin Hills that remained to me. At Mangkheng, the last halt before Falam, I spent some time searching for the grave of David Milligan. He had been killed there, and the Japs were said to have buried him superficially on the slope above the now ruined rest house; but I was unsuccessful.

Falam induced in me a desire to put it behind me as soon as possible, so my joy was unconfined when, a day or two after my arrival, I received orders to go out to India *en route* for sixty-one days leave in England.

Normally I would have been faced with the old westward trek of twelve days or more via Aijal or Lungleh in the

Lushai Hills, but hearing that at Indainggyi, near Kalemyo, there was now an operational air strip serving as a staging-post on the air-borne supply route between India and the battles now raging in Lower Burma, I decided to chance my arm on getting lifted out from there.

I marched out of Falam, most fittingly, with Norman Kelly. He now was in bad shape physically and was on his way out via Tiddim and Imphal to appear before a Medical Board. It was a sorry trek for both of us, with our memories of the sylvan progress that the traveller along the ridge top had once enjoyed. I wrote home:

Most of the attractive P.W.D. bungalows in the area, with their flower-laden gardens, simply no longer exist. Motor lorries are rotting down the khud sides, and Jap bunkers scar the slopes, where the jungle has been blasted out of existence.

In what once would have been the shade of the Fort White rest house, I said 'farewell' to Norman and watched his still-resilient stride carry him off towards the Tiddim that he knew and loved so well. I stayed long enough to identify from afar the slopes on which Peter Bankes had died, and then dropped down the road that led to the Stockades. As I marched I could not rid myself of the uneasy feeling that I should be escorted and armed with something more than a revolver.

The desolation that now was No. 3 Stockade almost reduced me to tears, and I hurried on down into the rising heat of the Valley and past No. 2. Just short of Tahan I paused to identify the patch of cover from behind which I had given the order to open fire when we attacked the village on Christmas Eve of 1942. I thought of Jack Oats and his disgust at having been thwarted from joining in, and I wondered if medical skill was doing anything for him. As I passed the tree from which our opening shot had dropped the Jap sentry, my mind curiously gauged the distance of his fall.

On, over well-remembered ground, my feet carried me into and through Kalemyo. The only building standing was the latrine-like edifice in which the Treasury cash had been safeguarded. Towards evening I arrived at Hpaungzeik, a mile or two short of my destination at Indainggyi. Finding here an undamaged rest house occupied by three officers of a Graves Registration unit, I accepted their invitation to spend the night with them, later regretting that I had done so.

All round the garden, leaning against the fence, were white wooden crosses awaiting their sad, individual stakings into the soil. The senior of the three officers was, of all things, a peacetime butcher; and the conversation over the evening meal was the most ghoulishly professional discourse to which I have ever been exposed—and I'm sure that it was not laid on for my benefit.

One of the three, who had got back from his day's work just before I arrived, launched into a description of the discovery—after many days of jungle searching—of a crashed fighter. In the most casual way he described how he had had to drive a bayonet into the pilot's distended stomach to release the gases of putrefaction before he could get the body out of the cockpit. Their subsequent apologies for causing my abrupt plunge into the garden to get some fresh air were profuse, but I wished that I had kept on marching.

I arrived at the air strip next morning simultaneously with an east-bound Dakota. I asked the pilot how long he thought I should have to wait to jump a ride west-bound.

'From now to eternity,' said the pilot. 'Only east-bound traffic follows this route. We fly back another way. What's your problem?'

'I'm trying to get to England,' I replied.

'Too bad,' said the pilot, 'unless you like to join me in delivering this lot at Meiktila.' And here he indicated through the aircraft's open door about forty drums of petrol. 'They're still fighting there, you know, but perhaps you'd like a last crack at the Jap before you pull out?'

'Not damned likely,' I replied, 'but if you can be sure of fitting me in on your return trip I'll take my chance and come.'

'Boy! You won't find me hanging around for a return load. If they don't hit me before this lot's out, you won't see me for dust once I'm unloaded. Sure you can come. You'll have the place to yourself.'

On which promising note I climbed aboard. What a fool! I might have been marching peacefully towards Aijal!

We took off and headed south-east. Within minutes we were bumping through the haze of heat rising from the plains of Burma. We crossed the Chindwin and the Irrawaddy just above their confluence, and soon were lurching down through a dusty pall.

As we rolled to a stop on the Meiktila air strip, Indian *jawans* came sprinting out from cover to unload. I weighed the respective merits of leaving the aircraft and risking being snaffled as a Heaven-sent answer to the problem of an officerless platoon, or of staying aboard and being caught in association with hundreds of gallons of petrol if we were hit. I left the aircraft.

I found I had little to worry about. The bursts of Japanese shells were observable to the south of the air strip, but there was that in the air that suggested hot-footed pursuit of a beaten enemy. How long it had been in coming! For one absurd moment enthusiasm suggested that I should dash off after all and offer my sword to the first taker. Sanity returned with the briskness of its disruption and, at a shout from the pilot, I boarded the aircraft and we took off.

I had for company this time a British sergeant, but he was no more communicative than the drums of petrol had been; and there was that stricken look about him that suggested compassionate leave to face an errant wife. I may have been wide of the mark, but I left him to endure the deadly cold of our westward journey with the same fortitude that I hoped I was displaying.

We crossed the Chin Hills well to the south of my 'stamping grounds' but, from my frozen stupor, I roused myself for an attempted view all the same. All I saw vaguely was hills and jungle, and there was nothing novel about that.

I left the aircraft at Chittagong and found my way to Calcutta. Having established that I was indeed bound for England and that air-borne departure from Calcutta, days or maybe weeks hence, involved of certainty a stop at Bombay, I applied to a chair-borne Staff Captain, whose consumption of pens I would suspect as having rivalled my destruction of boots, for permission to join my brother in Bombay and to be flown home from there.

The Captain assured me, with some asperity, that my absurd request was beyond the wit of the Army to arrange, and I was instructed to entrain for a place called Gaya, in the middle of Bihar, and there to report to a transit camp which, with an obsequious glance at my Major's crown, the Captain assured me catered for British officers of Field rank only.

Writhing under the lash of impotence, I boarded my train, removed myself from it at Gaya and sought out the transit camp 'for British officers of Field rank only'. I was marshalled through a sort of football turnstile, whereat I was handed a sheaf of forms requiring completion by myself. The topmost document was a neatly executed card that invited me to declare whether I was a rice or an *atta* eater. Sadly I deleted both, wrote in 'sunflower seeds' and pushed my way through the turnstile. The long arm of the Army had claimed me!

The war in Burma was moving rapidly to its victorious conclusion and, while in Calcutta, I had learnt that Steels had applied for priority in the matter of my release so as to get me on to a job of post-war reconstruction in Burma. I estimated that, by the time I returned from England, all might well be over bar the shouting. Inspired, therefore, by the atmosphere of the transit camp 'for British officers of Field rank only' I launched, no matter how prematurely, and in what I regarded as Kiplingesque vein, into a paean of demobilization, which survives as follows.

From way back they've passed an order, from on high the word has come,
   From the roll of serf and slave they've scored my name:
Without pomp, parade or pageant, drill, delirium or drum
   I am free to wander back the way I came.
Who can fathom what I'm feeling, who divine the dreams I'm dreaming,
   Know the rapture of the severed, sundered chain?
Don't attempt it, simply leaving me to planning and conceiving
   How to find my way down Civvy Street again.
     Chorus: I'm bowlered, benighted and bottled,
         I'm staggered and sunk and insane,
     I'm knocking the hell out of Colonels,
         A happy boxwallah again!

Five long years have I been waiting for the joy that now is mine,
  Sixty months of quarantine beyond the pale,
Scanning post and press and pamphlet, screed and scripture for a sign,
  As the shipwrecked con horizons for a sail.
Now, no longer conscientious to seem brutal and licentious,
  I've received O.H.M.S. a little chit;
Lacking anything contentious, it is plain and unpretentious,
  But, by all the powers that made me, this is it!
    Chorus: I'm bowlered, benighted etc.
Gather round and share my triumph, come and join the courts of song,
  There'll be beer in bulk and bottles, there'll be wine;
In the glare of glinting guineas this will be no thrifty throng,
  You'll have all the scope you want to shoot a line.
We shall dance and drink and wager round a flaming dummy Major,
  We shall fling all form and function on the fire:
And should aught of this enrage a red-tabbed regular up-stager,
  He had better stay away—or join the pyre!
    Chorus: I'm bowlered, benighted etc.

The officer commanding the transit camp was blessed with an independence of intelligence that contrasted notably with the Calcutta captain's lack of it. Having listened to the story of my frustrated attempt to join the home-bound caravan at Bombay, he gave vent to a loud, crude shout and got moving on my behalf. Within a few days I was on my way to Bombay, carrying minimum, lucid instructions as to where I was to report for the purpose of leaving an address that would find me at short notice.

At Bombay I located Jim. He was unable to put me up but, with the greatest of pleasure, I accepted for my first day or two the hospitality of 'Hutch' (of Lanywa, Indaw and Yenangyaung) and his wife. 'Hutch' was now Manager of I.B.P's Bombay office and I was delighted at the reunion after so many years. For the remainder of my stay, I moved into the 'Taj' where I had found that an old friend of my Guildford rugby football days was billeted.

Despite the misgivings of the pen-sucking captain in Calcutta, I made my connection with the York transport aircraft that was to take me home as easily as I had anticipated.

While flying over the Western Desert we received the news that Germany had surrendered and that next day had been declared VE Day. We landed in a London *en fete* and, before seeking our several homeward ways, another officer and I decided that we should not miss seeing the sights on such a historic occasion. We joined the dancing in the streets, cheered the King on his appearance on the balcony of Buckingham Palace and drank in innumerable pubs and bars with innumerable rollicking strangers. Our jungle green battle dress was an unfamiliar sight in London and we were allowed to pay for nothing. Our unit flashes, East Africans and Burma Levies respectively, excited no little comment; and one old dear expressed to me her surprised delight that a Jewish unit should be fighting with the Allies against the Japanese!

Worn and weary I forced my oft-impeded way to Waterloo and caught a train for Guildford. With his car laid up for want of petrol, my father met me at the station with my sister's pram (she being now a mother of a year's standing). Onto this novel transport I loaded my bedroll and trundled my way home—for the second time in eleven years.

19 Loose Threads

May 1945 to February 1946

Army administration operated in my favour in the matter of my leave. Arrangements for my return to the Far East were wholly overlooked, to the extent that sixty-one days leave that started with my arrival in England on VE Day terminated over three months later with my departure on VJ Day.

What this meant to my future can be gauged by the fact that, with sixty-three days gone, Maxine, constantly on the move in Europe, received from me a long-delayed letter in which I gave her the coverage of the sixty-one days and expressed the hope that she would be able to take some leave in England during the period.

Acting on impulse, she jumped a plane ride to England, called my home and found me on the other end of the line awaiting my marching orders! I told her to position herself underneath the clock opposite number five platform at Waterloo as soon as possible, slammed down the phone and raced for Guildford station. My parents were out of the house at the time, and when they returned to find an unknown American girl installed in the spare bedroom, they were somewhat nonplussed.

We had a week together, did the rounds of town and country, and were unofficially engaged when she returned to the Continent. We were married in Bombay rather more than a year later.

I returned to India by troopship, incurring during the course of shipboard activities a blistered foot that led to my being carried ashore with blood poisoning that put me into hospital near Bombay for several weeks.

From hospital I was sent to Hoshiarpur in the Punjab, which had become Headquarters for the Burma Army in exile. Maxine meanwhile had returned to the States from Europe and was out of uniform. Abortively, from my out-of-the-way location, I tried to plan the means of bringing her out to marry me somewhere or other. I did the minimum I could of the meaningless office work that was farmed out to too many of us, all boxwallahs *in suspensio*. I took three days leave in Lahore to watch a cricket match between the North Zone of India and Lindsay Hassett's Australian Services side, which I had already seen playing England in an unofficial Test Match at Lords while I was on leave. I fought boredom variously until the return of Burma Army Head-quarters to Rangoon called for the presence in Calcutta of an officer to arrange for the necessary shipping. With simulated distress in my face and a letter from Maxine in my hand I persuaded the Commandant to send me down.

In Calcutta I was better placed to make a nuisance of myself on the doorsteps of Steels, the American Consulate and the bank. I put up at the officers' transit camp at Alipore, and among those who came and went during my rather lengthy stay was my old friend, Frank Ford, whose command of the Chin Levies had so regrettably been terminated in 1943.

The Commandant of the camp was a cricket enthusiast and he and I bought season tickets for the Australians' unofficial Test Match against India at Eden Gardens. Unfortunately the occasion clashed with an outbreak of communal rioting in Calcutta, which found me, Tommy gun in hand once more, roaming the streets of the city with a platoon of British troops under my command.

Although we were supposed to be in camp and on call, the first day of the match dawned on a superficial lull in the rioting, and the Commandant and I sneaked away in a jeep to the ground. We were enjoying some interesting cricket (including three sixes in four balls from Keith Miller right over our heads) when there was an uproar from outside the fence and rioters started swarming over and onto the ground in thousands. They punctiliously escorted the players to the pavilion, while we feverishly battled our way back to where we belonged! Unofficial or not, at least I can say that I have seen a cricket Test Match stopped by a riot!

At intervals of about a week, I began receiving train loads of Burma Army personnel from Hoshiarpur, leading them in convoy across the city and marshalling them up the gang-ways of on-carrying ships. With the final detachment I sailed myself and, a few days later, was disembarking at the Sule Pagoda wharves in Rangoon, precisely where this my story had its Burma beginning.

It was New Year's Eve and, at opposite ends of the world, Maxine and I had agreed to announce our engagement next day. She, I knew, had arranged to have a party at her home in California. The ship that brought me from Calcutta had on board a strong contingent of the Burma Army Nursing Service, and a Burma Rifles officer travelling with me was announcing his engagement to one of the nurses as soon as we got ashore. We agreed, therefore, on a joint celebration, for which purpose we garnered a goodly harvest of gin.

We rounded up at short notice all the friends of either of us that we could locate, and we paraded about sixty strong in a Rangoon bungalow, Maxine being represented by a photograph of herself on a prominently positioned table. It was a great evening except for its final stages, when I found myself arrested by the Military Police allegedly for wrench-ing the lid off an Officers' Club piano as a protest against what I considered to be the piano's unreasonably early closure. The matter was settled amicably by my handing the M.P.s fifty rupees elsewhere to cover the cost of repairs. Whether or not this is entered in the Book as a bribe, at least the piano was in a fit state next time I viewed it.

While in Rangoon I did a sentimental but sorrowful journey round the various places that once had meant something to me in one context or another. The streets in the area of the docks and of Steels office were being cleared of bomb rubble by gangs of Japanese prisoners, strangely innocuous-looking little men against my memories of them as cunning and dedicated fighters in the jungle. The office itself was damaged and derelict, and my attempt to visit

'Merry Helenside' was thwarted by bolts and bars on the street door.

The Cathedral was being cleaned and redecorated in preparation for reconsecration after being desecrated by the Japs. With the dead bodies of its children strung out along the Hukawng Valley, Bishop's Home was shuttered and silent.

I visited the burnt-out shell of the Rangoon Gymkhana, pondered in the roofless silence of the long bar and retraced in memory the choreography of one of my cabaret numbers where the ballroom floor had been. Through long grass I wandered out onto the rugger field. Where I would have hoped to find it, my toe turned the tussocks this way and that in search of the residual trace of whitewash that might yet have marked the nearer touch-line; and my head rose to catch perhaps a dying echo of the last 'Long line, Steels!' But all was silent, as forever were the voices of some of those with whom I had scrimmaged. I walked away, alone with my thoughts.

'The Gin Palace' at least did something for my spirits. Practically unscathed, where scores of bungalows had been rendered uninhabitable, this stronghold of the bachelor male, this terror of the Rangoon *mem-sahib* with a nubile daughter, was now being adapted as married quarters! At first I was scandalized: the war surely had not been won for this! Then the delight of it began to seep through, and I moved on in the hope that it was a happy augury.

Alas, it was not long to be. Nothing was. Ever again.

At this point, near the end of my story, I am within a day or two of leaving Burma for the last time. It is a country in which I made more friends, other than of my own Anglo-Saxon kind, than I have made in any other land I have lived in. I like to think that some at least made friends of me. On the rare occasions now when I indulge the luxury of feeling homesick it is for Burma.

Looking back on it all, I both sympathize and criticize.

I sympathize because, having gathered the Burmese peoples under the panoply of the British Raj, we promised them, by implication at least, a mantle of protection against external aggression that was never anything more than illusory. True, we had the Frontier Force and the Military Police to deal with border incidents and opium smuggling, and the Burma Rifles to cope with brush fires; but there was no counter to foreign invasion and, though the land is studded with British and Allied graves, it was the peasantry who really paid and are paying.

I criticize because the post-war Burmese leaders, in an excess of self-pity, masochism, sterile nationalism—call it what you will, have so immured the country behind a curtain of distrust as to deny to that peasantry the restitution that could have been theirs, if not from Britain direct for reasons of *amour-propre*, then through the same international channels as have benefited other war-riven lands. As it is, large areas of the country are under the domination of rebel elements that defy the writ of the Government, while the foreigner is not tolerated as a resident. Fences are not mended in this way.

I sailed from Rangoon for Calcutta towards the end of January 1946, my release papers in my pocket for final processing on arrival. On reporting to Steels office I was told that, to help release dammed-up arrears of leave due to staff there, I was being lent for six months to their associate, The Attock Oil Company in Rawalpindi (whence I was to retire from service with Steels nearly twenty years later!).

My release papers were to include a military travel warrant to Rawalpindi, for which reason I declined with thanks an offer from Percy Salkeld of a civilian passage. However, on going along to collect my warrant, I was told that I would be travelling as O.C. of a troop train. I protested on the grounds that I was on release leave, that there were regular officers of equal rank travelling with their units, and that the job of O.C. properly belonged to one of them. I got nowhere and, being satisfied that I was the chosen victim of a piece of bloody-mindedness, I went back to Steels office, reclaimed my civilian ticket and left for Rawalpindi by the Frontier Mail four hours ahead of the troop train. I have no reason to think the troops did not get to destination safely.

However, I yet had to lose the last battle of my personal war. My release entitlements included, *inter alia*, one day's pay for every month of overseas service which, in my case, added up to sixty-three months. When my dues came to be paid to me, this useful accretion had been disallowed. On inquiring the reason, I was told that, as a pre-war resident of Burma, commissioned into the Burma Army (despite that my commission was 'British Army—General List'), I had spent the whole war in Burma and therefore could not claim to have been overseas!

I sent an appeal against this startling hypothesis to the appropriate body at G.H.Q., India, in whose name it had been spun. To my astonishment, the reply was a confirmation of fantasy!

My dander was now up and I sent a two-pronged representation to the Army Council in London and to Sir John Jarvis, the then Member of Parliament for Guildford. The latter replied reasonably promptly to the effect that he would be happy to take my case up. All the greater was my disbelief when the Army Council wrote me to the effect that under the definitions laid down by the Government Commission that had been set up to regulate payment of release claims, I was held to have had no overseas service and therefore had no claim.

Knowing what the answer would be, I nevertheless wrote back to the Army Council asking where lay my next court of appeal. Their reply, sure enough, enclosed a printed extract from, I believe, King's Regulations, in which an explanation that every officer had the right of a personal appeal to His Majesty was coupled with words of caution on the gravity of exercising such a right.

I had one more card to play. I wrote to the Army Council claiming that, by their own reasoning, I was entitled to the overseas allowance in respect of the three months leave that I had spent on my native shore.

They agreed, and I was paid!

The song is ended, but not, alas, the tale of violence.

George Wilson married after the war and returned to his

old haunts in Malaya, where he was managing a rubber estate. During the 'Emergency' he was ambushed by terrorists within a few hundred yards of his bungalow. His six-year-old son was with him. George pushed the boy off the road and told him to leg it for home, he himself staying to shoot it out with his attackers for long enough before he died to ensure the lad's escape and survival.

Jim Milne was dacoited and murdered in mid-river during a cash run up to the Mine at Yamone, whither he had returned to salvage the scuttled Dredge.

Moisey and Danny Higgins, whether with or without military enrolment and in what circumstances I have never been able to learn, joined some sort of armed foray from Mergui into Siam from which none returned.

Jimmie Cook was ambushed and killed by dacoits on the road up to Kalaw, whither he was making his post-war way on local leave.

Jack Oats wheels his crippled body about in Portugal, to the sunshine of which, for loss of blood circulation, he was ordered on medical advice. Undefeated by disaster, he is now qualified in Law, teaches English and has developed a talent for water-colour painting. Of recent years, when I was on leave in England and he was over for an annual medical check-up, we spent a weekend with Pru Bankes at her home in the New Forest. In health, in infirmity and by proxy it was a reunion of the Three Musketeers of No. 3 Stockade.

'Stooky' Seagrim, the doyen of the Burma Levies, surrendered to the Japanese in March 1944 on the promise that reprisals against the Karens for harbouring him would thereby cease. Whether or not he ever received it, apparently, is uncertain, but a letter addressed to him by the Japanese ended with the words—'I promise that you will not be killed but will be treated honourably as a prisoner of war'.

In his *Grandfather Longlegs*, Ian Morrison has described how, in the hell of the *Kempeitai* jail in Rangoon, 'Stooky's' radiantly Christian behaviour dominated the scene to such an extent that even the Japanese prison guards referred to him as the 'Big Master'.

On 3 September, pleading passionately for the release of the seven Karen Levies who had been sentenced to death with him, 'Stooky' was driven in an open truck to his personal Calvary in Kemmendine cemetery. A recommendation for a posthumous Victoria Cross (a decoration which his brother, also posthumously, had already won in North Africa) failed on technical grounds; but to the D.S.O. and M.B.E. which he had won in solitude was added the George Cross.

My last word must be of Burma. At the end of my story I have set a few lines which I dedicated to a teak tree whose transplantation I found myself sharing in after-years. The last three lines, I think, hold the key to sorrow for those of us who knew and loved Burma and gladly would have gone back there.

No children of ours or of our friends will send us pen pictures of jungle or upland scenes such as would liven our diminishing pulses with the warmth of vicarious participation. We write to and receive word from none, for that way lies the threat of persecution at the other end of the line. Scattered throughout the world, a shrinking band and potential bores to our neighbours, we comb our environs for those who are qualified to join us in warming our hands before the dying embers of Memory. The song indeed is ended, for even the sentimental visitor to Burma has been restricted until very recently to a stay of only twenty-four hours.

But the melody lingers on.

To a Teak tree in exile

Why hallow with exotic shade
    This unexpectant loam?
By what mishap were you betrayed
    In banishment to roam?
Your kindred crowd the Burma hills
And march beside the forest rills.
    Are they no longer Home?

Reflect I must — you never knew
    Old *taw chet's* early cry,
Nor watched *kya gyi* glide into view
    With hunger in his eye.
You never heard *thit kok thu's* shout
Nor feared the dah that rings about
    The boles of them that die.

No seed of yours is at your side,
    You live, you'll die, alone;
No echoes trembling down the ride
    Will mark you overthrown.
What requiem may charge the breeze
That sighs at even through the trees
    For one so quite unknown?

The Yomas lean against the sky
    And Irrawaddy swings;
About the *zayat* swallows fly
    On lissom, curving wings.
But how can each with each explore,
Why seek to enter Memory's door?
    You never knew these things.

Rawalpindi, June, 1958

Index